A NATION ON THE LINE

Call Centers as Postcolonial Predicaments

in the Philippines

JAN M. PADIOS

DUKE UNIVERSITY PRESS

Durham and London

2018

© 2018 Duke University Press
All rights reserved
Printed in the United States of America on acid-free paper ∞
Designed by Julienne Alexander
Typeset in Minion Pro by Copperline Book Services

Library of Congress Cataloging-in-Publication Data
Names: Padios, Jan M., [date] author.
Title: A nation on the line : call centers as postcolonial predicaments
in the Philippines / Jan M. Padios.
Description: Durham : Duke University Press, 2018. |
Includes bibliographical references and index.
Identifiers: LCCN 2017039420 (print)
LCCN 2018000176 (ebook)
ISBN 9780822371984 (ebook)
ISBN 9780822370475 (hardcover : alk. paper)
ISBN 9780822370598 (pbk. : alk. paper)
Subjects: LCSH: Call centers—Philippines.
Classification: LCC HE8789.P6 (ebook) | LCC HE8789.P6 P33 2018 (print) |
DDC 384.6/4—dc23
LC record available at https://lccn.loc.gov/2017039420

Cover art: Call center, Manila. Photo by Joerg Boethling/Alamy.

A NATION ON THE LINE

IN MEMORY OF DIXON CHIU

CONTENTS

ACKNOWLEDGMENTS

I wrote this book over many seasons and semesters; in half a dozen offices and apartments; in a few countries and time zones; and during significant life events. Although my solitary working style led me to isolation for most of that time, I was never alone.

From start to finish, the call center employees who generously agreed to take part in my research ensured that I would have no shortage of voices in my audio recorder during fieldwork or in my head later, when sitting down to write. While I hope *A Nation on the Line* can be read as one big acknowledgment of the lives and labor of these workers, I would be remiss to not explicitly express my boundless gratitude to each and every person who shared with me the stories and insights that became the basis of this project. They are a reminder that ethnographic knowledge production is a relation built on reciprocity between people and that it thus takes many forms, not simply those bound together in a book.

As an American studies master's and doctoral student at New York University (NYU), I had the great fortune of being taught, mentored, and advised by an exceptional group of scholars. Arlene Dávila, Lisa Duggan, Radha Hegde, and Andrew Ross—together with Robyn Rodriguez from Rutgers and later the University of California, Davis—were a remarkable dissertation committee for whom I am and always will be immensely appreciative. Arlene Dávila was an especially devoted dissertation committee chair and overall mentor whose invaluable support over a total of nine years meant the difference between surviving academia and thriving in it. Graduate school also gave me the privilege of taking seminars or doing qualifying exams with Adam Green, Philip Harper, Walter Johnson,

Crystal Parikh, Nicholas de Genova, and the late Neil Smith. Discussions and ideas from these experiences often return to me in moments of writing and teaching, reminding me that learning is anything but linear. Through the Asian/Pacific/American studies program at NYU, I also had the honor of learning from the marvelous Luis Francia and meeting Agnes (Bing) Magtoto, a warm and wonderful person who did translation for chapter 5.

In addition, NYU brought me a bevy of friends and colleagues whose brilliance has strengthened every fiber of my being, from my scholarship to my politics. Dinners and phone calls with Miles Grier, organizing and general rabble-rousing with Rana Jaleel, travel and revelry with Johana Londoño and Ariana Ochoa Camacho, and coffee and walks with Dylan Yeats have inspired and sustained me throughout the years. Thanks, as well, to Kari Hensley, Dacia Mitchell, and Zach Schwartz-Weinstein, who, along with Ariana, Rana, and Dylan, made up Mortal Kombat, a.k.a. my dissertation writing group; to Andy Cornell, for our conversations on autonomist Marxism; to A. J. Bauer, Emma Kreyche, Marisol LeBrón, Justin Leroy, and Zenia Kish for making the History of Capitalism seminar challenging and fulfilling, and for collaborations on conferences over the years; and to Vanessa Agard-Jones, Becca Howes-Mitchell, Elizabeth Mesok, and Ronak Kapadia, whose kind encouragement and astute comments on early portions of my dissertation during the workshop "Jumping Scales: Studying and Writing about Transnational Processes" (held at NYU's Institute for Public Knowledge and directed by Sally Merry and Nicolas Guilhot) helped make this project what it is today. Thanks, too, to all the friends and comrades I made through the Graduate Student Organizing Committee/United Auto Workers (GSOC/UAW) Local 2110. You sparked in me a political commitment to workers and labor issues that I have carried forward every day since leaving NYU.

In August 2012 I joined the Department of American Studies at the University of Maryland, where I have enjoyed an increasingly rare opportunity in the academy—the chance to stick around, grow intellectually, and enrich my scholarship. First and foremost, I thank Christina Hanhardt for generously lending me her time, attention, and advice. I am undeserving of the many ways Christina has championed me over the years, and I can only hope to do right by her support and return in some small measure her boundless humor, wisdom, brilliance, and friendship. Because of her, along with Janelle Wong, whose loyalty and support I feel at every benchmark and hurdle on the road to tenure review, my mentorship at Maryland has left nothing to be desired. To the other faculty members of my department, present and retired—Asim Ali, La Marr Bruce, Robert Chester, Jason Farman, Perla Guerrero, Jim Maffie, Nancy Mirabal, Sheri Parks, Mary Sies, Psyche Williams-Forson, Jo Paoletti, and Nancy Struna—thank you for creating an environment in which thinking critically, caring for students, and supporting junior faculty are the rules rather than the exceptions. Were it not for the work and confidence of the committee that hired me—Michelle Rowley, Christina Hanhardt, Psyche Williams-Forson, Jason Farman, Michael Casiano, and Tiffany Lethobo King—I, and most likely this book, would not be here at all. Moreover, Julia C. Johns and Tammi Archer have been great administrators who keep the wheels on the department, and although we can now only admire her from across campus, Betsy Yuen, our former academic coordinator, still sets the gold standard for administrative assistance and is still a wonderful friend. At Maryland I have also had the honor of working with a number of fantastic graduate students whose intellectual presence pushes me to be a better and more engaged scholar, teacher, and advisor. To the students of AMST 601, Transnational Political Economy and Cultures, and the Cultural Politics of Work and Labor, and to my advisees—thank you. To Sharada Balachandran Orihuela and Perla Guerrero: although we often wondered whether we had each made a huge mistake, I know that becoming friends with you has been one of the best decisions of my life. Thanks, too, to Randy Ontiveros for such easy camaraderie and conversation over the past several years.

For many academics, life's rhythm is marked by a seemingly endless cycle of applications, deadlines, submissions, and long waits, leading to various measures of exaltation and disappointment. I am fortunate to have received much financial and institutional support for my research and this book. At Maryland I received a Qualitative Seed Grant from the Center for Race, Gender, and Ethnicity; a Summer Research and Scholarship Award from the Graduate School; and subvention from the College of Arts and Humanities and the Department of American Studies. At NYU I was the recipient of the Mellon Dissertation Fellowship in the Humanities, a Torch Fieldwork Fellowship, the Henry H. MacCracken Fellowship, and numerous dean's fellowships from the Graduate School of Arts and Science, as well as a dissertation grant from the Council for Media and Culture. For every award that I received, however, there were perhaps half a dozen that I did not. However, through those experiences I found generous readers and terrific guidance in Deirdre de la Cruz, Martin Manalansan, Akiko Takeyama, and Ara Wilson. Thanks, too, to Sumanth Gopinath, Jason Stanyek, Carole McGranahan, and John Collins for editorial work on my publications; Sumanth especially has been a lovely colleague from afar.

Outside of my official institutional affiliations, I have found a scholarly and spiritual home in the Association for Asian American Studies (AAAS). The care, warmth, and brilliance of the scholars who constitute the association is humbling, to say the least. I presented an early draft of the introduction for this book at the AAAS Faculty Workshop retreat at Northwestern University in 2014, where Nitasha Sharma and Tina Chen, and the members of our breakout group—Jason Chang, Julian Lim, Kevin Escudero, Jeannie Shinozuka, and Melissa Borja—read it with rigor and offered encouragement. Over the years of attending AAAS, I have had the honor and privilege of presenting my work alongside Michael Paul Atienza, Fritzie de Mata, Josen Diaz, Robert Diaz, Valerie Francisco, Faith Kares, Victor Roman Mendoza, Joseph Ponce, and Joseph Allen Ruanto-Ramirez, and I have learned so much from Vivek Bald, Genevieve Clutario, Augusto Espiritu, Kale Bantigue Fajardo, Vernadette Gonzalez, Theo Gonzalvez, Allan Isaac, Martin Manalansan, Christopher Patterson, and Robyn Rodriguez. Stanley Thangaraj, whom I met through AAAS and who quickly brought me into the fold of a New York City–based writing group that included Griselda Rodriguez and Brian Montes, and, later, included Sarah Muir and Lili Shi, has been a sharp reader and enthusiastic colleague. In the Philippines I found generous support and friendship from Oscar Campomanes and Cori Perez, who gave me an intellectual home away from home at the Ateneo de Manila University, and brilliance, inspiration, and solidarity from Sarah Raymundo, from the University of the Philippines Dilliman.

In New York City I have wonderful friends and confidants who have responded to year after year of incremental updates about the book with unwavering excitement. Emily Clark continues to inspire my writing and other creative projects, while sustaining me through salad dinners on weeknights and afternoon hangouts on the weekend. Carolyn and David Hahn have shown me a level of warmth, caring, and kindness that I look forward to returning over a lifetime of friendship. Kavita Das and Om Aurora have been delightful dinner companions over the years, and I cherish the parallel progress of Kavita's book and my own; it's been fun having a friend and cousin-in-law to trade updates on drafts and the process as a whole. With Isra Ali I have enjoyed mutual cheerleading of our academic accomplishments and not an insignificant amount of fried chicken and pastry. With Amy H. I have shared so much of myself and received twenty years of love, peace, and refuge in return.

To my family: Sid Iyer helped secure the quiet space that I need to write but also made possible beautiful vacations and relaxing Saturdays that helped me forget about the book altogether, often by crowding out my neurotic thoughts with his brilliant humor and engaging conversation. Thank you, Sid, for reminding me that I can only ever do my best and hoping for my sake that I don't. My parents, Elma and Tony Padios, gave me the tools to not only write a book but *believe* I could write a book, which is half the battle. Elma Padios now knows more about how academic books get published than she ever expected, and her care, attention, and prayers have meant the world to me. My sister, Mae-Marie Coleman, could not have been a greater model of how to remain focused and persevere despite obstacles and adversity—something it turns out is quite important when writing a book! Also, let the record show that my sister was incredibly nice to me when we were young. People say it's the gap in our ages, but I know it's because my sister possesses magnificent powers of care and attention, a vitality I see at work with her husband and son, whom I am grateful to have as a brother-in-law and a nephew. Elson, Norma, and Megan Delid—always right across the Hudson River and always willing to take me (or my stuff) into their home—have shown me steady support since I made New York City my home over twenty years ago. The warmth and love of the members of the Maghinay family and the Padios clan—spread across many provinces, islands, oceans, and continents—have touched every aspect of this book; in many ways, they were its primary motivation. I do not exaggerate when I say none of this would have been possible without Mia and Dixon Chiu, whose care for me in the summer of 2005 was formidable; may Mia, Dylan, Damien, and Mckhyla Brielle get all that they wish for in life, for they surely deserve it. My cousin Tristan (Che Che) Dela Torre Capiendo has been a wonderful friend and informal research assistant to whom I owe a great debt of gratitude. Last but not least, Hema and Sivan Iyer have been well-wishers for my success for many years now. I look forward to finding more ways for us to connect as a family.

Finally, there is nothing like writing a book to remind you of all the people who showed you the treasures and joys of literacy. I had many (public school!) teachers—Shelley Sawyers, Denise Ousley, Barbara Walker, and Kristy Kosaka—and professors at Columbia University, especially Taylor Carman, who showed me how to love not only reading but rereading, not only writing but revising, not only books but scholarship. From there came a world of possibilities, including the chance to work with the remarkable Ken Wissoker, who saw this book from start to finish and offered expert guidance along the way; Olivia Polk, who provided invaluable editorial assistance and soothed my anxiety with her quick and thorough email responses; Jade Brooks, who shepherded the book in its early stages; Lisa Bintrim and Susan Albury, who managed the book project, including overseeing the expert copyediting for which Duke books are renowned; Bonnie Perkel, who helped secure subvention; Chad Royal, who set the marketing in motion; and Steve Cohn and Elizabeth Ault, who made *A Nation on the Line* available to Knowledge Unlatched, which will in turn make the book available open access. To them, the many staff members at Duke University Press working behind the scenes, the Duke Faculty Board, and the anonymous reviewers of this book's early drafts, I owe a great many thanks.

INTRODUCTION

In 2006 an unsettling event took place in my extended family. One of my young cousins in the Philippines, a nursing school graduate on the verge of obtaining her license and thus the chance to live and work in the United States, disappeared from home. As an adolescent, Jocelyn had been known for somewhat impetuous behavior; still, everyone worried. Weeks later, Jocelyn phoned her mother—a widow with three younger children—to let her know that she was safe, living on a neighboring island, and had gotten a job in a call center answering outsourced customer service calls for a U.S.-based cable company. The pay, she explained, was substantial. At ₱15,000 per month, she was earning more money than her peers who worked in fields like accounting or architecture, and although she was assigned overnight shifts, she had also made a lot of friends and could afford to rent a small apartment with three other women. Jocelyn also informed her mother that she would not be taking the nursing board exams as planned, because she did not want to migrate to the United States as many women in our family had done before her. In this way, my cousin's actions had emotional and financial repercussions of transnational proportions. Poor and without work, Jocelyn's mother had long relied on the remittances of her sisters-in-law living in America—the nurses whose path Jocelyn was expected to follow—and indeed Jocelyn's education and all her living expenses had been paid for with money these women sent back home with the expectation that, once working full time, Jocelyn on her own would provide for her mother and siblings. It was, as many in our family would say, her turn.

After the smoke from our little scandal cleared, I began to wonder about the job my cousin had taken as a call center agent. What did it entail? Why was she so drawn to it, despite our family's potential disapproval and her other options? And what did it mean that Jocelyn, who did not migrate to the United States for work, ended up employed by a U.S. corporation and serving Americans on the phone every night anyhow? A few months later, while spending the summer living in Metro Manila, I realized that Jocelyn's story was not at all unique. All around me, I saw young, college-educated, and English-fluent Filipinos eagerly lining up for jobs in the country's hottest new workplaces, where 1–800 numbers connect customer service and technical support agents like my cousin and her friends to homes and offices across America, as well as in England, Australia, and New Zealand. Tucked away in highly securitized office buildings and tethered to headsets and desktop computers, call center employees book airline reservations, troubleshoot wireless routers, or track insurance claims—all in the so-called neutral or light accents for which Filipinos are often known in the industry and beyond. Catering to customers in Western time zones, transnational call center work in the Philippines extends from dusk to dawn, cutting workers off from the normal rhythms of social life and fortifying not only their camaraderie but also the new night culture that surrounds them.

It did not take long for me to see that, in this former U.S. colony, call centers are a story with national and global proportions. Call center work takes place in office spaces, often quite large, where employees stationed at individual cubicles answer or make calls and queries on behalf of companies or corporations; such interactions can involve customer service, technical support, telemarketing, or debt collection. In the late 1990s, U.S.-based firms began outsourcing this work offshore to Asia, starting a competition among developing countries for jobs in global services. From a few hundred employees in 1997, the Philippine call center industry had expanded to 20,000 "seats" or positions by 2004 and then multiplied twelve times in a mere two years, reaching 240,000 employees by 2006. By 2011 the Philippines had surpassed India—a country with more than eight times the productive capacity—to become what a *New York Times* reporter referred to as "the call center capital of the world."[1] As 2015 came to a close, the industry counted 1.1 million people in direct employment and $22 billion in revenue—approximately 7.5 percent of the country's gross domestic product (GDP) and just $4 million short of the remittances from all 1.8 million overseas Filipino workers combined.[2] Indeed, what had started off as a few call centers in the economic development zones surrounding the former U.S. military bases known as Subic and Clark had transformed the urban landscape throughout the archipelago, marking the emergence of the industry as arguably the single most important social, cultural, and economic development in the country in the twenty-first century.

Along with this explosive growth and feverish enthusiasm have come seismic shifts in the symbolic economy surrounding the Philippines as well. The superlative success of the country in the global services market has come to support an overarching hope that the call center industry—or, more specifically, business process management, global in-house call centers, health information management, and knowledge process outsourcing— will advance Filipinos' march to modernity by steering the Philippines into the terrain of the knowledge economy.[3] Within this new national narrative, Philippine call centers are seen as counterpoints to the nation's decades-long employment crisis, its reliance on overseas workers, and the global perception of the Philippines as the economically feeble "sick man of Asia." Such optimism was further buoyed by what economic pundits described as the country's impressive economic performance during the administration of Benigno "Noynoy" S. Aquino III, from June 2010 to June 2016. For five of the former president's six years in office, the country saw real GDP growth averaging 6.1 percent a year; during Aquino's term, the country also earned investment-grade status for the first time in history, the Philippine Stock Exchange Index increased massively, and the nation paid off its debt to the International Monetary Fund.[4] Coupled with the U.S. financial crisis that began in 2007, these remarkable economic developments have fostered the image of an economically ascending Philippines that will not be left behind if, as many geopolitical watchdogs predict, the epicenter of the twenty-first-century global economy shifts toward Asia.

A Nation on the Line argues that the offshore call center is a touch-stone of the Philippine nation-state's aspirations for greater status in the global economy and, more specifically, a reconfigured relationship with the United States. Entailing more than just a set of jobs related to mundane matters like printers and mobile phones, call centers have been framed as a way for industry leaders, state actors, and workers alike to affirm the Philippines' readiness to compete in the neoliberal marketplace while challenging the economic and cultural hegemony of the United States. Like many of its neighbors in East and Southeast Asia, the Philippines' economic star has been rising, ostensibly granting it an opportunity to reinvent or revise its historical image as a third-world country and rework its material and symbolic relations with other nations—what Kimberly Hoang, writing about Vietnam, describes as "a platform to articulate new national ideals that challenge common representations of poverty in the Global South and the latter's oppressed relation to the West."[5] Indeed, I understand the Philippine call center industry as a canvas on which Filipinos attempt to project to themselves and the wider world an image of a new, technologically sophisticated, and globally competitive postcolonial country. Even more important, however, *A Nation on the Line* exposes the fault lines in this neoliberal terrain. The book demonstrates, for example, how this "sunrise industry" incites both national pride and deep anxiety about the nation's future and its colonial past; how call center agents, cast by the Philippine state as the nation's new heroes (*bagong bayani*), are simultaneously subject to intense scrutiny for their educational choices, consumption habits, and sexual practices; and how, despite its economic promise, the cultural and social value of call center work is anything but stable.[6]

The contours and contradictions of the Philippines' new national image come into even sharper relief when seen through the lenses of race, gender, sexuality, and ability. In the region and the world at large, the Philippines has long been marked as an easily exploitable source of feminized labor for nursing, domestic labor, or sex work. However, with their proximity to information technology (IT) and evocation of knowledge work, call centers enable state and industry actors to craft a counterimage of the country as a source of higher-order white-collar labor, or mental labor rather than labor in a bodily mode. Moreover, because the majority of offshore work originates from U.S. companies, industry enthusiasts see call centers as a sign of U.S. confidence in Filipinos' competence, professionalism, and dependability. In the triumphant language of the free market, Asia's sick man has not only been rehabilitated but is literally and figuratively called on to aid the United States and other powerful countries in a united partnership built on mutual trust and investment. The growth of call centers in the twenty-first century thus appears to signal the possibility that Filipinos could challenge—or perhaps even subvert—the racialized and feminized global hierarchies of labor and value in which the country has long been at or near the bottom.

Weaving between and gathering details from multiple call centers, including one where I applied and trained for a customer service job, *A Nation on the Line* tracks how this new national narrative and image of the Philippines is socially and culturally constructed in the everyday spaces and operations of the industry. At the same time, the book reveals the fragility of these ideological structures, as critiques of U.S. hegemony are destabilized by the demand for call center workers to speak American English and cope with customer racism and xenophobia, and the belief in the promise of call center work is undercut by its feminized and racialized status as the most routine and rationalized of offshore services. Nowhere are these tensions and anxieties more apparent than in the everyday lives of call center workers themselves. From their office cubicles to the intimate spaces of their homes, workers struggle to affirm, revise, or otherwise make sense of the unfolding global scene in which they are cast—and see themselves—as key actors, literally and figuratively performing the nation for many around the world. More specifically, the book details the intense efforts of call center workers, along with industry leaders and the state, to redefine and relegitimize the meaning and value of Filipino labor, culture, and value. One of this book's primary claims, for example, is that the relational demands of call center work—the imperative that Filipino agents identify and communicate with U.S.-based customers and therefore America as a material location and imaginary space—draw on and intensify an affective capacity I refer to as *Filipino/American relatability.* Culturally constructed within the affective architecture of U.S. empire, Filipino/American relatability encompasses the ways Filipinos and the Philippines have maintained an affinity with Americans and America—from popular culture to the educational system—during and since colonization. I demonstrate that, with the embrace of the call center industry, Filipino/American relatability has been transformed into a type of social capital and cultural resource fueling the Philippines' neoliberal aspirations and supporting its new national narratives, and thus a primary way the nation-state reconfigures the meaning and value of Filipino labor and culture in the contemporary era—but often with contradictory consequences.

In these ways, the burgeoning call center industry and the shifting ideological currents that it helps set in motion create the conditions for a new type of Filipino subject—one who performs proximity to America while simultaneously disavowing U.S. hegemony; who embodies productivity through work, consumption, and even intimate relationships; and who sees in the global economy a way forward for oneself, one's family, and the nation. Starting with a detailed look at call center labor processes and work cultures, and ending with an analysis of the queering of the Philippine call center industry, *A Nation on the Line* traces the outlines of these new subjectivities and the hope, precarity, and anxiety young Filipinos experience in and through call center work. Rather than attempt to resolve the tensions and anxieties it identifies, *A Nation on the Line* analyzes their construction—that is, how and why call centers constitute a social and cultural predicament in the contemporary Philippines and how workers negotiate these circumstances. As my opening story only begins to suggest, the book demonstrates how the Philippine nation-state's embrace of market-based priorities, projects, and narratives both relies on and reshapes the everyday lives and labor of Filipino call center workers, and thus shows how neoliberal globalization is reconfiguring identities, subjectivity, family, and nation. What I came to learn about these complex dynamics—and their deep roots in the history of U.S. empire, Philippine postcolonial struggles, and the postindustrial vicissitudes of labor and capital—constitutes the core of this transnational ethnography.[7]

The Philippines as a Site of Knowledge Production

With the advancement and intensification of capitalism around the world over the past twenty-five to thirty years, the logic and lexicon of the free market have become powerful but problematic tools for nations, especially postcolonial countries and other countries in the global south, to renegotiate or revise their material and symbolic status within the global economy.[8] Understanding this revision process provides a significant opportunity to assess the political-economic and discursive articulations of neoliberal globalization and thus the ways that these processes are reproduced through but also contingent on historically specific conditions and places. In the Philippines, state actors, industry leaders, and workers alike adopt the dominant rhetoric of the knowledge economy in an effort to transform uneven relations of dependence on the United States and the cultural legacy of American colonialism into relations with the United

States based on partnership, investment, and human capital—the watch-words of the twenty-first century. In this way, the Philippines conforms to what Monica Heller describes as a post–Cold War geopolitics in which re-lations between former empires and colonies have been reconceptualized "as collaborative rather than hierarchical and as aimed at economic devel-opment and competition rather than servicing the nation or the imperial center."[9] Within this neoliberal rubric, the legacies of empire—manifest, for example, in Filipino/American relatability—are reinterpreted as valu-able resources or assets within the capitalist marketplace. Demonstrated most clearly in relation to the English language, such symbolic shifts are not isolated to the Philippines. As scholars have recently shown, while for centuries the value of English has been derived from its association with colonial power, in the twenty-first century English is increasingly seen as a commodity owned by its postcolonial speakers, just one of many linguis-tic assets "to be discretely enumerated and labeled like items of jewelry or parcels of real estate" and valued for its promise of market access.[10] In the Philippines, which saw the domestication of American English into Phil-ippine English in the 1990s, a postcolonial nationalist ideology emerged that disavows U.S. cultural authority while simultaneously embracing the English language and the global economic arena whose doors it ostensibly unlocks. Within this new national narrative, Filipinos are not supplicant to the United States and global capital but rationally responding to the global market's demand for workers with exceptional affective abilities. *A Nation on the Line* thus unpacks these nested ideologies of nationalism and neoliberalism, revealing how they create new social and cultural possibil-ities while exacerbating or obscuring older problems and predicaments.

As a constitutive feature of the Philippines' neoliberal project and nar-ratives, call centers offer an exemplary and pointed perspective on the na-tion's larger efforts at repositioning and redefining Filipino labor, culture, and value in the contemporary era. Offshore call centers also offer a way to further understand how new arrangements of work and emerging work cultures in the global south change not only national narratives and aspi-rations but also the fabric of everyday life, modes of subjectivity, and facets of identity.[11] Like the textile mill of the nineteenth century or the automo-bile factory of the early twentieth, the call centers exemplifies the definitive features of its time: a fixation with language and information, 24/7 cycles of production that span the globe, and increasing labor precarity. Despite the complexities of call center work, however, scholars have either celebrated call centers as a "passage beyond the drudgery of factory life" and into the interactive and expressive realm of the new economy, or painted a "dispiriting image of a subjugated workforce" engaged in rationalized and highly surveilled tasks that offer little to no autonomy or authentic expression.[12] *A Nation on the Line* takes a different tack. I examine how the emotional and relational demands of call center work make possible both dismal toil and joyful camaraderie, thus defining call centers as spaces where capital reaches deep into worker subjectivity while creating more channels for affirmative communication and relations between workers.[13] The book also considers how many of the characteristics of the late-capitalist or postindustrial workplace in the United States—including no-collar culture, Theory Y management, "presence bleed," and the language of work-life balance—have made their way from American offices to call centers in Manila, Cebu, Bacolod, and many other Philippine cities.[14] Moreover, by paying close attention to the way that the meaning and experience of call center work extend beyond the call center proper and into the marketplace and home—linking it to the social reproduction of status, gender and sexual identity, and aspirations for the nation at large—the book traverses the conventional boundaries that separate the labor process or workplace from other aspects of workers' lives.[15]

By investigating life and labor at the other end of 1–800 lines, *A Nation on the Line* adds a new dimension to our current understanding of postindustrial processes by analyzing how they shape and are shaped by local cultures and identities, as well as national histories and ideologies.[16] The offshore outsourced call centers that have come to fill the Philippines' urban landscape were made possible by advances in technology as well as the increasing hegemony of neoliberalism as an economic philosophy and set of business practices that compelled corporations to get lean by shifting so-called noncore business operations to cheaper locales, such as Ireland and, later, India and countries of Southeast Asia. Often already primed by structural adjustment policies that pried open their economies for foreign investors, by the end of the twentieth century a number of poor countries were offering up land, labor, and state support to offshore outsourcing companies. Despite the global context in which they emerged, the disciplinary lines drawn around the study of call centers have made it difficult to see the meaning of these postindustrial workplaces within a larger arena of transnational power relations and postcolonial cultural politics. Where such scholarship has emerged, it has been bound geographically, historically, and culturally around India, even as it positions Indian call center workers as both national and diasporic subjects and thus reveals the cultural complexities of global service work.[17] Such scholarship also tends to focus on a particular range of policies, protocols, and experiences within call center work, especially the demand that Indian call center agents adopt Western accents, names, and locations as part of their service delivery, or the subjective liminality that results from Indian workers' negotiation between different temporal, geographic, and cultural zones. In contrast to this earlier work, *A Nation on the Line* is less focused on how call center workers' identities become hybridized or destabilized and more attentive to what call centers can tell us about a postcolonial nation and its citizens at a historically specific transnational juncture shaped by postcolonial relations of power. To these ends, the book seeks out the meaning and experience of call center work for Filipinos, who, unlike Indians, have been negotiating labor, culture, identity, and value vis-à-vis the United States for well over a century. By situating Philippine call centers within a broad context triangulated by the cultures of U.S. imperialism, postcolonial politics, and postindustrialism, *A Nation on the Line* analyzes how these unique workplaces are embedded in "colonial histories, class relations, and national interests," an approach other scholars have gestured to but not fully explored.[18]

By contextualizing the figure of the Filipino call center agent within the overlapping structures of transnational service work, Philippine postcolonialism, and the history of U.S. empire, *A Nation on the Line* forges an intervention within our larger understanding of how affect and affective labor are produced and deployed.[19] In tracing how Filipinos' subjective capacities are appropriated by the U.S. customer service industry, I develop the concept of relational labor, or the labor required to positively identify with, signal proximity to, and effectively communicate with others, particularly in ways that meet the demands of capital. I then move on to theorize Filipino/American relatability as an affective orientation and type of social capital that emerges from colonialist structures of power, including discourse about the English language as the basis of affective bonds between Americans and Filipinos and the ostensible benevolence of U.S. empire. The book understands Filipino relational labor as crucial to scholarly discussions of how social capacities are grounded not in essentialist or a priori human states but historically specific power structures, and thus how efforts to analyze the proliferation of jobs that require care, intimacy, and relatability must be grounded in an understanding of the ways such capacities have been extracted from particular racialized and gendered subjects over time.[20] As Nicholas J. Long and Henrietta L. Moore argue, the definition of human sociality as an innate capacity obscures how the ability to be social relies on the composition of a person's context and thus "ignores or presumes an answer to the question of why that capacity is deployed in the first place."[21] In this way, *A Nation on the Line* challenges the abstract language of ability and resource that underwrites the contemporary era's excitement about human capital and obsession with how to unleash it—language that inhibits critical inquiry into how relational or other types of intangible labor are always perceived and valued through hierarchies or ideologies of difference.

Finally, this project addresses itself to knowledge production within critical Filipino American and Philippine scholarship, taking up and building on the latter's predominant and often overlapping themes of U.S. empire and militarism in the Philippines; Filipino diaspora, labor, and labor migration; and the formation of national and transnational Filipino subjectivities and imaginaries.[22] This literature has not only recovered the Philippines and Filipinos from the silenced and hidden spaces of the past and present but also challenged structures of white supremacy, gender/sexual regimes of power, and the capitalist exploitation to which Filipino peoples have been subject throughout the nation's history of colonization and independence. Moreover, by focusing on key figures of Filipino labor, such as the Filipino nurse, sex worker, caregiver, seafarer, and factory worker, this scholarship has laid the groundwork for an understanding of the Philippines as a primary site for the production of workers and thus value around the world. *A Nation on the Line* places Filipino call center workers on a historical continuum with these other figures, tracing the way call center agents are imbricated within overlapping regimes of national, transnational, and global labor and capital, and asking what the call center worker can tell us about the constitutive role of race, gender, and sexuality in the operations of global capitalism and U.S. empire.[23]

However, while the book reveals how Filipino call center agents have much in common with other Filipino workers, it also makes clear the conditions that set them apart. Unlike previous generations of agricultural workers, nurses, or domestic helpers, Filipinos willing to work graveyard shifts and learn the byzantine policies of American customer service do not have to physically leave the country for higher wages abroad. "Abroad" has been planted in their own backyards, allowing U.S. capital to reap the benefits of Filipinos' labor without bodies crossing national borders. Indeed, Filipino call center workers' simultaneous physical location within and imaginative orientation outside the Philippines, their inclusion in postindustrial corporate workspaces, and the particularities of their social and class identities offer unique insights into the contemporary Philippines and Filipino subject formation. As Alinaya Sybilla L. Fabros writes, Filipino call center agents engage in "undervalued and hidden forms of work to overcome the global distance that the call center platform traverses," a type of social and symbolic work that entails "manufacturing proximity."[24] The desire and capacity to achieve this proximity, I argue, are grounded in Filipino/American relatability, which I understand not as a superstructural outcome of competition in the global labor market or as a sign of false consciousness, but as part of the structure of feeling surrounding the United States in the Philippine postcolonial imaginary and thus part of the material conditions of possibility of the present. At the same time, as a structure that rests on notions of benevolence and affinity, Filipino/American relatability also upholds the exceptionalist narrative of mutual and reciprocal U.S.-Philippine relations.[25] In what follows, I uncover how these narratives of empire and nation circulate within the Philippine call center industry, reinforcing the notion that Filipinos are affectively gifted and thus are reproducing a form of Philippine, as well as U.S., exceptionalism.

A Nation on the Line traces how workers, industry leaders, and state actors leverage the call center industry as a way to revise the twentieth-century narrative of U.S.-Philippine relations that casts the Philippines as culturally and socially inferior to its former colonizer and thus as a source of easily exploitable, cheap labor. *A Nation on the Line* documents how a complex and contradictory set of ideas, experiences, and feelings about Filipino identity, the Philippine nation-state, and the United States plays out in the Philippine call center industry. While much of the call center training I witnessed instructed agents in what Winifred Poster has referred to as "national identity management"—including how to subordinate Filipino cultural and linguistic traits that might be distracting to callers—employees forged an equally if not more powerful countercurriculum that insisted not only on the primacy and integrity of Filipino identity but also on the idea of a United States in decline.[26] Interrogating the many tensions and contradictions within these efforts, *A Nation on the Line* offers a critique of the way postcolonial nationalist ideologies become nested in the practice of neoliberalism. At stake in this investigation are nothing less than the nation, postcolonial or otherwise, as an imagined location and material entity; the narratives of progress, power, and freedom that press it forward; and the seductive image of capitalism and the market that binds it together. Uncovering the contradictions and problems inherent in each of these projects, *A Nation on the Line* reveals the need for new stories and trajectories by which Filipinos might live and prosper.

Backdrops and Origins

Sick Man, Mistress, Brother, Child: Narratives of the Twentieth Century

Twentieth-century Philippine history forms the critical backdrop for my analysis of culture, labor, and value as predicaments for the Philippine nation-state in the twenty-first century. The year 1898 saw the end of over three hundred years of Spanish colonization of the Philippine Islands, as Filipino revolutionaries rose up against the Spanish crown and the Catholic priests who wielded its power in the archipelago. As the final act of a crumbling empire, Spain ceded ownership and control over the Philippines, Puerto Rico, Guam, and Cuba to the United States, whose imperial designs already extended to the Caribbean and Latin America by the end of the nineteenth century. With the acquisition of the Philippines, the United States could maintain a strategic military outpost in Asia as well as gateways to new markets in the region, China being the most important of them. Yet the extension of U.S. sovereignty over the Philippines was met by violent resistance from Filipinos fighting to retain the independent republic established by General Emilio Aguinaldo in 1899, leading to the Philippine-American War. Officially ending in 1902—with ongoing battles continuing in the countryside until 1906—wartime gave way to the creation of an American colonial state whose goal was to modernize the Filipino people, integrate its economy into the growing global capitalist marketplace (of which the United States considered itself an emerging leader), and shape Filipino culture through the imposition of American democratic institutions, American education, and instruction in the English language. Endorsing the models of cultural racism emerging at the end of the nineteenth century, the American colonial state thus regarded Filipinos as an inferior people with the potential for development—that is, a race of children whose maturation it would be the burden of white Americans to set in motion.

From the occupation's start, the American colonists cast their control over the Philippines as exceptional in the way it braided authority with affection, and friendship with force. Writing from the executive mansion in 1898, President William McKinley instructed military commanders in the islands "to announce and proclaim in the most public manner that we come not as invaders or conquerors, but as friends, to protect the natives in their homes, in their employments, and in their personal and religious rights."[27] By grafting American institutions and culture onto Filipino life, the United States attempted to make the Philippines into its image, a project that Americans believed would lead to "confidence, respect, and affection" between Americans and Filipinos as two distinct "races."[28] In other words, the Americans endeavored to transform the Filipinos into colonial subjects who could *relate* positively to American people, institutions, and ways of life—that is, subjects who would see in themselves and their futures the outlines and fulfillment of American ideals and therefore would understand and identify with, rather than be alienated by, the social forces and cultural practices in which they were increasingly enveloped. Such relatability was also tied to communication. By instructing Filipinos in and through the English language, the American colonists created subjects whose ability to understand and speak the language of colonial power allowed that power to be exercised through shared, albeit drastically unequal, subjectivity.[29] Such efforts reflected the colonizers' desire to always be addressed in and on their literal and figurative terms and to achieve harmonious proximity with colonial subjects through a shared language. According to the Thomasites, American teachers dispatched from the United States to Manila on the ss *Thomas* in 1901, the United States had "found herself confronted by a great problem dealing with a people who neither know nor understand the underlying principles of our civilization, yet who, for our mutual happiness and liberty, must be brought into accord with us. Between them and us is a chasm which must be bridged by a common knowledge and sympathy; fellowship must be made possible."[30] Infamously referred to by Americans as their "little brown brothers," Filipinos were subject to a form of racism that presumed an affective, even familial, attachment between colonized and colonizer. In the paternalistic, exceptionalist framework of U.S. colonization, Filipinos and Americans were members of the same family.

U.S. colonization of the Philippines has long been understood as a project of American simulation. However, the colonial endeavor rested on the more fundamental idea that Filipinos were indeed *capable* of observing, understanding, adopting, and relating to American ways of life. In other words, to convince themselves and the world of their exceptional and benevolent rule, Americans were bound to the idea that their subjects had the capacity to be like their rulers in the first place—even if, as racialized colonial subjects, Filipinos would always find themselves coming up short in the rulers' estimation.[31] Filipino/American relatability—the capacity of Filipinos/the Philippines to become like Americans/America—thus became the cultural cornerstone of U.S. exceptionalism; without its promise, the ideology of American benevolence would be logically incomplete. In this way, the American colonial era allowed for the cultivation of Filipino/American relatability as an affective orientation that successive generations of Filipinos would come to understand as an exceptional aspect of Filipino subjectivity. From this affective economy emerged the belief in a special relationship between the United States and the Philippines—what Dylan Rodríguez refers to as a vernacular narrative of "historical congruence."[32] Within this narrative, World War II figures as a "genesis moment of political union and nationalist coalescence" between the United States as an allied power and the Philippines, which fought alongside it.[33]

The narrative of special or exceptional U.S.-Philippine relations in turn provided crucial cultural support for U.S. control of the Philippine economy in the later decades of the twentieth century. Following a period of post–World War II prosperity connected to the nationalization of industries and the growth of home markets, by the end of the 1960s the Philippines was on a course toward the economic crises, increased poverty, and indebtedness that gained it the moniker "the sick man of Asia." Upon his extralegal assumption of the presidency in 1969, Ferdinand Marcos turned to the International Monetary Fund and the World Bank for loans to cover the nation's extant debts. Together, Marcos, the World Bank, and the International Monetary Fund began to transform the Philippines into an export-oriented economy catering to U.S. and other foreign manufacturers in search of low-wage workers—especially women—for light manufacturing and assembly work. As in countries all over the developing world, these early neoliberal machinations sank the Philippines into a protracted debt crisis and created massive poverty. As a result, the nation's greatest export became Filipino citizens themselves. Filipinos went abroad in large numbers starting in the 1970s to work as nurses, domestic helpers, and contract laborers in the United States, the United Kingdom, Hong Kong, Singapore, and the Middle East, which was a process facilitated heavily by the brokering power of the Philippine state.[34] At the same time, the Philippines also saw the rise of a prostitution economy, spurred by the ongoing presence of U.S. armed forces in the islands following independence as well as the transnational migration of Filipinas as sex industry entertainers or mail-order brides.[35]

By the time of the People Power Revolution of 1986, the popular uprising that deposed Marcos and brought Corazon Aquino into power, the nation's external debt was just north of $26 billion.[36] Although a number of enterprises were privatized under Aquino's administration, the neoliberal reforms that further entangled the Philippines in the global economy, including the globalization of services, began with the Ramos administration in the mid-1990s. With its sights set on the Philippines becoming Asia's knowledge center, Ramos's staff of advisers—who had been trained in neoliberal economic and political philosophy in the United States—deregulated, liberalized, and privatized large sectors of the national economy, starting with the telecommunications industry.[37] From there, they strengthened the nation's information communications infrastructure, especially access to the Internet, through administrative orders and projects such as IT21—policies designed to advance the Philippines' integration into the knowledge economy and thus boost the national economy into the twenty-first century.[38] Yet the appeal of neoliberalism for the Philippine nation-state was not simply about economics but also cultural politics. Upgrading the Philippines through technology and knowledge was also framed as a way to make the Philippines a prime place of investment in more highly valued cognitive labor rather than the mere extraction of labor from Filipino bodies. Again, the metaphors of gender, sexuality, and ability through which these shifting geopolitical relations became legible cannot be underscored enough. For much of the twentieth century, the Philippines was the object of literal and figurative penetration by the United States, for which Filipinos produced pleasure in the form of surplus value extracted from them through bodily or manual labor.[39] With the economic reforms of the late 1990s, however, the Philippine state embarked on a plan that, as Robyn Rodriguez has described, signaled the nation's "invest[ment] in recuperating its feminized status through policy interventions that conform to hegemonic white, masculinized global conventions," including an embrace of neoliberal programs focused on technology and knowledge.[40] In these imaginaries, gender and sexuality are not "mere metaphors" for the operations of capital. Rather, they enable those operations by giving meaning to and thus further compelling the material relations on which capital accumulation relies.[41]

By the end of the twentieth century, the Philippine state had thus begun to assume greater authority with regard to overseas workers by framing labor migration as a development strategy, defining the privileges and responsibilities of labor migrants, and strengthening its overall powers as a labor brokerage state.[42] Moreover, the state's intense promotion and pursuit of IT at home allowed for a shift toward the race- and gender-neutral terms of the knowledge economy. Within this symbolic landscape, foreign investment loses the stigma of nonconsensual penetration and feminized dependence because the Philippine state assumes a masculine posture by brokering—that is to say, controlling and disciplining—transnational feminized labor while enhancing the possibilities of breadwinning from home. The hegemonic rhetoric of the market thus offers ways for the Philippine nation-state to assert autonomy because of, and not despite, the continuous flow of U.S. and other foreign capital into its economy—a revision process that is articulated in and through the development of offshore call centers.

Gender, Race, and the Invention of "1–800"
Since the tumultuous waves of U.S. corporate downsizing and restructuring of the 1990s, customer service outsourcing has held an especially loathsome place in the American imagination. As the shareholder revolution and corporate raiding destabilized the U.S. labor market at the end of the twentieth century, American workers disproportionately targeted their

rage about the loss of "their" jobs at the people on the other end of customer service lines. However, despite the heightened attention they received at the end of the twentieth century, call centers have been a fixture of the American service economy since the early 1980s. The term *call center* is in fact a generic name for a workplace where employees handle a wide range of outsourced business processes, such as medical billing or accounts receivable. In industry parlance, customer service or technical support call centers constitute just one component of business process outsourcing (BPO) or business process management firms, which provide back-office voice and data support to mostly North American, European, and Anglo-Pacific companies. While some U.S. companies still maintain their own in-house call centers, or contract with BPO firms located within the United States, late twentieth-century deregulation compelled many companies to contract with third-party outsourcing firms—often also North American or European companies—which set up offices in developing countries to fill these service positions at a much lower cost.[43] In a highly uneven arrangement both emblematic of global spatial-economic restructuring since the 1970s and reproductive of north-south colonial relations, offshore BPO firms benefit from low labor costs, the absence and/or repression of union activity, and nearly tax-free use of the land and infrastructure.

Today's call center is the product of two different but integrally related functions: telephone operations and customer service. Historically, both have relied heavily on female workforces. Indeed, at the turn of the twentieth century, telephone service *was* customer service, and the hello girls at the other end of the line—chosen for their adherence to Victorian bourgeois ideals of female civility, gentility, and servitude—assured its quality and efficiency, while also preventing male customers from expressing anger when the phone service overall was faulty.[44] Meanwhile, as the sphere of customer service grew after the Great Depression, it went from a type of work dominated by male shop clerks to one that employed women in greater and greater numbers.[45] By the 1950s, customer service jobs in the United States, especially in suburbs, were predominantly occupied by women who worked part-time for minimum wage, with no union representation and limited opportunities for career advancement.[46] From their early days, telephone and customer service were understood not only as jobs held by women but as positions specifically *for* women, and customers and employers alike came to associate these areas with the social pleasantry and caring nature they assumed women naturally possessed and exhibited. Moreover, the feminization of telephone and customer service—and their racialization as well—is integrally tied to how labor processes have been increasingly differentiated and automated, in turn requiring fewer and fewer skills of workers.[47] As Venus Green has demonstrated, until the 1960s most telephone operators in the United States were white, but as the work process was broken down into simpler processes (and integration made possible), the workforce became increasingly populated by African American women.[48]

Also by the 1950s, telephony and customer service had further merged as department store clerks began taking customers' orders and queries by phone. However, not until the consumer movement of the late 1960s and 1970s did companies begin to address consumers' questions and concerns in the highly systematized manner that would eventually launch the customer service systems we know today. This, too, relied on developments in telephony. In the 1960s, touch-tone phones allowed customers not only to call a company but to push a button to reach a particular department, while the creation of the Wide Area Telephone Service lines made possible the first 1–800 numbers. By 1981 General Electric had opened its "GE Answer Center," one of the earliest customer service call centers and an ostensible testament to the company's newfound belief in the loyalty that customer service could inspire in consumers.[49] Indeed, during the 1980s concepts such as customer satisfaction and customer loyalty became full-fledged corporate ideals pondered by men in boardrooms but increasingly left to women working behind counters and telephones to secure for the company.

The feminization and racialization of customer service continued with the emergence of telemarketing companies, one of the main forerunners of large customer service call centers. As a form of part-time sales work that required only a telephone and could be done from home, telemarketing quickly became an industry that employed women in large numbers.[50] By the late 1980s, major retailers reported that 50 to 80 percent of their workforces were composed of women and/or black or Hispanic workers.[51] By the late 1990s, customer service call centers in the United States made up a multi-billion-dollar business that employed "low-cost workers such as students, spouses of full-timers, military personnel, and new labor force entrants," full- or part-time, for average weekly earnings of around $400.[52]

The latter points to another facet of the feminization of call center work: its reliance on and production of worker precarity, or an insecure relation to wages and sources of employment that parallels women's experience in the workforce more broadly.[53] Such instability is further underwritten by the contractual and contingent relationship between outsourced call centers and their corporate clients.

As call centers expanded across America, so too did their technological infrastructure. With advances in computer telephony integration and customer relationship management tools, in-house call centers (customer service centers that were part of a company's operations) quickly became a thing of the past.[54] As early as 1978, third-party BPO firms were offering corporate clients their services in back-office functions like customer care, payroll, and sales.[55] The geography of customer service changed completely, however, with the advent of Internet-based communication network technology and the deregulation of telecommunications industries in countries like Indonesia, India, and the Philippines—developments that followed earlier outsourcing to Ireland and Scotland. These regulatory and technological changes made it possible for firms to move call center operations overseas and thus to pay workers in the developing world a mere fraction of what U.S.-based workers would be paid for the same work.[56] Thus, while the offshore outsourcing of customer service marked a watershed in the history of both customer service and telecommunications—yet another convergence of the histories of these already intertwined services—it also signaled another moment in which race, and now nation, became factors in the structure and value of customer service call center work. The gradual deskilling and feminization of customer service work thus cannot be separated from the shifting of these jobs offshore to developing countries: only because the work has been increasingly fragmented and automated can firms justify paying workers in the Philippines a fraction of the wages paid to workers in the United States. In this way, the transnational offshore customer service call center fits within a trajectory through which customer service workers have been deskilled, feminized, and racialized, producing the uneven structure of global customer service. At the same time, this abstract deskilling process is not enough to explain why call centers have emerged in the particular sites they have. While capitalists use technology to rationalize labor processes, deskill workers, and justify lower wages, they also use differences—in race, gender, nationality, or citizenship—to manage the workforce and select particular workers, such as those with an already existing affinity for U.S. culture and with so-called neutral accents.[57] Thus, the breakdown of call center work, coupled with the need for relational labor performed for a U.S. customer base, led many U.S. corporations to the Philippines at a time when national policies and aspirations were increasingly focused on the knowledge economy.

The Philippines, the Asian Century, and the Economy of Knowledge

Coined in the 1990s, the term *knowledge economy* points to the expansion of production processes that utilize and create knowledge, ideas, and information.[58] Yet the knowledge economy is not simply about a shift toward more immaterial, informational, communicative, or symbolic forms of labor. As Smitha Radhakrishnan argues, "knowledge" has become a powerful discourse of national development meant to signal a developing country's readiness for competition in a global world.[59] Moreover, as Aihwa Ong demonstrates, with the outflow of knowledge-driven jobs from the West to Asia that started in the late twentieth century, knowledge is "no longer the monopoly of middle classes in advanced capitalist countries."[60] The Philippine nation-state's turn toward the knowledge economy starting with the Ramos administration was thus part of a greater embrace of a new development model throughout the global south—one based on global services and manufacturing—as well as a way to affirm the postcolonial country's ascendancy within the world economy. As Walden Bello and colleagues note, the globalization of the Philippine economy has meant the disarticulation of the traditional sectors of the economy (agriculture, industry, and services) from one another, and the reintegration of the latter two sectors with global production and markets. By the early twentieth century, Filipino workers had therefore assumed three positions in the global division of labor: one on the assembly lines for electronic chips for export; another in the transnational flow of skilled, semi-skilled, and unskilled labor; and a third in the offshore sites of business processing activities from developed countries.[61]

Securing a firm place in the knowledge economy has, however, proven vexing for the Philippines, in part because most call center jobs have not required the knowledge, creative power, or technical acumen for which the Philippines aspires to be known. Indeed, the very conception of call center work and the BPO industry as a whole emerged in direct contrast to high-skilled knowledge work. When outsourcing began in the United States, it was often framed by CEOs and managers as a way for companies to focus on their core operations, such as research and development. Core functions were thus categorically defined as requiring the efforts and attention of the most skilled and thus most valuable workers, while the auxiliary, noncore, back-office functions—such as customer service, technical support, data entry, and payroll—could be shunted off to other companies or, increasingly, other parts of the world. According to the hegemonic definition of *knowledge* that emerged with the rise of the knowledge economy, BPO jobs were not necessarily knowledge-based jobs; rather, they were considered part of the vast array of service work that supported business functions that might or might not be geared toward knowledge. Defined by a facility with theory, technological skills, and credentialed expertise, knowledge work was thus increasingly distinguished from "routine information-processing activities in low-discretion environments," which in some definitions explicitly includes call centers.[62] Indeed, according to Paul Blyton and Jean Jenkins, the term *knowledge work* has obscured the full range of physical activity and mental processes that might count as knowledge, including experience and learned routines among workers at lower levels of organizations or within the service industry.[63] As a result, the knowledge required to undertake routine tasks, for example, has become illegible as knowledge work and therefore invisible within the global economy.

As a result, the rationalization of service work over the past thirty years has meant that call center work may, as Monica Heller has described it, "represent opportunity and access to globalization and white-collar jobs or at least economic opportunities that do not require massive labor migration" but at the cost of "the racialization and feminization used in the service of exploitation."[64] For scholars like Czarina Saloma-Akpedonu who have analyzed this complex context in the Philippines, the kind of national "self-imaginings" in which the country can and will attain high status in global IT and knowledge industries therefore requires "the suspension of disbelief."[65] Meanwhile, advocates of the Philippine call center industry wring their hands over how to leverage the country's success in the service industry into an opportunity for jobs that directly serve knowledge-based companies and thus might be properly defined as knowledge related, such as jobs in knowledge process outsourcing or health information management, which serves the ever-valued field of medicine. In this way, the aspirations and rhetoric around IT in general and call centers in particular in the Philippines contribute to the separation of and hierarchy between knowledge and service work. At the same time, call center industry advocates are careful (though not always, as I shall demonstrate) not to devalue customer service and technical support work, often idealizing Filipinos as naturally suited for affective, emotional, and relational labor and all but officially branding the country as a nation of service representatives. The result is a situation in which call center work is the source of both undeniable excitement and also anxiety about whether the Philippines will ever move beyond it to fulfill the aspirations generated by and constitutive of the knowledge economy.

Finally, any discussion of the knowledge-economy paradigm must acknowledge that although it has set the direction for various social and cultural goals at the national and even global levels, it is in fact an elite project that, as Radhakrishnan demonstrates, "tends to foster and enhance the development of an educated professional class."[66] The quest for knowledge-economy jobs thus leads to new ways of reinforcing old exclusions of class status and cultural capital, new functions for the industry to determine standards for measuring human capital, and new incentives for the national educational system to conform to the knowledge economy's standards. In other words, as the goals and the aspirations of the nation change in order to chase value up the chain, the value of labor and the identities derived from work are significantly reconfigured, even as they are propped up by entrenched social structures and blended in with enduring social imaginaries. *A Nation on the Line* tracks these processes within the everyday lives of Filipino call center agents, who are at the forefront of the country's postcolonial struggle and thus face its contradictions and complexities head-on.

Ethnography as Relational Labor

In one of my earliest experiences conducting research for this book, I found myself chatting online and over e-mail with Mia Mendez, a twenty-seven-year-old Filipina who had started an insightful and humorous blog about working in the Philippine offshore call center industry. The blog was based on Mia's several years of experience as a customer service representative and debt collections agent for a major European bank. As she and I communicated back and forth (mostly with me asking questions about her work and the industry at large, and she providing answers), I was struck by a familiar feeling experienced, I imagine, by most ethnographers: overwhelming gratitude that someone—a person halfway around the world whom I had never met, at that—would take time to offer detailed replies to my queries. Soon after our e-mail exchange began, however, I became somewhat concerned about just *how* quickly Mia responded to my e-mails and insisted that she need not rush to get back to me. In what months later (after we met in person) I came to see as her characteristically sharp manner, Mia not only responded to my latest round of questions without delay but also added, "I know you said 'no rush,' but being in the service industry for so long, I consider you as my customer. So I can't help it if I want to reply right away"—a statement to which she appended a smiley-face emoticon.

Mia's treatment of our interaction as a type of service delivery speaks to a number of significant aspects of ethnographic research broadly and my research in particular. First, as I was conducting an ethnography of service workers who have been trained to approach personal interaction and information exchange with courtesy and professionalism, the lines between the process of my ethnographic fieldwork and its content were often blurred. Like Mia, many of my research participants at some point or another seemed to project onto the interview process and researcher-informant relationship the very modes of communication and self-presentation that they were trained to deploy in call center work. For example, through a brief series of e-mails with Julian, a call center agent whom I met on Facebook, I sensed the register and tone of his message change when he self-corrected his initial assumption that I was a student and not a professor with a Ph.D. At first, Julian was apologetic about his error (which I assured him caused no offense on my part); then his language became more formal as he seemed to assume an official role as a representative of the call center industry and stated his interest in "being of service" to me. Indeed, in several fieldwork moments, especially those in which I was studying up by focusing on industry executives and government representatives, my attention and presence were treated as opportunities to sell me on the Philippines as a location for top-notch outsourcing, even though I attempted to clarify my role as a researcher and even shared the writing I was producing as a result.[67] This is not to suggest that research participants were never able to relate to me outside of these frameworks, only that their ways of knowing and speaking—in this case, though service delivery or marketing models—shaped various aspects of our interactions.

Second, Mia's explicit articulation of the manner in which she related to me at that moment caused me to reflect on the social structures and politics of location underlying even these earliest exchanges. Since anthropology's reflexive turn in the 1980s, ethnographers have been hyper-focused on the conditions of ethnography's production, including those moments when the process of ethnographic inquiry itself seems to provide the very content of research.[68] In other words, attending to the context-specific epistemological, ideological, and institutional foundations on which the researcher-subject relation rests is a crucial part of decolonizing ethnographic practice.[69] In my research, the necessity of practicing a decolonized perspective was perhaps most urgent when it came to the very language in which my informants and I communicated. As a U.S.-born Filipina with parents whose ideological positions and cultural investments diminished their desire to teach me their native language of Hiligaynon (Ilonggo)—preferences that undoubtedly reflect a racialized, colonialist hierarchy of values surrounding the English language and the marginal-ization of many immigrants in the United States—I cannot communicate more than rudimentary information in any Filipino language, let alone conduct multiple hours' worth of interviews. My informants, however, by virtue of this hierarchy and its reproduction in the very work that they do and that I set out to study, all spoke fluent English. In turn, these conditions lay the groundwork for my overall critique of colonial histories and postcolonial politics that enable the hegemonic valorization of the English language. The active generation of such critique, rather than passive recognition and confession of my privilege and positionality, to me represents the significance of reflective ethnographic practice.

Being Filipina and American, my identity also complicates the definition of *native* that has dominated the practice of ethnography. Like previous scholars, I question a worldview that sees an isomorphic convergence of people, place, and culture, as histories of imperialism and migration complicate any easy categorization of where someone is from and what culture they call their own. On one hand, having been born in the United

States and lived in the country my entire life, I am not at all native to the Philippines. On the other, because of my status and experience as a Filipina American who had spent the better part of my twenties connecting with my family in the Philippines and conducting my research, my participants seemed to consider me more native than they would a non-Filipino researcher from the United States. Rather than compelling me to stabilize my relation to nativity, these variable perspectives and the vicissitudes of history that they evoke allow me to see that the spectrum of nativity is a cultural construction that dangerously links place of birth to belonging, and identity to a static idea of place and culture. As the daughter of two Filipino immigrants who came to the United States with the force of nearly seventy-five years of U.S. colonization behind them, I have come to understand my belonging or being native to the United States as always already contingent on a racialized and imperial process that both separates me from and also tethers me to the Philippines.

From my early interactions with Mia, I also came to see that ethnographic research, like call center work, requires relational labor. In the next section, I describe the more logistical forms of this labor as I conducted it between 2007 and 2013. What I want to highlight here, however, is how I understand that labor in relation to the politics of ethnographic knowledge production and the practice of reflexivity as I have been discussing them. Throughout my fieldwork, and even more so during certain moments of writing this book, I perpetually asked myself: What is my relationship to what I am observing? What epistemological frameworks might already be guiding my understanding of my fieldwork? In other words, how, through academic training, Western ideological systems, or political inclinations, had I already come to "know" my subjects? As someone inclined to see capitalism as an inherently exploitative system in which difference and power shape ideas about labor, skill, and value, I often instinctively placed call center work in these terms, too. However, I sometimes found that my adherence to this dispiriting understanding of the global service industry was also an obstacle to my research and analysis. When people and places become legible primarily through subordination, it is difficult to see them as anything more than the end point of an exploitative process, rather than active mediators of their hopes and values. The goal of this book is therefore not to compile an endless compendium of ways that people are subjected to power beyond their control or to fulfill a desire to find informants who are suffering and thus sympathetic, but to offer an account of how people make meaning with both the tools they are given and those they shape out of the substance of their lives.

Another danger of bringing unexamined methodologies and frameworks to ethnographic research—if not other methods as well—is that such inquiries come to feel like ways to master the "real" conditions that research subjects live within. In this way, engagement in the field may entail modes of representation in which the very questions researchers ask reflect a closed, presumptuous, or otherwise problematic worldview. Writing about the challenge of understanding how immigrant women in low-wage domestic work could maintain hope for the future in the face of the social structures that seem to oppress them, Susanna Rosenbaum concludes that the question "How can they remain hopeful?" is a conundrum of the scholar's own making, one that places marginalized research subjects "in an unchanging present" that fails to consider their conceptions of success and value.[70] Following the lead of scholars committed to decolonized ethnography and feminist pedagogy, I reject the notion of scholarly mastery because it presumes that a scholar's job is to stand above rather than alongside her informants' reality, and because claims to mastery—always and already doomed to failure—contribute to the oppression and delegitimization of minority subjects in the academy, by the state, and beyond.[71] What counts as ethnographic knowledge within this book emerged from the logics, feelings, and aspirations that guided my participants' thoughts as we discussed them and from actions in which I often participated—not mere confirmation of what I already thought I knew.

Last, the relational work of ethnography also entails an awareness of and vulnerability to the ways my research participants tried to understand me as I tried to understand them—what John Jackson calls "ethnographic sincerity."[72] As many ethnographers know, informants and participants inevitably place researchers in their world vision, projecting onto them various ideas and criticisms, as well as hopes and demands. Throughout my fieldwork I was asked to opine on management problems, given many suggestions as to what my research should be about, and assumed to be a positive voice for the industry; my marital status, biological clock, and racial identity have also been objects of curiosity by research participants as well. As I discuss in chapter 3, as a Filipina American I was often interpellated into imaginaries and ideologies of U.S.-Philippine relations, an experience that ultimately underscored the larger dynamics this book explores. Such reflection on and insights about my engagement in ethnography further revealed the instability of objects and subjects, as well as researcher and research, while also enhancing my understanding of culture as not a static and bound collection of objects and constructs but a lived and open-ended set of practices.[73]

Ethnography as Transnational Labor

After spending portions of the summers of 2005 and 2006 conducting historical and other preliminary research in the Philippines, I began the research for this book in 2007. Since ethnography is grounded in the researcher's relationships with key individuals and/or sites, I started my project by expressing my research interests to people I already knew to be involved in the call center industry, such as Mia, whom I approached online. From these initial interactions, I came to know dozens of people working in various different call centers, in both Manila—the capital of the Philippines—and Bacolod, a midsized city in the central Philippines.[74]

The capstone of my fieldwork was my research at Vox Elite, a major global call center with locations in Manila and around the world. Started several decades ago, Vox Elite handles conventional call center functions— including customer service, technical support, and sales—and employs upward of 200,000 people in several hundred call centers worldwide. At Vox Elite I was able to participate in and observe the hiring and training process of potential and new employees.[75] Although call centers are notoriously securitized spaces, and Vox Elite is no exception, my access to the company's inner operations was made significantly easier by the personal interest that its vice president of human resources—a middle-aged Filipino man named Joel Partido—took in my research. Joel met with me several times, for several hours at a stretch, even though Vox Elite was busy with a large-scale merger with a major U.S. computer company at the time. However, by the time I was preparing for follow-up research with Vox Elite in 2013, security protocols at the company had changed such that I was no longer allowed access to the center. As the operations manager whom I spoke to over the phone from New York City explained (and as some of my research participants confirmed), heightened security was pervasive across the industry more broadly, but Vox Elite was also being particularly cautious because, according to the operations manager, it "had been burned" by researchers in the recent past. Taking this to mean that criticism of the industry and Vox Elite had reached a level that the company wished to avoid, I explained that the research I had conducted and wished to continue was not focused on the particulars of the company or its corporate clients but rather aspects of the work that speak to workers' experiences of their jobs. Still, my requests were repeatedly declined, but not before the operations manager in question expressed that, had things been different, he would have liked to bring me in and get my take on why the company had struggled to fill upper-level management positions with Filipinos! Alas, since my relationship with Vox Elite was severely hampered, I focused my energies in 2013 on interviews with call center employees at a different but similar large call center company I refer to as Premier Source.

My sense of the meaning of call center work and the way it fits into workers' everyday lives came from interviews and participant observation of employees themselves. I spent ample time with research participants in social settings such as shopping malls and restaurants, as well as more intimate settings like their homes. Although many of my questions and observations were guided by my interest in workers' culture and communication training, the practices and traits that are valued in the call center labor processes, and the social identities of the agents themselves, I mostly strove to understand the issues and concerns that were most meaningful to them, both inside and outside the call center. Given the length of time over which this research occurred, I was also able to sense changes in participants' views about call center work. Later interviews revealed more and more young people who were interested in call center work as a longer-term career choice, although the usual ambivalence about abandoning more conventional professional paths persisted. One of the most noteworthy changes between 2008 and 2013 was in workers' consciousness of the recreational sexual practices of many call center workers, the link between call centers and transmission of sexually transmitted diseases (especially HIV), and the stigma attached to the industry and its employees as a result—subjects I address in this book's final chapter.

In addition to engaging call center employees, I also studied up by interviewing or otherwise interacting with industry executives and representatives of the Philippine government, and by attending government- and industry-sponsored events, one of which took place in the United States.

Such research revealed the ideological links between the Philippine state and the call center industry, allowing me to build on similar work that insists on the relevance of the state in globalization.[76] To understand how the call center industry and its workers exist within a political arena with various allies, I also studied "across"—that is, followed nascent developments in organized labor, and the work of nongovernmental organizations which focus their efforts on call center workers. For this portion of my research, I interviewed activists of different stripes, from those taking a more industry-friendly approach to protecting workers' rights to one connected to radical and underground labor organizing groups.

A Nation on the Line keeps faith with American studies scholars' insistence that cultures of everyday life and the production of identity and difference are so multifaceted that they demand innovative and interdisciplinary approaches to studying them. In addition to multi-sited ethnographic research, the project thus also makes use of primary and secondary historical sources and a rich archive of media representations, television news spots, YouTube videos, comic books, magazines, and company ephemera. I also conducted original and secondary research on topics relevant to my questions about how call center work is linked to consumer culture, sexual culture, and service work culture in the Philippines. Finally, tacking back and forth between Manila and Bacolod offered me a unique comparative perspective on the Philippine call center industry, since Manila—a cosmopolitan urban environment considered saturated with call center work by the mid-2000s—differs culturally and politically from Bacolod, where social conservatism holds sway and call centers were a relatively unknown entity until around 2007. By 2013, however, industry and government leaders had officially designated Bacolod a "Next Wave City," signaling its readiness to expand its BPO offerings.

Book Outline

The chapters that follow examine the tensions, contradictions, and anxieties facing Filipino call center workers in everyday life, tracing these predicaments to the problems of labor, culture, and value facing the Philippines as a postcolonial nation-state in the twenty-first century. Following the interdisciplinary and transnational trajectories of my methodology, each chapter situates the Philippine call center industry within a different frame of reference, starting with postindustrial work cultures in chapter 1 and moving on in the subsequent chapters to the knowledge economy, postcolonial cultural politics of identity and language, the changing character of the middle class, and shifts in reproductive rights and sexual politics. While each framework reveals a different set of meanings of call center work for my research participants, together they reinforce my overarching argument about how the call center industry is a site of contestation over the status of the Philippine nation-state and the value of Filipino labor, a struggle that can and should be understood in racialized, classed, gendered, and sexualized terms.

Chapter 1 examines the call center labor process and work culture and the ways in which the call center, as a postindustrial workplace, blurs the boundaries between production and social reproduction, as well as work and worker. I examine the affective contradictions of call center work—that is, how the work comes to feel emotionally and physically damaging and draining, while also socially pleasurable, personally fulfilling, and fun. I then trace this contradiction directly back to the labor process itself. The chapter also introduces two concepts: relational labor, or the labor of identification, proximity, and communication; and productive intimacy, which is the form close relationships between coworkers take when made productive for capital. Finally, chapter 1 demonstrates how my research participants interpret the demands of call center work through norms of Filipino relationality, such as *pagkatao* (personality/humanity) and *kapwa* (unity of self with others), allowing them to feel that the work is "very Filipino" despite its Western origin.

Having examined the intricacies of call center work proper, I then move on to analyze its broader class and cultural contradictions in chapter 2. I examine the contestation over the skill and value of call center work, linking these debates to the fear that the work reproduces, rather than transcends, the racialized and feminized labor for which the Philippines has long been known and thus is an obstacle, rather than a pathway, to entry into the knowledge economy. I also carefully detail how the unstable class status of call center work in the Philippine context is shaped transnationally, through the global social relations that make call center work a precarious job associated with racialized and feminized servitude. Chapter 2 then discusses the contradictory cultural logic of call center work by looking at colonial recall—the ways in which the industry raises the specter of U.S. colonialism—and Filipino/American relatability. I close-read moments within my fieldwork in which elite industry actors attempt to make sense of the colonial power dynamics that shape call center work, resulting in a contradictory politics that aligns with global capital while contesting the power of the United States. I pay particular attention to how this contradictory dynamic manifests within the shifting politics and meanings of the English language and Filipino identity. Most important, however, chapter 2 demonstrates how workers, industry leaders, and state actors mediate and negotiate the uncertainties of call center work through an appeal to market logic, thus emerging as active participants in the making of the nation-state and its neoliberal narrative.

Chapter 3 draws on my participant observation of the call center hiring and training process at Vox Elite. Building on the first two chapters, it takes an in-depth look at how class contradictions, racialized and gendered service, and colonial recall shape the structure and experience of call center work from the minute a person begins filling out a job application. Unlike previous ethnographic accounts of call center hiring or training, I extend my analysis beyond the question of how national identity is managed or how call centers reproduce colonial relations of control. In addition to understanding these important facets of call centers, I also critically examine how the presence of white male American corporate trainers, and of myself as a Filipina American, shaped the training experience for Vox Elite employees, in part by implicitly inviting the latter to affirm the symbolic integrity of Filipino identity or to challenge U.S. economic dominance. This chapter presents call center training as the site where the postindustrial struggles of the American middle class—represented in the aggrieved whiteness of white male American trainers—converge with the aspirations and growing confidence of Filipino workers, thus complicating the terrain on which Filipino/American relatability plays out.

Chapters 4 and 5 look more closely at the predicaments of labor, culture, and value as they revolve specifically around cultures of consumption and sexual politics. Picking up on questions of class contradiction discussed in chapters 2 and 3, chapter 4 looks closely at the cultures of consumption and credit in which Filipino call center workers are increasingly entangled, in ways both pleasurable and precarious for workers. I critically interrogate the perception of call center work as a gateway to a middle-class lifestyle, as well as the moral reproach leveled at their conspicuous consumption.

Building on discussions of productive subjects in chapter 1, chapter 4 also examines how cultures of consumption and finance reinforce a productivist ethic and thus the cultural construction of call center workers as what I call "productive youth"—young workers whose very sense of self is measured and determined by their ability to produce multiple forms of value. Finally, chapter 5 examines how contestations over the social and cultural value of call center work are complicated by the association of the workforce with gender and sexual deviance, as well as sexually transmitted disease. The chapter first describes how Philippine call centers have been culturally constructed as nonnormative and specifically queer sites, tracing this construction to a wide range of factors, including liberal hiring and promotion policies, the sexualization of global media assemblages, shifting sexual cultures among Filipino youth, and the industry's valorization of relational labor, which creates occupational opportunities for *bakla* and transwomen as performative individuals.[77] I then consider the discourse of deviance surrounding the recent rise in the number of call center workers testing positive for HIV, a trend reported in media outlets starting in 2010. Like the concerns about educational achievement or class mobility examined in previous chapters, I understand the concerns over workers' sexuality and sexual practices as articulations of fear and uncertainty about the social value of call center work to the nation. In the book's conclusion, I draw on some of the last moments of my fieldwork and reflect back on earlier moments to highlight insights related to a number of the book's questions and themes, including the power of national narratives to shape everyday life, and the pitfalls of the knowledge economy.

A Nation on the Line traces the connections that make up the business of customer service outsourcing to the Philippines, following the flow of capital, corporate culture, and customer demands from the United States toward its former colony, and Filipino workers' affective labor as it recrosses those same boundaries. Yet the book is a transnational account not simply because it tracks movements of capital and labor across national borders, but because it stresses the ways that transnational political economy and culture transform the meaning and identity of the Philippines as a nation-state. As over two decades of transnational scholarship in American studies and Asian American studies have made clear, the term *transnational* applies not only to the empirical—that which actually crosses national borders—but first and foremost to a standpoint of critique of the nation-state as an entity socially and culturally constructed in relation to other nations, whose material and ideological borders are established or displaced through imperial and military action, and whose imagined community includes or excludes various peoples based on geopolitical priorities.[78] By directing its focus to the Philippines' struggles to stabilize its status within the global economy and the ways new national narratives emerge as a result, *A Nation on the Line* uncovers how the Philippine nation-state is always in question—and in ways that involve the United States, although not always predictably. Neither solely an account of U.S. corporate power and empire in the Philippines nor a static portrait of the Philippines in the postcolonial era, *A Nation on the Line* merges the horizons of Asia and America, strengthening a key thread in an ongoing conversation about what transnationalism as a method does, and how one might go about doing it.

LISTENING BETWEEN THE LINES

Relational Labor, Productive Intimacy, and the
Affective Contradictions of Call Center Work

June 2013. At ten minutes past eleven at night a small flashing icon near the top right corner of her computer screen told Diana Pilar—a twenty-three-year-old customer service representative for Premier Source's account with Air Anima—that a new call had been routed to her line. Having earlier removed her headset so that she could speak with me more freely, Diana now replaced it so she could take the call. I, too, donned a headset so that I could listen in, a process usually reserved for managers and trainees, and appropriately referred to as *barging*. As I did so, I noticed that the brightly colored knitted muffs covering the earpieces of Diana's headset were one of three personal items in the small blue cubicle where we were seated. The other items were a photograph of Diana's two younger brothers and an advertisement for a Coach purse torn out of a fashion magazine. Just before the new call came in, Diana had been explaining to me that with her earnings she was able to cover the tuition and living expenses for her brother Terry, who was studying computer science in college and would soon be applying for jobs at several call centers, including Premier Source. When I asked about the advertisement, Diana smiled and said that it lent her inspiration for her mother's upcoming Coach-themed birthday party, which Diana was organizing.

The new call—Diana's ninth since her shift started two hours earlier (a rare slow night on the floor)—did not come directly from an Anima customer but from another call center agent working for Navigate, the online travel agency through which the customer had booked her Anima flight. The Anima customer, a woman from Texas, had called Navigate to inform them that the sixty dollars she had previously paid in baggage fees to Air

Anima had not been refunded or credited to her when she later changed her flight to a different time and day. The Navigate agent then explained to Diana that she was going to bring the customer onto the call. One click later, all three parties—the customer, the Navigate agent, and the Air Anima agent—were all virtually present, while I listened in the background.

On the right side of Diana's computer screen, a clock displayed the amount of time that had elapsed since the call's start; below it was an inbox containing an interoffice memo from Diana's team leader stating that the account's current average handling time for calls that shift had been six minutes but needed to be lower. From what I had already learned about how long even a simple exchange of information between agent and caller could take, I suspected that having not one but two people on the line would increase Diana's handling time on the call; indeed, Diana was left hanging while the Navigate agent and the customer exchanged more words. Finally, the Navigate agent—undoubtedly trying to manage her own handling time and service delivery—decided to return the sixty dollars to the customer but then informed her that her credit card would be charged the sixty-dollar baggage fee for the new, changed flight. The call reached an emotional tipping point as the caller shouted, "Fuck this, I'm canceling *everything! I'm not giving anyone any more of my fucking money! I've been on the phone with you people for four hours! You are both complete idiots who should be fucking fired!" At that point, Diana calmly apologized to the customer but made clear that she could not assist her further and disengaged the call, just as her timer reached seven and a half minutes.

This window into Diana's work life reveals the kind of labor that customer and technical support call center agents in the Philippines do on a daily basis, as well as the way call center work fits within the larger context of workers' family lives, their consumer cultures, and transnational structures of power shaped by race, nation, and class. Diana's ability to support her family financially points to her earning power; her confidence and competency in communicating in English illustrate the cultural capital the job requires; and her exposure to and management of feelings—both her own and the customer's—demonstrate the intense emotional labor call center agents engage in as an inherent condition of the job. Moreover, Diana's ability to strategically maneuver through the demands of Air Anima, Premier Source's corporate client, and the immediate circumstances of the call, suggests the tedious mental labor the work entails. Afterward,

Diana shared her logic and savvy with me by explaining that because the customer's problem originated with a Navigate agent's failure to transfer the baggage fee payment to the new flight (a mistake she could detect from the database she accessed during calls) she didn't want to use her call time to explain the problem to either party. She maintained that it wasn't in her interest to do so: the sixty-dollar fee was going to be paid to Air Anima no matter what, so instead of making herself a target of the caller's anger and spending more time on the call, Diana terminated it, saving her time and energy. "It was their fault," Diana proclaimed. "I don't want to save their ass or be the one to tell the customer what went wrong." When I asked Diana how she felt about the customer's shouting and cursing, she replied, "Sometimes customers, they get like that. I just tell myself to not take it personal [*sic*] and keep doing my job, keep being professional. That's already automatic for me, when I get to the production floor."

Diana's situation also reveals some of the contradictory experiences of labor, culture, and value embedded in call center work, and thus the kinds of tensions this book identifies and situates within the Philippine nation-state's postcolonial struggles to gain a foothold in the postindustrial knowledge economy. Although she did it well, Diana's job handling customer service for Air Anima reflects call center work's highly rationalized nature, in which back-office and customer-facing work is divided into relatively repeatable and routine tasks. As the call further demonstrates, call center jobs also require intense performative and emotional labor in a highly surveilled environment driven by a quality control system that measures nearly all aspects of workers' activity. Call center agents make airline reservations, troubleshoot wireless Internet devices, and check credit card statements, all while nervously aware of the ticking clock, their customer's mood, their supervisor's demands (for faster call resolutions, more sales, more pleasant service, etc.), and their own exhaustion. Not apparent from my observation of Diana, however, was the larger work culture in which Philippine call center labor takes place. Although Diana spoke to me about the stress involved in dealing with customers and clients, she also described her working environment as highly enjoyable, citing the many friends she made at work and opportunities they have to, in her words, "decompress from all the pressures we face on the floor." Even her mother's birthday party, she said excitedly, would be attended by many of her friends from work, including her team leader.

This chapter focuses on the subjective demands of the customer service labor process—especially its appropriation of emotional, affective, and relational labor—while detailing how these intangible performances are measured and evaluated by management. I also demonstrate that the rationalized relational labor of call center work is linked to a work culture that fosters positive social relations among coworkers. These relationships take shape through both the formal corporate culture and official management practices, such as *coaching* and *developing people,* as well as the informal intimacies that emerge between coworkers. Philippine call centers, I argue, create and maintain an internal realm of social reproduction that allows for the regeneration of relationality as the raw material of call center work. This renewal process is all the more important in Philippine call centers, where the imperative to work overnight dislodges workers from the normal socially reproductive rhythms of social and familial life. By analyzing the labor process and work culture in the same frame, this chapter brings into sharp relief the striking contrast between the often damaging physical and psychological repercussions of call center work, and its capacity for fun and camaraderie between coworkers. Rather than dismiss the social and pleasurable aspects of corporate work culture as merely another mode of workplace control, or assume its potential for unbridled radical solidarity—the two primary ways that aspects of the humane workplace have been framed in the past—I try to understand why Philippine call centers have this contradictory characteristic and how workers experience it.[1] As I demonstrate below, such contradictions can be traced to the call center's hypervalorization of productivity and reliance on human relationships, which, in the Philippine context, enables the subsumption of Filipino modes of sociability and relational practice by capital while also enhancing the value such modes have for individual workers.

The Panopticon at Pyramid Processing

February 2009. The street outside my apartment building was dark and deserted at half past midnight. As I settled into the back seat of one of Metro Manila's ubiquitous white taxis, the driver lowered the sound of Billy Joel singing "Honesty" on the radio so I could direct him to our destination: Emerald Avenue. Just an eight-minute drive from where I lived in Makati—although it would easily eat up thirty minutes in regular daytime traffic—Emerald Avenue is home to dozens of call center companies and therefore the nocturnal beating heart of the commercial and business district known as Ortigas. As we approached Pyramid Processing, where I had been observing the production floor and interviewing workers for a few weeks, the slumbering city suddenly awakened with activity: young people walking briskly into and out of office building lobbies, or standing together in circles while the smoke from their cigarettes wafted upward into the amber light of street lamps. A string of convenience stores and small restaurants were open and ready to serve, hot dogs turning on metal trays in the window and energy drinks chilling on refrigerated shelves. All around Metro Manila—especially in thriving commercial zones like Libis and Bonifacio Global City—late-night scenes like this one were unfolding, as call center workers carried on yet another night of transnational service work.

Upon arriving at Pyramid's offices, I made the requisite stop at the guards' desk to register my name and the company I was visiting in a thick but meticulously organized logbook whose every entry displayed the flawless handwriting that many Filipinos are schooled in using. On this day, I was scheduled to meet Antonio, a Pyramid Processing quality assurance (QA) manager, who had agreed to walk me through an employee performance evaluation process. Behind me, employees quickly flashed identification badges at the guards and then made their way to the bay of elevators ahead of us. Moments later I joined the fray and waited patiently as people disembarked on various floors of the fifteen-story building.

When I arrived at one of the three floors Pyramid occupies, I checked in quickly with another guard; it would be another year or two before the company automated its security system, eliminating the need for these quiet armed men. As was always the case at that time of night, the large production floor was buzzing with energy, and the temperature was near frigid. Of the one hundred or so cubicles spread out before me, about two-thirds were occupied, with the remaining empty cubicles awaiting a batch of rookie agents who would be starting on a new account in the next two weeks. Directly in front of me, trainees were undergoing their first night of fully supervised calls—a stage of training referred to as *nesting*—on an account for a national car rental service in the United States, and the sound of their nervous discussions with neighbors and trainers charged the space around them. Meanwhile, team leaders on the other accounts paced along the rows, making themselves available when their agents had a question or when a call needed to be escalated because of a problem. With their restrained colors, plain office chairs, and desktop computers, agents' workstations seemed indistinguishable, yet above them hung colorful banners and other decorations, with a different theme or color scheme providing a visual outline of each account on the floor. Bright poster boards announced the mission and vision for various teams of agents, with imperatives and mottos like "Deliver Excellence!" and "Performance Is Power" that employees had written by hand in big block or bubbly letters. As I stepped to the side and looked for Antonio, a steady stream of agents began trickling onto the floor, their demeanors relaxed yet purposeful as they settled into an eight-hour shift.

Seconds later, I spotted Antonio standing at one of the workstations for managers, where he was talking to another employee about some papers he was holding, most likely a printout detailing how well the account was doing relative to the goals set by the corporate client during their last meeting. As soon as he finished the conversation, we walked to a small room near the back corner of the floor, where we would listen to a customer service call recorded from an Internet provider account and Antonio would train two junior QA managers to evaluate the call. This opportunity was significant because it promised a unique perspective on the two most talked-about things among my research participants: performing emotional and affective labor, and performing in general—that is, attempting to meet the various metrics established by management and corporate clients, including call handling time, first-call resolution, and customer satisfaction scores. Indeed, very few of my research participants could talk about their jobs without expressing great exasperation, and sometimes deep distress, over the panoptic surveillance to which they were subject and the tedium of responding calmly and empathically to callers' challenging questions or their demeaning comments. "The metrics," as workers ominously referred to them, could spell the difference between promotion and demotion and thus held great power over workers' everyday lives. "There would come a point," a Premier Source employee named Billie explained, "wherein you would go to sleep and dream about your scores."

The four of us—Antonio, the two junior QA managers (Damien and Megan), and I—squeezed together in the room where all the QA equipment was housed. After a minute or two, Antonio queued up a call by an agent named Elson, who had been with the account for a little over a year. Although Elson's call itself was chosen at random, his particular team was being evaluated at the request of the client company, a small provider of Internet service in New Zealand called Keen. In Keen's most recent meeting with Pyramid's account managers, they had shown concern over poor results on its customer service survey and wanted Pyramid to develop a plan to improve these scores. In telling us this information, Antonio also added that he had heard a rumor about Pyramid "shaking things up with their third-party providers"—meaning their call centers in the Philippines and elsewhere—as they were attempting to grow their base of broadband customers. Antonio wanted Pyramid to be on the right side of this shake-up, receiving more of Keen's business and not less, and therefore was eager to get the company the report it had requested.

Antonio handed me a clipboard and a copy of Pyramid's customer service evaluation tool, the Comprehensive Quality Assessment (CQA) survey, so I could follow along with their discussion. For the particular account Elson was working on, the CQA contained thirty-six questions about an agent's performance. Divided into subcategories, the questions ranged from how the agent handled the caller's private information, to how well they identified the problem the caller was having, to whether or not the agent paced the call according to "the customer's style and technical level of knowledge." Each question was given a numerical value, such as twenty or fifty points; however, twenty-one of the thirty-six questions only allowed agents to receive the full point value, zero points, or an "auto-fail"—meaning an automatic failure for a given subcategory of evaluation should the agent not perform correctly. Thus for much of the survey, there was little to no room for error if the agent wished to "pass the scorecard."

The playback began. On the line was a woman who wanted to know why her e-mail account was deactivated. From the start of the call, the woman seemed both tired and irritable, perhaps because of the young child crying in the background. She grew even more annoyed, however, after Elson asked her to verify her e-mail address for security purposes, a step so crucial to the corporate client that QA managers will auto-fail agents if it is done incorrectly. In attempting to remember her e-mail address, the caller gave one that was similar but not identical to the one the company had on file for her. The discrepancy caused the agent to ask another series of questions to verify the caller's identity, to which the caller responded, "Look, that e-mail address is most likely mine. I don't use this company's web browser that often, so it's highly understandable that I made a slight mistake in remembering the e-mail address for the account. Why don't you just use common sense?"

Elson remained quiet despite the caller's slight to his intelligence and simply repeated that he had to ask the security questions to verify the woman's identity. After this step was complete, Elson surveyed the caller's account using the Keen database (a process that was visually recorded and thus subject to scrutiny by QA managers) and realized that the woman's e-mail service had been rendered inactive because, as he informed her, "of a problem with her bill" that she could resolve only by speaking directly with someone in the company's billing department. The caller expressed irritation over this inconvenience, which only redoubled when Elson informed her that the billing department was closed at the time. Elson, however, mistakenly offered to connect the woman to the billing department—a foible perhaps caused by exhaustion (this call occurred near the end of his shift, around six in the morning) or a desire to end the call—to which the caller responded in a voice of irate and condescending disbelief, "This is idiotic. Didn't you just say they were closed?!" Again, Elson did not verbally acknowledge the woman's response. Instead, he told her that she would have to call back during the billing department's hours of operation and closed the call.

"Okay," Antonio said as he turned to the CQA survey, "the agent clearly conducted the opening spiel and the security checks correctly—so full points there. Now, what about 'Customer Experience'? Did the agent 'Provide the caller with clear and easy-to-follow instructions'?" I looked up at Damien and Megan, whose eyes are nervously pinned to their clipboards. After a few seconds Damien suggested that Elson be given full credit for the question because, as he saw it, the agent knew that it was a billing issue and told the woman to call back the next day when the billing department would be open. Antonio then challenged Elson's perception of the call by saying, "Yes, but does *the customer* know the reasons she has to call back and speak to the billing department? The agent had that information right in front of him [on the computer screen], but he didn't tell the caller what the problem was exactly. He just told her to call back. That means she doesn't know what's going to happen when she does. I would give Elson

'Needs to Improve.'" Damien and Megan nodded in silent agreement. Elson would not be given any credit for that portion of the call.

During the QA scoring session, it quickly became clear to me that the agent's score on "customer experience" was determined by an interpretation of the customer's subjective state in relation to what the agent communicated. When reviewing the call, for example, Antonio listened for how the agent related to the customer and then determined the customer's state based on that information. Thus, even though the customer did not actually complain or otherwise inquire about her bill while on the phone with Elson, he was given a "Needs to Improve" score on the question. By asking what the customer could possibly know about her bill based on Elson's communication, Antonio demonstrated that, unlike Damien, he was listening for not only what the agent said but also how what he said affected the customer. Later, Antonio clarified this way of evaluating agents by saying that some of the metrics have nothing to do with an agent's knowledge of a product or a process but his or her ability to "think like a customer"—something he did not believe Elson succeeded at during the call. Moreover, from a QA point of view, one of the most problematic aspects of Elson's performance was his lack of a verbalized empathic response when the customer expressed irritation or frustration. Rather than saying something along the lines of "I understand your frustration with this process" or "Yes, I did say the billing department was closed, I understand how that can be confusing," Elson simply remained silent. Because he did not demonstrate that he was relating to the customer during a moment of tension, Elson was given "No/zero" on the question of whether the agent used empathy to manage irate customers. Furthermore, he was given "No/zero" on the question related to his professionalism and enthusiasm because, according to Antonio (and here Damien and Megan agreed right away), there was too much "dead air," that is, silence on the part of the agent during the call, and because Elson's apparent interest in the caller's problem never seemed to rise above the level of sober indifference.

The intersubjective demands of call center work can thus tell us much about the appropriation of human affect and emotion by and for capital— that is, the emotional economy in which call center labor produces value. The scoring session made abundantly clear that subjective capacities— what QA managers at Pyramid Processing refer to as the "human element"— constitute a call center agent's most valuable tools for producing customer satisfaction. All across the industry, agents are trained and evaluated for two human elements in particular—rapport and empathy—both of which Elson ostensibly failed to mobilize during the call. To achieve rapport, agents attempt to establish a harmonious interaction with callers in which the two parties exchange information with ease. In addition to setting the tone for the personal identification process, rapport is also part of transparency, wherein agents let customers know why they are asking questions, what steps they are taking to address customers' problem, and, most important, what callers stands to gain from these procedures. Rapport is not simply about seeming pleasant or making customers comfortable, however. More fundamentally, it promotes the idea that agents are there to help customers rather than to defend the corporate client or blame customers for the problems they are calling about. As suggested by the call that opened this chapter, agents can also learn to restrain rapport when the blame or failure can be shifted elsewhere. Meanwhile, in the emotional taxonomy of call center work, empathy means understanding the expectations and frustrations that a person experiences with a product or service, including the customer service delivery process itself. To help foster empathy, agents are told to be active listeners by letting customers speak, probing for details about callers' problems, paraphrasing what customers say, and understanding the customer's tone of voice. Agents are trained to display empathy by using phrases like "I understand" and acknowledging a customer's position as someone who, for example, desperately needs to resolve a billing issue. Empathy requires what Arlie Hochschild calls "deep acting," or the use of the trained imagination to actually feel the feelings one is displaying—or, at least, to narrow the gap between what one feels and what one displays.[2] By not displaying empathy with the caller, Elson failed to properly acknowledge the customer's frustration.

Empathy and rapport are therefore understood as important emotional tools that influence how callers feel and behave, in turn mediating how callers relate to the company in question. Call center work thus clearly requires affective labor, or the labor employed in shaping someone's mood or state of mind. More specifically, however, call center work requires relational labor, which includes agents' effort to relate to customers in a way that manages their overall relationship to the client companies or businesses in question; in this way, agents are charged with reinforcing callers' submission to the forces of capital.[3] This concept of relational labor points to more than just the agent's need to identify and communicate with the caller; it also highlights the pressure on the call center agent to identify with not one but two companies—the call center and the corporate client. This need to shift perspectives between callers, companies, coworkers, and even technological systems is a defining feature of outsourced call center work and was clearly on display in the call that opened this chapter. During my time as a participant and observer at various call centers, I was struck not only by how workers speak but also how they orient themselves, both psychologically and physically, in various different directions. By *orient* I mean something more than the fact that agents must pay attention to many things and multitask; I mean that agents must learn to identify with the intentions of others, including "the corporate 'other.'"[4] Moreover, by appropriating and then directing an agent's affective state into a specific relationship with a caller, the call center labor process literally values some affects and emotions over others. Elson may very well have registered the customer's irritation and chosen a disaffected response as a way of coping with the caller's subsequent rude and insulting comments—what Martin Manalansan describes as "a kind of managed alienation and a tempered hostility to the regimes of power and nurturance"—but such a response did not earn him a positive score on the CQA.[5] Indeed my research participants made abundantly clear that negative feelings were always boiling beneath the surface of their trained performances. As one Pyramid Processing employee told me, "you have to have the highest level of EQ [emotional quotient] to be here. You have to manage what [the customers] are going through, and you have to manage yourself. When I go to work, I always bear in mind that I have my locker where I can keep my excess baggage. And I count to ten before I get irate. To cool myself down."

The Social Reproduction of Relational Labor

It is difficult to overstate the extent to which call center work that involves direct verbal communication with customers drains agents of morale and motivation. Night after night, week after week—and, for some, year after year—agents are literally at the beck and call of customers and clients, their every word and click of the mouse the objects of disciplinary surveillance, measurement, and control. Despite—or, as I argue, because of—

these conditions, call center work offers employees abundant opportunities for emotional solidarity and social bonding. This dynamic is rooted in the affective and relational demands of call center work and the work culture to which it gives rise.

After the QA scoring session, Antonio and the others broke for lunch. I took my leave, too, because I had arranged to meet some agents from Integral, a neighboring call center, at a nearby outdoor food market that catered to the many call center employees in the area. Introduced to this group by a friend, I had been invited to hang out with them during breaks and after work; five people in the group had even formed a rock-and-roll cover band cleverly named Calvin and the Talent—"talent" being an industry word used to refer to call center employees—and I had seen them perform a few times. Calvin was their warm and friendly band manager, the son of a Filipina and an American serviceman, who often joined them during breaks. Calvin didn't work in a call center, but he hardly ever missed an opportunity to socialize with his friends.

When I arrived at the market, I found Erica, Macky, and Stephen sitting together, still waiting for the others to arrive. Erica, who had gone to high school in Australia and had studied communications at one of the city's most prestigious colleges, had been working at Integral for six years as a language and cultural trainer. Stephen had worked in a local resort just outside the city before getting a call center job; he had studied to be a pilot, but since the on-the-job training took several months and would actually cost him money, he did not pursue it. Then there was Macky, the youngest of the group; he and Stephen were two of the band members. Macky had worked in one call center before Integral. Normally quite talkative, that evening he looked distant and glum.

"He had a lot of bad calls at the beginning of his shift," Erica explained. Knowing that Macky answered no fewer than 150 calls a day—he took orders on a contact lens account for a major pharmaceutical company—I was worried about how many was "a lot."

"It wasn't that many," Macky interjected, as if he had read my thoughts. "It was just a couple that really, really pissed me off. One was seven minutes long. Normally, I can take, like, ten orders in that time, but this lady—this one lady, everyone on the account knows her—she kept asking me for a big order size, and I kept telling her it's not possible, she has to get a special approval for that. She keeps . . . she kept arguing with me. I really wanted to disconnect that call." Stephen asked if he had escalated the call to his team leader.

"I had to," Macky sighed. "My TL [team leader] was okay about it. We laughed afterward, but still. I won't be laughing if I resign."

Stephen put his hand on Macky's shoulder and said, "Huwag mag-resign, okay? [Don't resign, okay?] We'll have a jam session later, and you'll feel better." Just the reminder of the band's existence seemed to relax Macky a little bit, at which point he and Stephen got up to buy something to eat while I stayed with Erica.

As Macky's description of his feelings suggests, workers' resistance to their psychologically harrowing conditions is constant. Indeed, the agents I interviewed gave me rousing examples of their defiance at work, including finding ways to disconnect calls without being penalized, and managing to spend their downtime between calls in the cafeteria with friends rather than at their workstations. While not insignificant, these surreptitious modes of insubordination make up only a small part of a larger tableau of struggle and solidarity unfolding nightly among call center workers. As the caring exchange between Stephen and Macky implies, agents often manage the stress of their working conditions by turning to one another for emotional support and psychological decompression. In fact, many of my research participants spent significantly more time speaking of positive interactions with their coworkers than negative interactions with callers, leading me to see the importance of the relational efforts transpiring among them, both at work and outside of it. Harold, another member of the Integral crowd and a staff person in the company's recruitment department, described it this way: "With us, we sometimes end up working fourteen, maybe fifteen hours in a row, and we will still get a couple of bottles [of beer] after, because it becomes a stress reliever. I would even sacrifice sleep to go out and talk about work. That's important. So, I guess . . . you are bonded by stress." The practice of morning happy hours has become so ubiquitous that Tagalog speakers have even coined a new word to describe it: *inumagan,* which combines the words *inuman* (to drink) and *umaga* (morning).

Call center agents' workplace relationships point directly to the ways that capital subsumes subjectivity through relational labor, and thus the reason that call centers are at once dismal and fun environments. *Sub-*

sumption names the process that transforms particular and concrete labor (e.g., a person's efforts to assist another person with a problem) into abstract labor, or labor for exchange (e.g., the selling of these efforts to a call center company, which in turn sells this labor to a corporate client). In bringing together workers willing to sell their labor, disciplining that labor through routine scripts and management policy, and directing it through technological and information systems, call centers exemplify "real subsumption," in which social relations and labor are purposefully organized according to the dictates of capital.[6] While there is debate about the extent to which emotions, affect, and subjectivity can ever be completely subsumed or absorbed by capital, it is significant that the call center labor process involves human capacities and forms of social life, or what Kalindi Vora calls "vital energy."[7] By converting these subjective resources into labor power for exchange, call center work depletes and diminishes their supply, hence the language of "feeling drained" or being "burned out" used to describe the effects of a night's work. Furthermore, because of the specific subjective resources used in call center work—care, kindness, empathy—and the way they are constantly tested by callers and measured by management, call center employees actually lose the willingness and even ability to meet these challenges over time and thus burn out and resign. In this way, a call center's figurative proximity to a factory becomes more pronounced, in that the manual labor required in the latter actually depletes the very capacities that workers need to complete the job. Like workers on a repetitive and disciplinary assembly line, call center agents do not simply get bored with or exhausted by mounting emotional challenges. They may experience an emotional breakdown altogether. The most extreme versions of these breakdowns lead to workers needing what one employee described as "looney leave"—an extended break to calm the nerves, if not seek professional psychological assistance—or, as I often witnessed during my fieldwork, a visit to the hospital to treat the physical manifestations of stress, such as high blood pressure or gastrointestinal distress.

The most everyday example of resource depletion in call center work is, however, demotivation. If motivation describes an affective state in which someone is willing to act toward a particular end (after all, one can desire something without being motivated to do anything about that desire), then a lack of motivation means not wanting to do something—not wanting to be friendly to a customer, handle calls efficiently, or even show up to work. Workers often spoke to me about the challenges of staying motivated in such a highly critical and demoralizing environment. It was not uncommon, for example, for employees to express gratitude for their jobs and a few beats later declare their desire to resign because of the constant stress they experience. Imagining oneself exercising the power of refusal is a common way that agents cope with work's intensity; it is exhilarating and empowering to imagine just hanging up the phone, telling off an operations manager, or simply not coming to work. Yet these feelings can and do amount to more than just mental escapes: attrition due to worker burnout is a real problem that managers are always desperate to prevent because, as everyone in the business knows, it is more expensive to train new workers than to retain existing ones. Workers' engagement in affirmative relationships is therefore crucial for keeping up productivity and combating attrition and, as such, are built into the corporate culture and official roster of management practices through lighthearted employee events, one-on-one coaching, and team-building exercises. Since the emergence of Theory Y management, many American managers have become convinced that fostering positive relationships between coworkers, and between employees and the company itself, goes a long way to retaining labor and maximizing its productivity.[8]

Yet these techniques of managerial control are not simply an American export to the Philippines. Unlike in the United States, where call center workers can enter and exit the workday in a rhythm that more or less matches those around them, Filipino agents' overnight schedules cut workers off from affective attachments to family and friends that under normal circumstances would provide them with the emotional energy needed to face yet another day at the office. Indeed, descriptions of being disconnected from one's normal social and familial life were a constant refrain among call center agents, as were stories of how call center work ruined their romantic relationships with non–call center workers.[9] "You never see your boyfriend or girlfriend," one agent explained to me. "After a while," he went on, "the relationship just . . . dies. It's really hard for the other person to understand what you are going through, with the hours and the stress. It becomes easier to break up than to stay together." Such frequent references to their social and familial disconnection, coupled with my understanding of the emotional and relational demands of their work, thus exposed yet another important tension at the heart of Philippine call centers. Call center work requires constant social reproduction of subjective capacities. However, not being allowed to take part in these reproductive processes in a normative way means that workers and the workplace need to set these processes in motion internally.[10] By reproducing the very social capacities of call center agents on which the capitalist accumulation process depends, employee relations and corporate culture thus function as the call center's own internal realm of social reproduction.[11]

My understanding of these socially reproductive workplace practices was honed through my research at Global Invest, an in-house call center for a major European bank of the same name, and my interviews with workers at Call Control. I was invited to see Global Invest by Bryan Aclan, one of the company's assistant managers and a coworker of Mia Mendez, one of my main research participants. Having been educated for some years in Canada, Bryan had returned to the Philippines right before entering college at the University of the Philippines Dilliman. After graduation, he started off as an entry-level agent at Global Invest but then quickly rose through the ranks when he applied for and received an assistant manager position. A consummate booster of the call center industry, Bryan had clear aspirations to continue moving up the Global Invest corporate ladder as swiftly as possible. Bryan's two younger brothers also worked at the company and had similar goals.

As we passed through the gates of the meticulously manicured office park where Global Invest is located, Bryan explained that the company "has a strong corporate culture" to which new hires were introduced very early on through such activities as all-expenses-paid overnight trips to local resorts. Such attributes gave Global Invest what Bryan described as a "country club" feel. However, walking through the brightly painted corridors lined with lockers and bulletin boards, I was struck less by the air of well-heeled society and more by the feeling of being on a college campus. One of our first stops on the tour was the cafeteria, where among the fast-food stations and cushioned booths were computer terminals for surfing the web, a foosball table, and a Magic Sing karaoke station, all of which smacked of a university student center. Another part of the building held an auditorium where award ceremonies and employee-appreciation events such as fashion shows took place, and along the hallways hung the kind of community-building message boards that plaster the walls of college dormitories. However, instead of pictures of student leaders or upcoming campus activities, Global Invest's boards boasted news of the company's corporate sustainability projects, pictures of its "most productive employees of the quarter," and images of the management staff accompanied by some tidbits from their personal lives—the latter a reminder of the center's commitment to relaxed managerial hierarchies. Aside from these perks, Global Invest also had the call center basics: shuttle service for employees, twenty-four-hour places to purchase food, and sleeping quarters.[12]

Bryan and I stopped periodically during this tour to discuss Global Invest's approach to employee relations, which I knew was not unique to the company (although as an in-house call center, Global Invest did spend more money to uphold its corporate culture). When I asked him why the company offered all of these services, Bryan explained that "working in a call center is very stressful, but companies realize that if they don't have [these kinds of bonds between employees], they won't have a hold on their people. I guess that's one thing that motivates people—being happy with your coworkers. Because if they're not happy, they don't treat the customers right, and if the customer is not treated right, the client will pretty much get worried that all hell will break loose." In a nod to the recent financial crash in the United States, Bryan then added that "fun makes people happy, and people can do anything if they're happy. Regardless of how negative the environment is—there's a financial crisis, the economic future is vague—as long as they enjoy their work, they're willing to go the extra mile to sustain the company." By drawing a direct line from the emotional state of a call center agent to the customer, and then to the corporate client and call center as a whole, Bryan made clear how the power of capital operates at the level of subjective experience and through the regulation of workplace relationships to "take hold" of people. In this context, we might understand Bryan's insistence on the need to be happy *with* your coworkers to not only or even primarily mean "to be made happy *by*" one's officemates but to experience happiness and stress relief in a collective manner, *alongside* them. In this way, a call center agent's constantly decreasing motivation, as the manifestation of resistance to workplace stresses and demands, signals how ostensibly compassionate innovations in management theory seek to quell workers' internal conflict with capital and therefore function as forms of counterrevolution that normalize workplace distress.

By creating social areas outside of customer-agent relations, such as company-wide athletic competitions or company-sponsored dress-up days, elements of social reproduction are brought into workplaces, in effect organizing social relations to better facilitate their appropriation by capital. At times, this socially reproductive function expresses itself in a literal way with events like Global Invest's "family fun" days, which consist of a daylong series of entertainment and games geared toward employees and their families, through which the company addresses the affective losses incurred as a result of workers' harrowing schedules, while also reinforcing that the company itself is like a family. As Bryan clearly articulated to me, "this is the time that the company can show gratitude to the families of its employees, who have sacrificed so much, so much time with their loved ones, to go to work." Overall, however, the collegiate feel of companies like Global Invest goes a long way in capitalizing on the easy camaraderie among young workers thrown together in a highly intense setting where they are evaluated constantly. Because so many Filipino call center agents are recent college graduates, their work-based cooperation can be grounded in attachments to what Filipinos call a "batch," or the class with which one proceeds through and graduates from high school or college. People I interviewed sometimes articulated this link between call center work and the college experience explicitly, as when Mary Rose, a Global Invest employee, explained that "in college you're used to pulling all-nighters, so the transition to call centers is not that hard."

Productive Intimacy

A call center worker's ability to experience intense personal distress alongside moments of social diversion stems from not only the need to reproduce affective resources but also the call center's reliance on human relationships and its hypervalorization of productivity. One of the most remarkable and yet least discussed characteristics of call center work is the sheer volume of work that call center employees do. The hours are long—especially for anyone in a managerial position—and the tasks are seemingly endless: not only must customers' orders be filled, their bank accounts opened, or their cable boxes reset, but mid- and upper-level management must constantly consult one another, write and read statistical reports, or train and coach other employees. Representatives of client companies, always coming and going, must be assured of results and cost-effectiveness while also wined and dined. If call center workers' minds are anything like their computer screens—multiple open windows and various chats occurring at once—then the activity they are involved in, especially the communication with others, is constant. Two Call Control operations managers I interviewed, Paulo and Charlene, had each worked in the industry for about eight years; by the end of their tenure, they were pulling twelve- to fourteen-hour workdays, with Paulo having to spend many of those hours with clients from the United States.

Call centers are thus quintessential places of postindustrial production not only because they create value through intangible and ephemeral forms of labor but also because they compel the intensification of and increase in work that characterizes contemporary capitalism. When research participants explained to me that call centers are really unique places—"different than the traditional office" is how several people put it—they were speaking in part to the pace and volume of the work. Yet the more I talked to and observed employees, the more I saw that call centers are not just about productivity but productivism—an orientation toward work in particular and life in general that sees in purposeful, goal-directed activity the highest ethical value and the measure of a person's or life's worth. As Kathi Weeks argues, productivism has become more prevalent in postindustrial society, as work has come to govern our lives.[13] Furthermore, because work has become what Weeks describes as "an avenue for personal development and meaning," productivity is increasingly tied to the very substance of our identities and our subjectivities.[14] By compelling us to work more, and to derive personal pleasure from that work, the ideology of productivism is a technique of biopower available to capital for increasing and intensifying accumulation. When activated in a workplace that relies on and fosters close relationships among coworkers, productivism creates the conditions for productive intimacy to take hold. Productive intimacy is the form that close relationships take when they are made productive for capital; when used as a form of corporate biopower, productive intimacy allows capital to govern workers from within their relationships, putting their affective attachments to use in the creation of exchange value and surplus value.[15] Productive intimacy signals the way that call centers blur the boundaries between production and social reproduction, relationships of equality and relationships of control, and work and workers.

Furthermore, productive intimacy involves learning to make one's attachments and relationships productive for capital, thus marking the pinnacle of value for relational labor. My interviews with employees of Call Control in Bacolod were crucial in allowing me to understand how productive intimacy works through teams and the labor of coaching. Comprising anywhere from five to fifteen people who are supervised by a team leader, teams of rank-and-file agents are one of the most important techniques for building affective attachments among workers; although agents are evaluated on an individual level, the team as a whole is responsible for meeting the client's metrics, thereby solidifying their bonds. In other words, through their affective attachments—which are constantly reinforced through team-building activities such as taking day trips to a nearby resort or decorating the team's stations with a particular theme—agents become invested in the cohesiveness of their team, which benefits workers individually while also compelling their continued productivity and cooperation with the demands of the workplace.[16] Everyday teamwork thus becomes the primary method for achieving productive intimacy, especially through coaching sessions between a team leader and an agent. Such sessions involve one-on-one interaction in which the two review the agent's recent performance (in general or on a particular call), discuss problems the agent had or encountered, and strategize solutions to these problems.

My best sense of coaching work came from Ronnie, a senior team leader at Call Control. Sitting across from him at the fast-food restaurant Jollibee, I asked Ronnie what methods he would use to coach and motivate me if I were one of his agents. Ronnie replied, "First I have to find out the real reason that you are not motivated. Is it the metrics? Are you having a hard time? Are you not being helped? You also have to go back to the reason you are here in the first place. When you applied for the job, did you think about having fun, or the salary, providing for your kids? If you tell me that you really want to wake up excited to go to work, then I have to give you options. What do you think I can do, or we can do, to make you feel excited? Do we have to do team-building [activities] and have some fun? Things like that."

Noticing that Ronnie started from the premise that an agent he is coaching would *lack* motivation, I followed up by asking, "What's a common reason for agents to be unmotivated?"

"Most of the time it's really the pressure of a certain account, of balancing and passing all their metrics. Some agents really do crack under pressure. So I ask them, 'What do you need? What can we do?'"

"It sounds like you ask your agents a lot of questions," I said.

"Yes, most of the time, I let the agents speak more than I do. Most of the time, I am listening. I almost never give suggestions; I am always giving options. Because that way you get them to think. These people are college graduates; they have bachelor's degrees. They are not stupid. Sometimes they know the answers but are just denying it or not aware of it unless you give them options. So you get them to think, which makes them accountable. Then they start finding their faults and start working on it [by] themselves. You empower them. When they become empowered, they become motivated, they perform."

Ronnie's responses to my questions contain a treasure trove of modern management gems. Practices like listening, gauging frustration levels, mustering excitement, and encouraging self-discovery all keep faith with Theory Y and its principle of worker autonomy and empowerment as a means for greater happiness and thus productivity. His descriptions of this work also make clear how personal identification with his agents operates as a form of control. Describing himself as a "middleman" between the company and its rank-and-file agents, Ronnie explained that he makes sure

> to really talk to my agents, establish my investment in them, make sure that they are one with me and my goals . . . work on them. But I just get angry if the metrics from the previous day are bad, or if I received e-mails and reports of escalation. I guess I am only human. I need to let it out. But I guess letting it out will [make the agents] feel that I also care for the metrics—it's not all about them, it's not all about the people, it's all also about the metrics. Because I am a team leader, basically I am a middleman.

Crystallizing the principle of real subsumption—in which social relations are configured in a way that creates subjects for capital's needs—Ronnie then proclaimed, "I need to take care of [my agents] as people, but I also need to take of the business, because without the business, there's no people."

At one point during our interview, Ronnie and I were joined by Pamela, one of the agents Ronnie had supervised at Call Control. As a way of learning more about how Ronnie interacted with agents, I asked Pamela what had made Ronnie such a great team leader.

"What made him so good? Because, if you have a request, he is willing to do things for you. He is willing to go beyond what he needs to do, even if he has to bribe someone!" Pamela replied with a laugh. "So, as his agent, you would be ashamed not to perform well. It's like a give-and-take relationship between him and his agents."

Ronnie's and Pamela's descriptions of their relationship demonstrate how the intimate interactions between team leaders and agents are compelled by the imperative to produce value for the firm, in turn blurring the boundaries between the objects of labor and the objects of attachment: coaching, as Ronnie describes it, requires working on people, while the metrics and the business are things to care about. Moreover, by "get[ting] them to think," Ronnie compels his agents to work in line with company goals, illustrating how capital "takes workers' subjectivity into consideration only in order to codify it in line with the requirements of production."[17]

The need for coworkers to relate to one another and for managers to relate to their subordinates was a recurring topic in my interviews. Sitting with me at a Starbucks, a Call Control operations manager named Janice expressed this in terms of an antiauthoritarian ethos. "I think at Call Control, we are not trained like, 'I am the manager; therefore, I am the boss.' No, you have to know how to make that relationship work. You have to know your people." When I later asked Janice whether she felt that working at Call Control for eight years had changed her personality in any way, she responded by explaining that she had learned to better relate to and communicate with coworkers. "Especially when I became a manager," she said, "I learned that I have to really adapt to the different types of people and [that my words should be] more sensitive, more compassionate, more appealing to their senses. You have to take into consideration their ego, their pride." Indeed, with all the relational work that call centers seem to require, it is no surprise that even the lowest-level managers refer to their work as akin to relationship-based professions. During an interview with Edgar, another operations manager at the company, and Genevieve, a Call Control sales coach, I asked them to tell me about their most memorable experiences from coaching. In response, Genevieve described not a single interaction or coaching session but the entire experience of dealing with agents who are either having trouble selling to customers and/or believe they don't know how to sell. "I'm not only a coach," Genevieve explains, "but sometimes, too, I am a psychologist. Because you really need to understand the root cause as to why the agents aren't selling. Sometimes they say, 'I am afraid to receive a rejection, because I hate rejection.' So that's a psychological issue of the agent, and I have to deal with that." Edgar echoed this idea: "We're psychologists, we're counselors, we're a lot of people. . . . We're spiritual advisers." Even the way Ronnie speaks to agents is fundamentally relational: although he asks what agents need, he follows up with the question of what *we* can do, as if the solution to an individual agent's problem necessitates a collective effort by the agent and manager.

Although the relational labor among coworkers contributes to a sense of intimacy among them, it, like the relational labor conducted with callers, must be harnessed, rationalized, and evaluated as well. This was made clear after Ronnie explained that, to my surprise, he had twice failed the review process for promotion to senior team leader. When I asked Ronnie why it took him three attempts to get the promotion, he explained that he "was having a hard time answering the question 'Why are you such a good team leader?'" and that the reasons he gave were "not enough for the senior management." I asked him to elaborate. "The reasons I gave," he went on, "were about people management, about making sure that people are motivated, that I talk to them every day, basically to make sure they are taken care of. Basically that's what I *really* do. But they wanted to know more. Because if you become a manager, it's about the data analysis, about what percentage of what you've done affected your agents' performance." Ronnie then went on to explain that Call Control's senior management expected him not only to properly motivate his agents but also to demonstrate an empirical correlation between the number of times he coached them per week and their overall increase in performance, so that he and others might reproduce his methods. Thus, while management was convinced that Ronnie was excellent at his job, his initial inability to both quantify his management method and communicate it to others stalled his upward trajectory in the company. He eventually received the promotion after creating an action plan that demonstrated links between his contact with agents and their ability to achieve the desired call metrics.

Coaching is just one element in management's larger effort to "develop people," another sanguine-sounding mantra that I heard throughout my fieldwork. While developing people often simply meant training them for new work (Paolo was "developed" by being sent to the United States to participate in instructional seminars for a big client), it also meant finding ways that an employee's particular skill set could best be used by a team or the company. By evoking personal discovery, *development* also carried with it the positive affect of coaching or "getting to know your people"; indeed, many employees understood it as a way that a company shows that it cares for employees, and thus it strengthens employees' affective attachment to or identification with the workplace. Another research participant, Mike, attempted to describe this state of mind by expressing how the best people for Pyramid Processing are the ones whose intrinsic motivation is completely in line with the demands of the work. When Mike talked about going out with his coworkers after work, he described not just the stress relief he experienced but a sense of surprise at how fulfilling it was to get together and "not complain about the boss" but talk about the structural problems with the company, such as problems with particular accounts. Mike further explained that call centers need people "who are going to be happy even if you ask them to work on the weekends or on rest days [days off]. These are not just people who speak good English and have a lot of experience working in a call center but people who will perform well and at the same time will really, really be happy. People who are driven to work, who really enjoy the work." Mike then went on to describe his coworkers at Pyramid: "We have a couple of supervisors here—I've seen them—they sometimes help out with the hiring and interviews, and I [came] to find out that they pulled double shifts to do so. And one manager here, she applied for vacation for three days, just so she could help out with the interviews in recruitment, which is not even her department."

Even more striking about Mike's description of his working environment was his description of intrinsically motivated performers as still "rare" in 2009. Continuing to describe the exceptional manager, he explained, "For example, if an agent doesn't end up getting the pay they were supposed to get, she [the manager] will really be harassing payroll on their behalf. In most companies here [in the Philippines], you won't see that kind of person." While this part of our conversation highlighted Mike's growing acculturation to and admiration of a productivist work ethic, something he mentioned later revealed his awareness of how this ethic might be shaping a new generation of workers. "Call center work," he declared, "it changes you, it changes your outlook on things. Before, when I was in high school, I had more time on my hands, and I did a lot less. But after working in this industry, I learned to do more and manage my time better. Time becomes like gold. So maybe this discipline should be advertised in the media and in school, to promote call center jobs. This is what parents want for their children, right?" In his enthusiasm about call center work, Mike thus began to imagine a new kind of Filipino, one whose inherent motivation for work and compliance with capital could help discipline a country long thought of by many of its citizens as an unruly place where capitalist accumulation and democratic culture are undermined by a lack of order and political corruption. Yet discipline did not seem to be the only thing on Mike's mind. In his eyes, call centers were the opposite of corrupt, as they produced individuals who actively enhanced the advantages of those around them, rather than take advantage for themselves.

Filipino Consciousness and Relational Labor

By way of concluding this chapter, I examine the way my research participants understood relational labor through specifically Filipino relational modes of consciousness. Tracing how Filipino call center agents made sense of call center work through already existing cultural constructs not only reveals how global labor processes intersect with localized identities and ways of life but also prepares us to see how relatability in general, and Filipino/American relatability in particular, are activated and harnessed in transnational call center work. While this chapter grounds the remainder of the book in a description and analysis of call center work and work culture, it is important to understand these processes as inextricably tied to and categorically shaped by my participants' understanding of Filipino subjectivity and cultural practice, rather than as simply a set of processes brought in from outside the Philippines and transplanted there unchanged. In contrast to frameworks that represent Filipino collectivist culture as clashing with Western management styles, I offer a more nuanced account of how a Filipino emotional economy constituted by unity, reciprocity, and an acceptance of unequal power relations finds new expression in a form of postindustrial and transnational work.[18]

Just as call center agents often spoke more about relationships with coworkers than their dealings with customers, they also, surprisingly, spoke more about how call center labor appealed to Filipino sensibilities rather than conflicted with them. It was very common, for example, for workers to point out that call center labor and work culture, with its intense emphasis on relatability, emotion, and mutuality, are more aligned with Filipino cultural norms than are traditional workplaces in the Philippines. Employees referred to their working environments as very "personal" and therefore more comfortable to maneuver in. Lara, for example, was a Premier Source team leader who had previously worked in sales for a transnational corporation in the food processing industry. Although coaching and teamwork were important in her previous job, Lara explained that "it's not personal the way it is in BPOs. Because of the process of coaching, it's really personal. Your manager really knows you, not just your performance. And if you know the agent personally, it makes it easier. You know how to push for performance when you know what's keeping the agent from doing well. You know how to approach the person when coaching him." Lara went on to say that approaching people in a more personal way "was very Filipino," thus suggesting, paradoxically, that these American/Western environments were in fact more Filipino than other, older workplaces.

Indeed, there were many moments in my interviews and research in which it became clear that call center workers interpret their workplace culture through a specifically Filipino consciousness. At one point during my interview with Ronnie, the Call Control team leader, and Pamela, his former agent, we were discussing how Ronnie's willingness to, as Pamela put it, "go the extra mile" for his agents made them feel obliged to maximize their performance on the job. To confirm what Pamela was saying, I asked, "So you feel accountable to him as his agent?" But before Pamela could answer, Ronnie added, "Although I don't really remind them that they have *utang [na loob]*. What I tell people is that they *don't* have to pay back."

Pamela nodded in agreement and continued, "And what's good about Ronnie is that if he's mad at you, he's mad at you just at that time. After he gets it all out, he's good with you." Turning to Ronnie with a smile, Pamela asked, "Remember that time you made me cry because I didn't handle that call properly? You came back after an hour, and we were already laughing about something totally different."

"I think that's the pattern that people under me notice," Ronnie remarked. "What they say is, during the first half of the shift, I'm 'untouchable,' because I am looking at and deal[ing] with the metrics. I look at all the things I have to do, I tell my agents the things they need to improve on, and that they need to prove to me that they can do it. But in the second half [of the shift], I change moods."

"Yeah, it's like he's okay again," Pamela added.

Ronnie continued, "Because I want agents to end their day on a good note. The first part of the day, even though I started it by being angry, I'm going to make sure things turn around. I'm going to make *bawi* (a retraction). And whether *they* make bawi or not, I make sure they will go home and go to sleep with a good feeling."

In this conversation Ronnie described some of the relational skills for which he is known among Call Control employees, in particular his personal investment in his agents and his interest in keeping their emotional fuel tanks filled up so they have enough affective energy for the next day of work. What is striking is Ronnie's invocation of Filipino terms to describe some aspects of the relationships he has with agents, suggesting that he understands workplace dynamics through Filipino social and cultural constructs and that the latter shape his approach to management. Like Ronnie, many of my research participants turned to Filipino terms to describe ways of approaching coworkers and the job itself. One agent explained that call center work made her more attuned to how service workers in general "handle their jobs," which she attributed to their *pagkatao,* or "how they interact with people." Many more described the relational and personal nature of call center management as "very Filipino" in that the harmonious relationships that coworkers seek with one another are an expression of *kapwa,* or the "unity of self with others," as well as *pakikiisa,* which emphasizes collective equality and emotional collaboration.

Exploring my informants' use of these terms helps to shed light on two ways that Filipino modes of relatability are put to use in call centers as postindustrial workplaces. *Utang na loob*—sometimes referred to as a "debt of gratitude"—names a social exchange that strengthens bonds between the giver and taker even as it implies that the latter is indebted to the former. *Utang na loob* thus operates by linking the *loob,* or "inside" of a person, to another; the concept is thus deeply relational, intimate, and personal and speaks to what Fenella Cannell has described as a distinctly Filipino emotional economy that seeks to transform hierarchical relations rather than simply reproduce them.[19] Ronnie evinces this transformative mode when he uses the phrase *make bawi* to describe how he recovers the affective losses caused by his draconian demands on agents' abilities. Although the retraction of the critical statement is important, perhaps the operative word is *making,* for making bawì points as much to the person's act of redeeming the negative situation for the sake of the relationship between two parties as it does to the erasure of the original offense. In this way, making bawì is an attempt to achieve harmony with the recipient of one's harsh words or criticism. When Ronnie speaks of *utang na loob* and making *bawì* as ways of relating that he must manage, measure, or contain, he implicitly refers to the kind of power negotiations Cannell describes in her work. In other words, despite being in a managerial position that requires him to treat agents as subordinates (both to himself and to the dictates of capital), Ronnie also works to transform his own feelings about his agents and their performance in order to equalize the power dynamic as much as possible. In these ways, Filipino call center workers interpret the call center's demands for relational labor in a way that reinforces Filipino relational practices and modes of identification.

At times, Filipino cultural constructs are elevated to the ethos of a company as a whole, even across lines of cultural and national difference. In a profile of an Indian CEO of a Philippine company, SPiGlobal, the author writes, "Parekh's belief in the Filipino people comes across as he uses a local value as one of SPi's own: *malasakit.* Loosely translated as compassion and care for others, *malasakit* has become an SPi core value that is behind the company's every move and action. *Malasakit* together with the values of meritocracy and being apolitical are the core values at work in all SPi locations across the globe."[20] In this example, the Filipino concept of malasakit becomes the basis of an entire organization's humanist ethos and thus an example of how capital, as Timothy Mitchell describes it, draws "parasitically" on cultural resources.[21] In this situation neither the feeling of malasakit nor the drive for productivity exists independently. Rather, as co-constituted and mutually reinforced, they demonstrate how a familiar system of interpretation—that is, an aspect of Filipino culture—is mobilized to make sense of the powerful social relations of capital and labor in which workers are intertwined. As a result, the capital-labor relation gets grafted onto and then reinforced by these cultural systems. While I was observing operations at Premier Source, for example, the assistant site director Araceli Ramos explained to me that workplace dynamics at the company were like those of a family, in which the American site director, Jerry, was like everyone's father. Describing her motivation to work while on vacation ("when on vacation, you work, you want to work"), Araceli explained that it was because of her feeling of malasakit, or "protective concern" for the company as if it were a family.[22]

By pointing to the centrality of Filipino cultural constructs within call center work, I do not mean to reproduce the reductive notion of Filipino core values that render cultural and social modes as objective and static. Rather, I see in these constructs what Sarita See describes as "a particular economy of values based upon reciprocity (ethical, political, cultural, philosophical, and material)," which gains new meaning in the context of transnational and postindustrial service work, often in ways that produce surplus value, worker consent to long hours, and a reinforcement of corporate culture while also making call center work a site of fulfilling personal relations and commitments—the affective contradictions of call center work that this chapter set out to explore.[23] On one hand, Araceli's use of malasakit demonstrates how call centers require a type of productivity that relies on affective relations that, because they are personal and relational, are experienced as real and, because they feel real, can be described in the same way as other real affective relations. Indeed, Araceli spent a great deal of our interview describing the congenial, trustful relationship she has with her supervisor, Jerry. Echoing other research participants, Araceli reminded me that "Filipinos are very relationship oriented" and that "it's more important to be happy with who you're working with than other factors about the job." On the other hand, Araceli's use of malasakit demonstrates how understanding things in a Filipino vein naturalizes the incessant productivity and full submersion in work that call centers seem to compel. Of course, no part of this process is natural or automatic, although it often appears that way.[24] Subjective capacities and practices such as kapwa, utang na loob, and bawi are not simply there for the taking; rather, they are shaped into raw materials for capital by the call center labor process and work culture. As Araceli would later tell me, she sometimes finds having to "make lambing with some coworkers"—that is, to show them fondness or affection—an utterly exhausting process.

CONTESTING SKILL AND VALUE

Race, Gender, and Filipino/American Relatability
in the Neoliberal Nation-State

A common refrain among many call center employees I interviewed in the Philippines, especially those who had joined the industry in its early years, was that they had only a vague impression of what the work entailed, even at the time they applied for the job. Primarily attracted to the substantial compensation the industry offered, these young college graduates often knew little about call center work beyond its very basic descriptors like "answering phones," "speaking English," and "working at night." As I came to learn, the ambiguity about call center work stemmed in part from its novelty in the Philippines, where local customer service lacked many of the standards developed over the past fifty years in the United States—including the use of toll-free 1–800 numbers—but it was also significantly rooted in the call center's uncertain connection to the corporate world. Because of their location in high-rise office buildings in business districts, as well as their association with technology and English, call centers were initially regarded by many Filipinos as a type of conventional office work, or what one former employee described as a "Makati-type job." Yet despite the white-collar exterior, the kind of skills required of call center employees and the range of professional advancement available to them were often unclear. A call center agent could be employed by a global powerhouse like Citibank but not in the recognizable positions of financial analyst, account manager, or even teller. Or one could work for a tech giant like IBM but not design or develop systems or hardware.

Instead, as all agents quickly learned, their tasks are highly specific and limited, pertaining to only one product or service at a time (such as troubleshooting cable boxes or handling insurance claims), and thus part of a larger spectrum of labor that is routine, precarious, low-wage, and feminized. What's more, in servicing customers in the United States and other advanced industrial countries, rank-and-file agents found themselves having to negotiate racial and national difference by conforming to the standards for accent and English imposed by management and finding ways to cope with customer racism and xenophobia. To confuse matters even further, call center agents earned more in entry-level positions than in comparable or even higher roles in more normative professions: a first-time customer service agent in a Philippine call center might earn anywhere from ₱10,000 to ₱15,000 per month while the monthly salaries of entry-level architects and accountants were less than half that, hovering around ₱3,000 and ₱6,000 per month, respectively.[1] Indeed, with its stringent requirements for English language skills and a full or partial college education, the call center industry was in fact more exclusive than many initially imagined it to be. Thus, my research participants understood that, structurally speaking, they were cheap labor, but they often did not perceive themselves as such.

This chapter looks closely at the social and cultural contradictions of call center work for workers, industry leaders, and the state, and the ways the latter entities attempt to resolve these problems. I argue that the tension and anxiety about the skill and value involved in call center work are the everyday expression of a larger set of questions about the symbolic and structural place of Filipino labor and culture in the global economy circulating throughout the industry. With their proximity to technology and knowledge, do call centers pave the way to a bright future or a dead end? Is call center work an opportunity to capitalize on Filipino/American relatability, allegedly one of the country's greatest resources? Or does it reproduce colonial relations of control? In keeping with the book as a whole, I do not aim to provide resolutions to these deliberations. Rather, this chapter examines the racialized and gendered terms in which the questions and ensuing debates are articulated, the stakes of the debates for various actors, and the ways of thinking and new practices—such as intensified market logic, investments in biocapital, and a renewed commitment to American English—to which these challenges give rise. In so doing, I demonstrate that the contestations over call center work arise in part from the symbolic investment that the state, and industry leaders, place in the call center industry as the means of fulfilling a new narrative about the Philippine nation and Filipino subjectivity—a narrative in which the ontologically secure, decolonized Filipino subject delivers the Philippines into a post-racial and postgender international arena where the nation competes in the battle for knowledge and information. In other words, this chapter demonstrates that the problem of call center work is in many respects a problem of the Philippine elite's own making, in that attempts to discursively transform the class, racial, and gender complexities of transnational call center work into a boon for the nation make the irruption of these complexities all the more palpable and problematic.

Global and Local Social Relations of Call Center Work

It is difficult to fully grasp the range of tensions linked to offshore call center work in the Philippines without mapping the global and local social relations on which the work is premised and in which it is embedded, as well as the significance of these relations in terms of race, class, and gender. Like nearly all offshore outsourced jobs, call center work has been moved to the developing world as a result of global labor arbitrage, the process by which corporations take advantage of differences in national or subnational wage scales and what is benignly referred to in economic parlance as the *cost of living.* Yet if the latter names the socially determined cost of maintaining a life beyond mere subsistence, then paying wages consistent with (or even slightly elevated above) the lower costs of living in the developing world reproduces the uneven material relations between nations and the devaluation of life on which different costs of living are based in the first place—dynamics in themselves produced by histories of colonialism and neocolonialism.[2] In other words, that labor is cheap in the Philippines is not a natural fact but a social relation; without the differential value of Filipino life, the entire process of call center outsourcing to the Philippines would not be possible. Offshoring call center jobs would also not be such a lucrative option for foreign corporations were it not for high rates of surplus labor among college-educated Filipino workers—a surplus that also results from uneven economic and social relations that have their roots in neocolonial relations of control by the International Monetary Fund and World Bank. As a manifestation of the already asymmetrical social relations between the U.S. corporations that are in command of the global value chain and the Filipino workers seeking work within it, call center jobs are thus both a source and a symptom of social contradiction.

Social relations at the global and national scales come to bear on the meaning and experience of call center work for Filipinos in everyday life in ways contingent on their class positions. Call center work has consistently drawn from the Philippines' top four socioeconomic classes—nebulous categories referred to as classes A, B, AB, and C, with class A representing the most affluent and elite group.[3] Yet, for members of classes A and AB especially, and to some extent class B as well, call center work's ambiguous relation to conventional educational fields and markers of professional status, not to mention its instability, raises questions about such work's ability to reproduce their social positions and class identities. Such anxieties are expressed in references to call center work as a "dead end" and "last resort"; indeed, almost all my research participants described business processing work as a far cry from their first choice of careers in fields like physical therapy, business administration, or engineering but the only meaningful choice available to them in the Philippines' narrow and constrained labor market. When I first met Mia in person in 2009, she had been having an ongoing dispute with a friend, a former call center trainer named Sophia, about long-term professional prospects in call center work. Mia was convinced that there was room for growth in the industry—"most people treat it as temporary, but it doesn't have to be," she claimed—and it was not until Sophia's brother started working in a call center that she began to see the possible legitimacy of Mia's perspective. Mia's defense of call center work was interesting to me because, as a self-identified member of class A, she in fact had other options for employment, namely, to take over a thriving business her mother had started. Members of other classes—B and C especially—tended not to have such equally rewarding opportunities.

One of the primary groups giving voice to the class contradictions of call center work are workers' parents, who often see the job as a distraction from their children's future studies or careers. Moreover, given the low autonomy and the sense of indebtedness that young Filipinos tend to have vis-à-vis their parents, many college graduates interested in call center work often find themselves negotiating between their narrow range of choices for employment and their parents' expectations for their social mobility. Many of my participants worried about their inability to reciprocate their parents' efforts in providing them with an education and therefore maintaining not only their class status but also the familial harmony that comes with honoring what they consider their parents' sacrifices. A Premier Source agent named Maricel, a college graduate who had studied architecture, explained the dilemma quite clearly: "I feel guilty working [as a call center agent] knowing that my parents worked hard and spent a lot to bring me to college and pay for what I wanted to be, so it's like, for me being in [a] call center, even though it pays for everything for me, I would like to pursue my career still." Moreover, as the story of my cousin Jocelyn that opened this book illustrates, choosing call center work can be particularly hard for young people who originally pursued nursing. Because nursing has been a primary means of social mobility for generations of Filipino families since the early 1970s, an individual's decision to desert nursing can instigate particularly intense anxiety on the part of family members, especially those who have provided the resources for pursuing this path.

In this context, the social anxiety about call center work as a dead end clearly stems from concerns about the social reproduction of class status based not just on income but also professional identity, proof of educational achievement, long-term economic stability, and cultural capital. John, a human resources employee I interviewed, explained that in order to support a young person's desire to pursue call center work, "They [parents and educators] have to be convinced that this is not just a job, but that it's going to be a good job"—meaning something that is stable, imbued with responsibility and respectability, and that creates value from parents' investment in children's education. I saw these worries most clearly in Bacolod in 2009, when call centers were just starting to proliferate there. According to the head recruiter of a top BPO company at the time, the applicants who possessed the skills required for the industry were the least likely to need or apply for a call center job, as their parents could support them while they pursued other career options. In many cases, parents in these families did not encourage their children to work in anything less than high-level professional jobs or family businesses, if they encouraged them to work at all. Such aversions are further bolstered by the history of locally situated class identities. Bacolod is the capital of Negros Occidental, a central Philippine province where for much of the twentieth century life and labor were organized around the cultivation, production, and export of sugar. Although its production has precipitously declined since the heady days of the 1970s, the image of the bourgeois landowning family whose children do not have to seek wage labor remains powerful. As the recruiter further explained, this local history resulted in an overwhelming number of applicants who, unlike the sons and daughters of affluent families, were in dire need of jobs but were considered underqualified for call center work.[4]

Instability also contributes significantly to doubts about the value of call center work. While call center wages are comparatively high, the jobs themselves are contingent on corporate actors whose decisions to pursue or cancel a contract with a BPO firm can change with little to no warning. "The thing that really scares me," a Premier Source employee named Victor proclaimed, "is the job security. Because we know our contracts are really tied to the client, so if the client pulls out, then you don't have work. It's in your contract that you are 'coterminous' with the account you are handling. So in terms of stability with work, we don't have it, because it's really, really easy for a call center to just pull out and . . . they're gone. And what are you going to do with the millions and millions of Filipinos who are working in the call center?" While not conveying accurate statistics about call center employment in the country, Victor's comments reflect his anxiety about being a part of a highly contingent workforce and his sense of the economic devastation that might befall call center workers if corporations decide to look elsewhere to fill call center seats. One way workers respond to these precarious conditions is to mirror the flexibility and speculation they see in the market.[5] A woman named Tess, whom I met in 2009, told me that after being let go from two accounts in which the corporate client abruptly discontinued the contract with the BPO firm, she had recently started another job handling life insurance claims for a more stable Canadian company. Although the job paid less than the previous two, Tess and her parents had decided that it would be better for her to take the more secure job at lower pay than to risk staying with an unstable account. Even though she had worked in the call center industry for five years, her parents still frowned on her line of employment because of its disconnection with her college education and its instability.

The tensions that call center work poses for young college-educated Filipinos thus amount to more than a personal dilemma or an uncomfortable conversation with a parent. Along with its affective and service-oriented purpose, call center work's precarity, lack of clear opportunities for professional advancement, and routine nature bear all the markings of feminized, low-status work, at the same time as it pays relatively high wages. In this way, the anxiety my research participants experience in everyday life points to how gendered and racialized global processes shape perceptions of skill and value, and thus the way class identities are socially constructed both locally and transnationally. At times, the various scales of these conflicts converge around the question of what constitutes a normative social exchange for a member of the middle or affluent class. In one of my many discussions with Joel Partido, the vice president of human resources at Vox Elite (and, in his forties, one of the oldest people I had met in the industry), he explained the following about Cobalt, the prepaid mobile phone service offered by a major wireless company in the United States that was one of Vox Elite's corporate accounts:

> Cobalt cater[s] to the lower-class folks in the U.S., so normally [agents will] be talking to blacks or Hispanics [sic]. You know, it's very slang, very loose, and it's very direct, no room for "Ma'am, Sir." So if an agent, suddenly he or she—let's say she—gets a caller who says, "Yo, dude, I ran out of minutes, blast me thirty bucks!" it would make them think, "Is this something that I'd like to do for a living? Talk with those dudes?" And, you know, once we are not able to serve them or resolve their problems, they use very colorful language. . . . I'm probably stereotyping some agents who are middle-aged, coming from a conventional family and not so used to slang and American street jargon. But let's say for the more toxic accounts or programs, where it's normal for you to get shouted at, the Filipino tries to rationalize everything and say, "I've not been raised by my family to be shouted at from someone halfway around the world who I don't even know, and I'm supposed to resolve his problem?"

Joel's description of the Cobalt clientele implies that this racialized encounter with low-income, nonwhite Americans might be perceived by Filipino call center agents as below their social location. His comments further suggest that racial identity, intersecting with class position, is perceived as having a bearing on not only speech but sociability writ large: black Americans and Latinos of the "lower classes," according to Joel, eschew polite formalities and resort to cursing when there is a problem resolving their customer service needs. Constructing an economically marginal black or Latino man ("those dudes") as the subjective *other* to a middle-aged Filipino woman, Joel's description also demonstrates how interacting with customers perceived to be black or Latino and lower class is imagined as the limit of agents' social capacities and thus their class positions. Within this cultural logic, the kind of treatment an agent deserves is legitimized by the conventional institution of social reproduction and class status (a family), but such interlocutors, by using speech linked to a space imagined as devoid of formal institutions (the street), frustrate agents' class-based expectations. In turn, these interactions reveal how class identities can be constructed transnationally through intersections of race and gender, but also how Filipino agents attempt to recuperate a perceived loss of status by undermining American authority in a way that relies on the vilification of the poor and nonwhite.[6]

Contestation and Negotiation in the Public Eye

The anxiety that workers feel about perceptions of their choices and status was palpable throughout my fieldwork and interviews. In fact, seeing me as someone with an audience for my scholarship, my research participants were often extremely keen to clarify many aspects of their work for me.[7] Their eagerness made sense in light of the periodic public contestation over call center work's value to the nation. For example, in March 2013 Juan Miguel Luz, the associate dean of the Asian Institute of Management, delivered a commencement speech to the graduates of Bacolod's prestigious University of Saint La Salle. After waxing nostalgic about his early days teaching at a mission school in one of the city's working-class settlements, Luz described the Bacolod that he sees in the present, focusing exclusively on the call center industry. He began by mentioning Bacolod's status as a Next Wave city, which marked it as one of the country's premier hubs for information and communication technology outside of Manila, and then ran through the standard descriptors of call center work: global connections, overnight shifts, American English, and happy hours that begin at six in the morning. What Luz said next, however, struck a dissonant chord with the crowd. Describing call center work as a "highly competitive" world, a source of signing bonuses, and a chance to make lasting friendships, he proclaimed, "But call centers are also the lowest-paying, least skilled jobs in the knowledge-processing industry. And if the Philippines (and Bacolod) do not move up the skills ladder to more knowledge-based work (as opposed to voice or call agent work answering simple questions or problem-solving online), call center work will move elsewhere to a lower paying jurisdiction or country. Such is the nature of the BPO industry." Luz then encouraged the students to keep in mind that should Bacolod move up the knowledge-processing ladder, away from the "transient" call center industry, it would contribute to the recent economic growth for which the Philippines had become "respected again abroad."[8]

When I arrived in Bacolod in June of that year to conduct my research, the memory of Luz's speech still lingered in the minds of many call center workers. Here was a leading educator and prominent businessman, my research participants said, who was trying to make the Philippines more globally competitive—"as we all are," added one person—but who clearly knew nothing about the trials and tribulations of the workers on the front lines of the industry. On the Facebook page where the speech was posted, call center employees angered by Luz's description of their jobs as low skilled and low paid thus mounted a defense of their work. Many eagerly pointed out the strenuous demands of the job, their bountiful paychecks, and the "excellent, competitive, smart, and strategic" qualities of call center employees. "The BPO [industry] has long been stereotyped by those people who haven't been there," wrote one commenter. "They will always think people who work in a call center don't know much; [are] not qualified [for] their suppose[d]-to-be-career so then they opt for call centers." Another person summed up these sentiments by simply saying that "the speech discredited the value of the people working for the BPO industry." In response to this collective protest, Luz issued a public apology for the offense and "misimpression" his speech had caused. In the apology, Luz revised his description of call center work, referring to it vaguely as "all about knowledge-processing" and more specifically as "a service industry" and therefore "built on individuals . . . who bring on board two distinct skill sets (if not more): English communication skills and technical skills in a wide range of disciplines." He ended the apology by explaining, "As rightly pointed out to me by call center agents themselves, the work is tough, the ability to 'think on one's feet' and 'out-of-the-box' is paramount, and the need to stay calm in the face of demanding clients is difficult to master, but this they do with great ability."[9]

Luz's speech and the intense discussion that ensued highlight the way call center workers tend to respond to the charge that their work does not require skill or lacks long-term value. While pointing to the social and cultural demands on their labor, workers also turn to the language and logic of the market, specifically through the discourse of professionalism. In my conversations with call center employees, professionalism was invoked in a variety of ways, but the most prevalent was as a way of creating emotional distance from racist and xenophobic customers. As previous scholars have documented, call center work subjects agents to the policing of racial and national boundaries by customers for whom a non-American accent becomes an occasion to delegitimize a call center agents' skills (by asking to speak to either a supervisor or an American) or accuse agents of stealing American jobs. Kiran Mirchandani, following David Theo Goldberg, refers to such acts as expressions of neoliberal racism in which customers display their entitlement to racist behavior on the basis of consumer preferences or choice.[10] In this context, professionalism means being nonreactive, not taking customer racism personally or overidentifying with it, and thus not disrupting the course of service delivery. In other words, the discourse of professionalism allows call center agents to see dealing with racism and xenophobia as simply what the market demands of them, or what Mirchandani describes as a "job-related skill."[11] This discourse also perhaps helps explain why most of the questions about dealing with customer racism that I posed to interviewees were met with rather flat responses. While perhaps initially upset by a caller's aggressive remarks about their accents or location in the Philippines, my informants shook these experiences off by saying things like "That's just how some people are" and "You just have to know how to deal with them, mostly by ignoring them."

Professionalism was also invoked in ways that challenged the idea of call center workers' jobs as menial. In the later years of my fieldwork, for example, the concept of call center workers as subject-matter experts emerged, recasting workers into knowledgeable roles where their value came not from the breadth of their skills or their theoretical knowledge but their familiarity with a particular subset of information about a product or service. Similarly, by reiterating the call center industry rhetoric about options for advancement and permanence, the language of professionalism also helped workers negotiate the pushback about their jobs being dead ends. Call center agents quickly learn the corporate hierarchy on which outsourced call centers are built, starting with rank-and-file agents and moving up to team leaders, account heads, and operations managers; indeed, many of my informants became team leaders and midlevel managers faster than they had anticipated and before they even really understood what the jobs entailed. "In this industry," said Bryan from Global Invest, "you can be promoted as fast as you can climb the ladder." Similarly, Billie, an agent whose initial impression of call center work was as something "anyone can get into," realized that "there's a future here," a notion she started to gather from her company's human resources representatives on her very first day of training.

For many, the value of call center work could also be recuperated in relation to its demand for advanced speakers of English. Even though English-language instruction is extended to all Filipinos through public education, only those whose social positions and material resources allow them to hear and practice the language stand a good chance of being able to command it at the level used in call center work. Such cultural capital is derived from formal education but is also inherited through parents or other family members whose jobs and/or education necessitate high-level English language skills. In turn, such privileged families have better access to cultural products that help refine one's language skills, such as opportunities to travel to English-speaking countries or expensive cable networks that broadcast American television shows. It was no surprise to me, for example, that Mia, who had attended elite private schools in Manila, had experienced such speedy upward mobility in the industry. Similarly, after attending school in England and working for a few years at a resort in southern Florida, Mia's friend Sophia was so adept at English that she moved from the position of rank-and-file agent to trainer in a matter of weeks. The class contradiction of call center work could thus not be clearer: what many consider a low-skilled occupation fit for cheap labor turns out to be a job that requires a type of cultural capital that correlates strongly with economic privilege.[12]

Luz's speech also points to the way elite industry leaders' abstract and detached understanding of the global value chain eclipses the everyday toil of actually existing workers, even if both share the same aspirations and vision for the future of the nation-state. Workers indeed understand that as customer service or technical support representatives they are considered less skilled than workers higher up the global value chain, often expressing their awareness of their structural status through descriptions of their jobs as ones that "Americans don't want to do," a statement that I believe speaks less to an empirically based understanding of the actual jobs people in the United States are willing to take on and more to their awareness of how U.S. corporations seek to pay workers the lowest wages possible and therefore move jobs overseas. Their outcry against Luz was thus not a result of ignorance or misrecognition about how value is constructed and perceived within the global economy. Rather, workers objected to the framing of their labor as a mere preliminary space in their nation's march toward modernity, one in which they indulge in juvenile desires for fast money and a good time. This meant, however, getting Luz to see their struggle as racialized and feminized cheap global labor that nonetheless contributed to the nation with their knowledge-based skills. Luz evoked this ostensible contradiction in his apology, in which he subsequently described call center work as, vaguely, "all about knowledge-processing" and part of the service industry. The contestation over Luz's speech thus demonstrated how Filipino call center workers grappled with the complex process of valuation and devaluation involved in service work in the postindustrial global economy— that is, how many service industry jobs draw on mental acumen but are nonetheless classified, and classed, in ways that devalue workers' labor.

Public discussion of the social and cultural value of call center work also periodically emerged from the other end of the political spectrum, among those critical of the state's complicity with the forces of global capital in general and the United States in particular. Standing before the Philippine congress in 2005, Raymond Palatino, a representative of the radical Kabataan (Youth) Party, excoriated the government for using foreign jobs as a palliative against the country's chronic labor crisis. Voicing concerns about how call center workers are degraded by BPO companies, Palatino referred to the workers as "honor students [and] student leaders who graduated from the best universities in the country" who are "relegated to answering calls from customers whose problems most of the time can be fixed by even a toddler."[13] By characterizing the work as fit for children, the speech played on the powerful metaphor of the Philippines as the object of infantilization by more powerful countries, suggesting that the call center industry reproduced this colonial discourse in the contemporary era. Yet descriptions like Palatino's also elide the nuances and complexities of call center work, in part by perpetuating the image of call center agents as mere casualties of neoliberal globalization's advance.

Blamed by Americans for stealing jobs, criticized by elites for lacking aspiration, and painted as subjugated victims by critics of globalization, call center workers are thus caught between the misplaced grievances of the American populace and the frustrations of contemporary Philippine nationalisms. In response to this explicit and implicit outing—a revelatory discourse that seeks to expose the supposedly true value of call center work—call center workers insist on the challenges and professionalism that their work entails. My research participants were adamant, for example, about the difficulty of their work, which they describe not as strictly or even primarily stemming from what scholars call work's effort—the particular task at hand—but from work's intensity, or the conditions under which they do these tasks.[14] Time and time again the call center employees I interacted with underscored the importance of their affective efforts, the pressure to perform, and the work's strain on their social lives. For most of my research participants, the combination of these demands—managing feelings while getting through all the service delivery steps in a timely manner—proved to be the most taxing aspect of their work. "It's hard," one Call Control worker explained to me, "because you want to build rapport with [the customer], but in less [sic] time possible, and if you're not assertive, you'll end up with more complaints from them, the call takes longer, and [they won't find you] convincing anymore. . . . Then the person will literally run all over you. You can't let them take control of you. You have to always be on top and be pleasant at the same time." Call center workers thus attempt to revalorize their feminized and racialized labor by not only calling attention to the efforts involved in emotional interactions but also highlighting the struggle for power that each call entails. Moreover, this revalorization is an attempt to revise the signs of gendered, racialized, and sexualized servitude that, in public discourse, are linked to call center work: rather than being completely ruled by customers' desires, workers point out that they are actually the ones who have to "be on top."

Yet there are inconsistencies, tensions, and contradictions in workers' defenses as well. As I discuss in more detail in the following chapter, when it comes to racism and xenophobia, the discourse of professionalism is merely one of containment rather than confrontation or critique, thus leaving transnational racialized structures of power intact. Similarly, the language of expertise in the title "subject-matter expert" obscures rather than acknowledges the potential difficulties of finding future work based on the very limited knowledge that such expertise represents. Moreover, while workers highlight the potential for advancement in the industry in order to contest its dead-end status, they just as often refer to the work as temporary so as to present themselves as serious people not swept up in the industry's hype and emphasize their desire to move on to the more normative professions for which they were previously trained or educated. A Call Control employee named Charlene articulated this position most clearly when she described the job "as something transient," despite having worked in call centers for eight years. "For most grads, it's the last option. I was a clinical dietician before I got into the industry. Call Control was paying the highest, so I grabbed it. It's the first time to earn your own money . . . but you won't want to stay there." After hearing sentiments like Charlene's throughout my fieldwork, I began to ask people more directly about whether or not they had plans to continue working in the industry. In a group interview, Valerie, a single mother, responded, "I just hope to stay here in the meantime," then explained that she was interested in returning to her original choice of careers, in marketing. Valerie added that in the four years she had been working in the industry, she had never heard of anyone making a long-term plan to stay in the industry for good. "This place is temporary, really. This is more like a ways and means for a short period. This is not a place wherein you anticipate becoming a manager."

Again, rather than understanding my research participants' discrepant descriptions of call center work as a sign of confusion, I understand them as active negotiations of the social and cultural contradictions of the industry and their own ambivalence about being part of it. In attempting to alleviate their parents' and their own anxieties about the value and skills involved in call center work, agents could, for example, always point to the ample compensation they were receiving. Making assertive and declarative statements like "There's no other industry that will pay you the same" or "I'm really earning a lot in this job," my research participants often spoke of call center work as a kind of trump card in the country's educational and employment gamble, and the only way they could make a substantial contribution to their family's survival, growth, or well-being. Such sobering economic logic is of course difficult to dispute. What I found intriguing about such claims, however, is how my research participants themselves were never quite willing to accept that this type of rational market logic *should* dominate their thinking or their lives—only that it did. Indeed, although I was not surprised to find that most of my participants' parents acquiesced to their decision to work in the call center industry once they witnessed their children's earning power, I also learned that such deference to money could not be assumed. Within a cultural matrix in which class status is attached to education and the perceived social value of one's work, for some families income alone does not automatically justify a digression from a more professional path. By voicing the desire to pursue different lines of work, my research participants and their parents were thus not only making efforts to recuperate a perceived loss of class status but also expressing hopes that one day Filipinos would be able to choose their line of work based on something more than just income. Thus, it is possible to interpret statements about high earning potential as affirming the industry's rewards in the face of those who criticize these workers' choices but also lamenting the uneven social relations in which their lives were clearly enmeshed.

Industry Anxieties

Given the Philippines' attempts to gain a firm foothold in the knowledge economy, the sense that call center work entails feminized and racialized forms of service, is structurally precarious, and maintains an ambiguous relation to educational achievement presents a problem not only in the everyday lives of workers but in the ideological imaginaries and material practices of industry leaders as well as the state. Steered by industry leaders who, as elite actors, have a strong influence on its objectives, the Philippine state since the late twentieth century has played a major role in what scholars describe as the disarticulation of industry and services from the national economy and their reintegration or rearticulation with transnational political-economic structures that serve global capital.[15] Both state and elite actors also significantly shape the reproduction of the nation-state as a symbol and a story, in which Filipino labor and culture come to have significant meaning in the everyday life of the nation and within the international arena.[16]

Given their aspirations, business leaders and the state are thus caught between the need to support the existing call center industry and the need to relentlessly upgrade the Philippines and its citizens. On one hand, for example, industry and state actors concede that there are not enough people to fill call center jobs, recognizing this as a problem that industry leaders must face head-on. On the other hand, these same parties insist that the Philippines can move up the global value chain to higher-order and more complex service work. Indeed, since the call center industry's emergence, BPO business leaders have been clamoring for more jobs in knowledge-processing outsourcing and health information management, leading to a pervasive anxiety about the nation's store of human capital, and a stark contradiction between the optimism about the Philippines' place in the global service industry and the fear that its failure is inevitable. In article after article in *Breakthroughs!*—the newsletter for the Information Technology and Business Process Outsourcing Association of the Philippines (IBPAP), an umbrella organization for the industry that facilitates offshoring outsourcing to the country—observers express considerable concern about a gap between the growth of the industry and the skills of available workers. In 2007 one writer worried that there might be an "insufficient quantity of suitable and willing talent to fuel growth" of the call center industry.[17] Several years later, after the Philippines had already surpassed India in voice services, another declared, "Unless something dramatic happens very soon, the Philippines will not be able to meet demand for educated and talented people by next year."[18]

Industry organizations attempt to handle this shortage of talent in a number of ways, one of which is to intensify efforts to generate biocapital, or the labor power and thus potential profits from the cognitive and emotional capacities appropriated in call center work.[19] Such efforts take the form of government-sponsored programs, including ones that train individuals marked as "near hires"—candidates who have passed an initial screening by potential employers but still need to develop certain skills to qualify for employment.[20] Often marking a person from a lower economic class and/or one who lacks proficient English language skills, the category of a near hire reveals how proximity to the call center industry and the chances of landing a call center job are contributing to new constructions of class in the contemporary Philippines. But the efforts to produce biocapital for call centers extend across the educated populace at large. One of the best examples of this drive is the Global Competitiveness Assessment Tool (GCAT), which assesses competencies relevant to service work, including a person's verbal and quantitative skills, computer literacy, and visual-spatial acuity. The GCAT also has a behavioral component, which "tests a BPO candidate's service orientation," including "responsiveness, empathy, interpersonal communication, courtesy, reliability, and learning orientation."[21] Evoking the standardized tests for entry into graduate degree programs in the United States, such as the MCAT, LSAT, and GMAT, the GCAT thus functions as a credentialing and professionalizing technique that addresses the stigma of outsourced work among middle-class and elite educated workers by codifying the exclusivity of the labor market for call center workers in the country and measuring a person's competitiveness within it. The assessment also evinces the aspirations of the industry and the state to move up the global value chain: "What the GCAT emphasizes," states an industry newsletter, "is that the IT-BPO is not limited to voice services" but can expand to include more knowledge process outsourcing and other professional services.[22] To top off these efforts, in 2013 the BPAP added the term "information technology" to the organization's original name (the Business Process Outsourcing Association of the Philippines), creating the Information Technology and Business Process Outsourcing Association of the Philippines (IBPAP). The additional reference thus emphasizes the organization's ability to "provide the whole spectrum of world-class services . . . including corporate and complex services, creative processes and products, customer relations and health care information management, and software product development"—that is, not just support for customer service call centers.[23] In fact, the idea for the GCAT started with the IBPAP, which referred to it early on as the BPAP National Competency Test.[24]

Like call center workers, industry leaders also see the discrepancy between call center work and educational achievement as an obstacle to its growth. In another issue of *Breakthroughs!,* IBPAP executive Martin Crisostomo declared that "the task is to market the IT-BPO or call center job as a worthwhile and long-term career in order to attract more qualified applicants."[25] Part of these efforts have been targeted at overseas Filipino workers, whom business leaders hope to entice to return home to fill call center seats. To do so, however, industry leaders must be able to demonstrate that call center work constitutes a massive improvement on overseas work. In an article entitled "It's Time for Heroes to Come Home," Crisostomo told the story of a single mother working in domestic service in Saudi Arabia who was able to return to the Philippines and raise her two children with a salary and benefits comparable to what she had been receiving from her previous employer.[26] "As a domestic helper for years," Crisostomo explained further, "English was the only way she could communicate with her Arabian [sic] employer—and this honed her speaking skills, which probably helped her qualify in our industry." In a different article, Crisostomo discussed another domestic worker, employed in the United States, "who is now CEO of her own IT outsourcing company in Davao—with one of its clients being no less than U.S. president Barack Obama."[27] Such stories suggest a reconfigured hierarchy of labor, in which call center work's proximity to technology and ostensible pathway to ownership of the means of production elevate it above overseas Filipinos' work abroad, which is rendered into mere preparation for the more cosmopolitan and corporate world of call centers.

Stories of overseas Filipino workers who return to the Philippines to pursue call center work thus stage several resolutions to the ideological problems challenging the Philippine nation-state, including the problem of labor migration. The narratives suggest that after decades of failing to generate jobs within the country, the Philippine state is finally able to reclaim the bodies of its citizens, though not necessarily the surplus value they produce. By knitting together the threads unraveled by globalization, the call center industry becomes the site of an imagined return of overseas Filipino workers to the Philippines, and thus a reassembly of the nation as home. Such stories also consistently convey—however inaccurately—that call center work allows Filipinos to withdraw from a sphere of dependence that revolves around the United States. Crisostomo went on to write about a Filipino nurse who, "on getting her visa and complete papers for working in the States, just turned her back and decided to stay home in exchange for a great opportunity in healthcare information management outsourcing."[28] Another IBPAP newsletter article profiling people whose lives have been transformed as a result of their employment in the BPO industry is about Peachy, "a registered nurse who wanted to work in an American hospital" but who sought call center work when the U.S. financial crisis struck. For the author, "Peachy proves that you need not stray too far from home to find fulfillment and prosperity."[29] The inherent irony of these narratives is that most call center jobs in the Philippines not only are for U.S. corporations but also sometimes succeed in bringing Filipinos in *closer* proximity to the United States, as was the case with the domestic worker–turned–CEO cited above. Yet this does not stop industry leaders from using these notions to brand the industry as elevated above overseas work and therefore recruit new workers.

In its attempt to project the image of a technologically advanced Philippines ready to take on complex offshore work at home rather than sending citizens abroad, the Philippine state affirms and supports industry aspirations. An early iteration of this state-generated national imaginary was the Arroyo administration's project for the Philippine Cyberservices Corridor (PCC). Modeled after the miles-long stretch of office space in Dallas, Texas, that houses major IT companies like Ericsson and AT&T, as well as Malaysia's Multimedia Super Corridor, the PCC would cover six hundred miles, connecting cities in the northernmost and southernmost regions of the country.[30] The economic goal of the PCC was to encourage foreign and local investment in IT-enabled services in general and, in keeping with the Arroyo administration's aspiration for greater inclusion in the knowledge economy, to move the Philippines beyond BPO work and toward knowledge process outsourcing and health information management. Yet the image and rhetoric surrounding the PCC did cultural work as well. By linking the nation's super regions through technology, the PCC contributed to what Neferti Xina M. Tadiar calls the "dreamwork" of national development in the age of neoliberal globalization, a fetishization of the Philippine state's desire to produce an unimpeded flow of information and capital.[31] Moreover, as a backbone on which the national economy hangs, the PCC enhances the representation of the Philippine economy as rehabilitated, economically virile, and able to be penetrated by foreign capital with the integrity of a consenting partner protected by the ASEAN—its family and economic pack—rather than a victim of the aggressive advances of stronger, wealthier nations.

In this way, the PCC reinforced the notion that in the twenty-first century exploitative relations of dependence between the global north and south have been reconfigured into relations of investment and partnership. The nation is thus imagined as a postracial, postgender space in which Filipino labor is intelligible through the neutral register of human capital rather than the differential language of race, gender, and ability. The workers I interviewed evoked this imagined equitable partnership between the Philippines and other nations. One such person was Bryan Aclan, the midlevel manager for Global Invest who had given me a tour of the bank's call center in Manila. After we talked about Bryan's ambition to climb the corporate ladder from his starting position as a customer service representative, we then discussed the ideological conflict in the Philippines between those struggling for the development of national industries and those, like Bryan, who believe that the Philippine government ought to court investment from other countries as much and as often as possible. According to Bryan, the Philippines "can no longer afford to be insular." "We live in a global society," he elaborated. "The world is so small. Being too patriotic doesn't suit us as a growing nation. Even China had to open up—it's the largest country in the world, but it realized it needs other countries, too." Bryan's comparison of the Philippines (a country of 90 million people with a GDP hovering around $250 billion) with China (with 1.4 billion people and a GDP of $12.4 trillion) reveals how the post–Cold War rhetoric of national partnership enables an understanding of countries as occupying an even ethical terrain even as they inhabit radically different economic territories. It also points to the allure of the market logic through which many people attempt to resolve the contradictions of call center work.

Filipino/American Relatability and the Contradictions of Colonial Recall

My interest in industry actors and the state has less to do with the efficacy of their efforts in solving the problem of the talent gap and more with how the problem of call center work is socially constructed and imagined, including how it is rooted within a longer history of the Philippines' structural subordination within the global economy and of the racialization and feminization of Filipinos as subjects of U.S. colonialism and U.S.-led neoliberalism. Many of the ideological contradictions and national anxieties related to call center work emanate, I argue, from the recapitulation of these dynamics, or what I refer to as *colonial recall*. After outsourcing jobs to Europe and then India, U.S. companies flocked to the Philippines not only because Filipino workers command lower wages but also because the latter could offer what I have called Filipino/American relatability as an affective and communicative resource. References to this ostensibly distinct Filipino capacity abound in the Philippine call center industry's marketing literature and research reports. An account of Philippine services written in 2005 insisted, for example, that with the takeoff of call centers, "the country stands to gain from its cultural affinity with the major major that is the United States" and that "a result of this affinity, strengthened through the country's public educational system patterned after that of the United States, is the functional level of English-speaking skills of the Filipinos."[32] Using greater rhetorical flourish, a more recent "Investor Primer" produced by the IBPAP boasts that "when a North American client's customer makes a reference to the New York Knicks, Lady Gaga, or upcoming national elections, the Filipino knowledge worker always relates."[33] Nor is the discourse of relatability limited to these official spaces of representation; my research participants also often spoke of this ostensibly distinct Filipino quality as well.

It is possible to read the rhetoric of relatability as yet another instance in which elite labor brokers and workers, desperate for capital investment in the country and decent jobs in general, essentialize Filipino identity to secure a comparative advantage in the global marketplace. In this way, colonial recall entails an instrumental evocation of the colonial past that sanitizes it for the purposes of global capital and the neoliberal national project.[34] Beyond this, however, we might ask what ideological purposes and effects these claims about the affective features of Filipino subjectivity actually serve and set in motion within a larger narrative about the Philippine nation-state. In other words, it is worth noting how everyday claims about Filipino social capacities are embedded within a kind of vernacular understanding of the colonial past and in turn become part of the material conditions of possibility of the present. When workers, industry boosters, and state actors refer to an exceptional affective relationship between Filipinos and Americans, they refer to what I call *Filipino/American relatability*, or an intimate form of power crafted by American colonizers, in which the latter extracted cooperation and communicative capacities from Filipino subjects as a means of both disciplining them to the colonial order and also achieving the cultural proximity and so-called fellowship between the United States and the Philippines on which the colonial project relied. Moreover, as a technology of power that was justified on the basis of Filipino racial difference, Filipino/American relatability was also a racialized mode of sociality in which the colonized subject's proximity or likeness to colonial authority—that is, Filipinos' ability to relate to Americans (or Americans' demands that Filipinos relate to them)—was a crucial way in which imperial influence and control were wielded through affective, social, and communicate capacities. Filipino/American relatability is thus a manifestation of colonialism in its cultural and most subjective forms, and it is recalled—that is, brought to mind but also transferred back to its source—in the structure and substance of offshore call center work. The appropriation of Filipinos' affective capacities, the imperative to speak American English, the need to orient the self to American customers and corporate clients, and the vexed invitation to think of oneself as part of American domestic spaces—all of these aspects of Filipino/American relatability reemerge in call centers, creating unsettling moments in which the demand for subservient imitation and internalization of American culture and rules of order emerges in the present.

Within the postracial and postgender discourse of the global economy, however, Filipino/American relatability is seen not as a technique of power but as a source of empowerment, a cultural attribute and affective orientation of the Filipino people defined by an exceptional ability to understand and forge cultural connections to Americans—in other words, not as a problem but as a kind of social capital. Within this ideological landscape, the Philippines' apparent success in call center work indexes the ontological security of "Filipino" as an ostensibly decolonized, postconquest identity.[35] Former colonial subjects whose ability to relate to Americans was intimately tied to their very subjugation, and who had the English language imposed on them from above, Filipinos could now be neoliberal subjects for whom relatability is a form of commodified affective labor that proves not their subservience to the United States, but their necessity and value to the global economy; not their imitation of American culture, but their flexible command of it; not their colonially induced confusion over Filipino identity, but their unique ability to adapt to other cultures as a result of it.

The clearest articulation of this cultural logic was presented to me in 2009 during a series of meetings with BPAP executives Melvin Legarda and Joseph Santiago, men in their forties who, unsurprisingly, treated our encounters as just another opportunity to market the Philippines by reiterating the cultural qualities that ostensibly make the country and its citizens ideal for call center work.[36] In one portion of our discussion, Joseph, the senior of the two, described a commercial that BPAP had developed to market the Philippine BPO industry to corporations with a U.S. customer base. According to Joseph, in the commercial a white male customer service agent smiles and speaks "perfect English" to a customer over the phone. At the end of the call, the audience sees the white agent peel off a mask to reveal that he is really Filipino, clearly suggesting that Filipinos are so adept at sounding like native English speakers with American accents that the usual disruptions in communication that come with differences in language and accent would not be a problem with Filipino agents on the line. Importantly, however, Joseph explained that BPAP decided to drop the commercial after the organization realized it no longer needed to convince potential U.S. corporate clients that Filipino agents could affect an American accent to service a U.S. customer base. At a certain point, Joseph explained, BPAP executives came to believe that agents could simply "be themselves" while on the phone with customers, which "made for the best [training] programs."

Joseph's explanation that managers began to discard the practice of training agents to mimic national accents—replacing it with accent-neutralization training—points to a real policy shift in the industry at large that started as early as 2004. A number of issues precipitated the change. First, training in neutral accents was a response to U.S.- and U.K.-based customers who felt angered by the perceived insincerity and foolishness of the mimicry and thus became distrustful of the companies the agents represented. Indeed, in my training experience at Vox Elite we were warned that "Americans can always detect a foreign accent so don't bother trying to fake one." Another reason relates to cost cutting and flexibility: accent-neutralization programs allow staff to move easily among accounts that are linked to different parts of the world and therefore reduce the cost of training. Moreover, language experts had finally managed to convince call center managers and trainers that miscommunication was not necessarily due to an agent's accent but their lack of proficiency in conversational and colloquial English, and therefore that more attention should be given to those aspects of speech, rather than culturally specific modes of pronunciation.[37] Antonio, the QA manager at Pyramid Processing, articulated this point to me when he explained that "most customers know that his or her service calls will be thrown somewhere in the third world." The "real" source of customers' frustration, Antonio explained, was not the agents' accents but their lack of facility in the English language.

The idea and practice of accent neutralization has received greater attention from scholars in recent years, given its increasingly widespread use in offshore call centers.[38] Whether an accent can ever in fact be neutral and what such attempts at neutrality might mean are pertinent questions that echo similar uncertainties about the concept of global English, which I discuss below. For A. Aneesh, accent neutralization is a significant part of a larger process of "unhinging" people from the particulars of place, identity, and biological clocks; neutrality and standardization are thus key to understanding globalization.[39] To Joseph Santiago, however, the implementation of accent-neutralization policies allowed Filipinos to further express their particularities *as* Filipinos. Emphasizing that with neutral accents Filipinos could just "be themselves" (since they had what he called "light accents" anyhow), he offered a nationalistic interpretation of the policy changes. In other words, Joseph's understanding of the policy shift created an interpretive opening in which he could reinforce the ontological security of Filipino subjectivity within a transnational labor process that demanded that Filipinos speak for U.S. corporations in the language of a former colonial power. Within this cultural logic, the idea that "we don't have to sound like them" to be good at our jobs became a powerful confirmation of Filipinos' unadulterated and undisguised presence on the world stage. It also further reinforced that if call center agents learned to speak American English, it was because American English is what an account— that is, the market—demanded, not because it was a naturally superior language. Indeed, Joseph's brief but illuminating interpretation of the accent-neutralization policy suggested that the meaning of Filipino/American relatability had shifted from a sign of colonial control to one of neoliberal cultural capital, and thus that Filipinos had moved past mimicry as a way to relate, literally and figuratively, to America and Americans. In this way, I saw how, as an umbrella organization whose managers and staff interact with potential clients from around the world and which services the whole industry, the IBPAP plays an important role in maintaining the ideological apparatus on which Filipino citizens might hang their aspirations for the nation-state. For example, in his requisite talk about the Philippines' labor power or "talent supply," Melvin cited the nation's annual graduation rate (then 400,000 graduates per year), as well as its strength in English and IT. Knowing what I did about the deskilling that outsourced customer service work represented, I asked Melvin how training in IT would help an employee in the industry, but he did not answer my question directly. Instead, he parlayed the question into an opportunity to herald the Philippine government's support for building IT infrastructure and thus greater digital connectivity across the country through the PCC.

Moments like these reveal how industry leaders themselves struggle to make sense of the narratives they have a role in creating. At one point, for example, my conversation with Joseph and Melvin turned to competition between India and the Philippines within the global market for back-office work. Echoing a popular topic in many of my interviews with other people, Joseph began to speak about the cultural traits that make Filipinos far better suited for customer service work than Indians. When I asked why he thought this was the case, Joseph responded, "There's an exact set of rules to service in India. They are more utilitarian. Filipinos are compassionate," to which Melvin added, "We are good at working with the heart."

Joseph continued, "It also has to do with our deep immersion at the bottom of the ladder for so many years. We were a colony of Spain, and then the United States, the Japanese invaded us during the war, and then poverty really pushed us under."

"What do you think is the effect of these experiences?" I asked.

Without missing a beat, Joseph replied, "Benevolence. You know, the Philippines is the only place that you can see a Japanese, American, and Filipino war memorial in the same place." Again, Melvin interjected by saying, "Also, our religion."

"Yeah," Joseph agreed. "We are for loyalty and equality. Just go back to basic nature, and you have your answers. I even told someone from an Australian collections account that the Philippine psyche is perfect for helping them collect on debts from customers. We know what it means to be in debt. We present ourselves as part of the solution, as someone who can help manage their money. We are not targeting customers, attacking them [as scary debt collectors]."

"Do you talk to investors this way, about these kinds of details, like the Philippine psyche?" I asked.

"Yes, we are very detailed," Joseph insisted. "We talk about history."

Again, at first blush, these vernacular accounts of Philippine history and Filipino/American relatability seem like yet another way that elite Philippine actors, responding to competition with other developing countries, attempt to establish the "value proposition" that Filipinos can ostensibly offer corporate capital—what Anna Tsing calls a "niche-segregating performance."[40] Yet in offering up a version of Philippine history in which Filipinos are gifted with an incomparable capacity for compassion, empathy, and understanding, Joseph and Melvin also reproduce and extend the exceptionalist narratives on which U.S. imperialism and the American colonial state in the Philippines relied. It is significant, for example, that Joseph uses the term *benevolence* to describe the Philippine psyche. In so doing, he evokes the key word and sentiment President William McKinley used to describe the American colonial project in the islands in 1898.[41] In recalling this narrative and citing the coexistence within the country of memorials and cemeteries that mark the respective deaths of Filipinos, Americans, and the Japanese during World War II, Joseph implies that Filipinos have inherited the benevolence of their former colonizers. Evoking World War II as what Dylan Rodríguez calls "another genesis moment of political union and nationalist coalescence" between Filipinos and the United States, Joseph reinforces a "historical congruence" between Filipino subjectivity and the United States as an exceptional nation whose benevolence compels and deserves the allegiance of the colonized.[42] In such a framework, Filipinos' relational capacities are treated as the outcome of the colonial past, now domesticated within Filipino identity; Filipinoness, in other words, is defined by exceptional affective capacities that emerge from the Philippines' exceptional history. For Joseph in particular, "the Philippine psyche" is conflated with Philippine history, and has become especially attuned to the plight of others as a result of decades of subjugation and war. Such ideas are articulated and elaborated on elsewhere in the IBPAP's literature. In a *Breakthroughs!* article entitled "Filipino Qualities as Competitive Edge in This Crisis," Jonathan de Luzuriaga writes:

> The one quality that our clients have treasured in the Filipino BPO worker, and which they are hard-pressed to find anywhere else, is our customer-service orientation. The average Filipino BPO-IT worker, especially those in the voice sector, genuinely wants to serve their clients and are more than willing to go the extra mile. And, may I add, they can weather the harshest demands with a smile that turns an irate customer into a happy, long-lasting one. That kind of sunny service comes from within and would be difficult to duplicate. Another related quality is the legendary Filipino resilience. This is something that we as a people laugh at among ourselves as an inside joke, yet ironically it is an emotional and spiritual resource that we have not yet fully valued or capitalized on. Poverty does not faze us; the threat of an impending job loss would not drive us to suicide.[43]

Luzuriaga further underscores these statements by also attributing Filipino resilience and hospitality to "attitude," which, he explains, "is something that is far more difficult to emulate, because it is embedded deeply in culture, seeded by history, and nurtured over a long span of time."[44]

The language of "spiritual resource," "value," and "capitalization" in the above excerpt also speaks to the way industry leaders transform the meaning of culture and identity through their use of market logic. Yet Melvin and Joseph were also careful to distinguish between Filipino or Asian approaches to the capitalist marketplace and American or Western ones. In another meeting Joseph expressed his frustration with the assumed superlative value of Western business practices. He explained that "there are actually people within this industry who tell me that I should be more Western. I say to them, 'Look, you are the ones who came here for our help, and you are telling me I should be more Western?'" In 2009, when I first met Joseph and Melvin, it was common for my research participants to regard U.S. outsourcing to the Philippines as a sign of a United States in crisis and in need of Filipinos' assistance. This idea was integral to Joseph's understanding of why Western companies were drawn to the Philippine call center industry in the first place. During our interview he explicitly argued that Americans fundamentally misunderstand capitalist enterprise. "Jan, you are from New York, right? Well, don't mind me saying so, but the way Americans think about capitalism is all screwed up," he said. Further explaining that "the beauty of capitalism is in innovation, not blowing the competition out of the water," and that "the Americans forgot that when they went to India," Joseph went on to denounce Americans' supposedly misguided obsession with the crass concerns of cost cutting rather than the lofty goals of added value.[45] He topped this off by remarking that the Philippines "fight[s] on a level playing field. We are a global player. As a culture, it is deeply embedded in us to forgive easily and not take competition too seriously."

For Joseph and other industry advocates, the value that the Philippines offers the United States is tied in part to workers being Filipino. Moreover, this Filipino *being* to which Joseph attests ostensibly comes to fruition when the United States, and Western powers more broadly, leave global capitalism's center stage to make room for "emerging" Asian nations and their subjects.[46] As if to hammer home his point about the rise of Asian countries in the wake of a U.S. decline, Joseph noted that many American families had begun living in extended households as a response to the global economic downturn, which he interpreted as "Americans beginning to see the beauty of the Filipino and Asian concept" of sharing space and resources as a family. Within this cultural logic—a logic that upholds a neoliberal postcolonial imaginary—Filipino compassion in general and ability to relate to Americans in particular are not signs of Filipinos' continued subjugation to dominant world powers but rather proof of their modern subjectivity and their readiness to lead the global economy with both technical skill and affective acumen.

Having Your English and Speaking It, Too:
The Problem of Market Logic

As my interviews and observations make clear, Filipino industry leaders and call center workers, reinforced by the state, lean firmly on the logic of the market to stabilize the often unsteady social and cultural connotations of call center work. By way of closing this chapter, I explore how this process operates on the shifting terrain of local and global English-language politics, which play an important role in the neoliberal ideology nesting within postcolonial Philippine nationalism.[47] Doing so reveals some of the ideological pitfalls of and problems with the post–Cold War notion of the global economy as an even and collaborative playing field and thus the interpretive framework in which the Philippine call center has come to have meaning for many involved in it.

In the late 1980s, Filipinos of the middle and elite classes began a cultural nationalist project to decolonize the English language—that is, "to reclaim it not as a sign of colonial dependency but as part of the national culture."[48] This reclamation manifested itself as a rejection of American English as the standard-bearer for the language and thus the recognition of Philippine English as a distinct and autonomous form. Filipinos were not alone in these efforts. With the emergence of the concept of world Englishes, many people around the world began to emphasize that different varieties of English had developed their own legitimate identities, thus establishing a postcolonial reconfiguration of the dominant hierarchies of the language.[49] Moreover, this decentered approach to English became part of a postracial vision of language in which "the racist attitudes prevalent during the colonial period" are thought to "have mostly given way to more rational approaches to cultural diversity," in which more varieties of English are considered not only acceptable but are welcomed additions to the linguistic repertoire.[50] The decolonization of English has thus been crucial to a middle-class and elite cultural nationalist project as a kind of linguistic modernity in which Filipinos can have English as a national language and speak it, too. These efforts also set the stage, I argue, for the kind of thinking espoused by the IBPAP executive Joseph Santiago, who saw the call center industry's turn toward neutral accents as part of the disavowal of U.S. cultural hegemony.

What does it mean, then, that most call centers I visited, and the one in which I trained, required agents to speak American English? What will become of the Philippines' project for linguistic modernity under these circumstances?[51] For many, the resolution to this problem of colonial recall is to not see it as a problem at all. As with the challenges posed by customer racism, which I discuss in the next chapter, the issue of American English is construed as one of market demand and not colonialism's return. This framework of interpretation is made possible not only by the concept of postcolonial world Englishes—in which the United States and United Kingdom allegedly cease to be the source of the language's legitimacy—but also by the rise of English as the undisputed language of the global information society.[52] In this hypercapitalist context, English has value not because of its proximity to former colonial powers but because of the possibilities of mobility within capitalism that the language ostensibly offers. The postracial shift from imperial English to world English thus reinforces a neoliberal narrative of the global economy as a marketplace in which capital and communication flow smoothly owing to English's putative ability to function as a linguistic currency with no particular national origin. In turn, what Rey Chow refers to as the "neoliberal attitude toward multilingualism" discursively transforms languages into individualized commodities, "to be discretely enumerated and labeled like items of jewelry or parcels of real estate."[53] Within this logic, capitalism in general, rather than any nation in particular, makes English worth speaking. These points are not lost on the Philippine middle and elite classes, who, as Vicente L. Rafael argues, since the 1990s have often experienced "periodic panic . . . regarding the deteriorating ability of Filipino students to speak English and thus compete in a global marketplace."[54]

Yet there are fault lines in this ideological terrain. While Filipinos might very well own their brand of Philippine English, its value in the global marketplace is still defined by transnational U.S. corporations and the Philippine elite who accommodate their demands—thus, American English has remained the standard and the norm for transnational call center work.[55] The question of English's value is thus an ever-present reminder that colonial recall is not just about how the Philippine call center industry is built on the structures of empire but also about how the specter of U.S. imperialism incessantly demands that Filipinos account for the substance, boundaries, and value of Filipino identity and the Philippine nation.

INSIDE VOX ELITE

Call Center Training and the Limits
of Filipino/American Relatability

March 2009. Joel Partido was a slim and smartly dressed man in his early forties, making him one of the oldest people I had met in the call center business in the Philippines. As we shook hands in a crowded Starbucks on a Friday night, I quickly took in Joel's friendly if fairly harried demeanor. As the vice president of human resources for Vox Elite, Joel was in the midst of the company's major acquisition of an Elphin call center in the very building where we were meeting. Elphin, a major U.S. computer company, had long maintained a large in-house call center in Metro Manila along with several onshore in-house centers in Florida and South Carolina. Several years earlier, however, Elphin had begun shutting down its centers in the United States and outsourcing that work to Vox Elite in the Philippines; after the financial crash hit hard in 2008, Elphin went forward with plans to turn over its last remaining in-house call center, the one in Metro Manila, to the third-party company. Almost overnight, thirteen hundred Elphin workers would become employees of the already large Vox Elite, and Joel had to oversee this transition as well as the addition of sixty additional employees to the human resources department. As I talked with Joel about the changeover, it seemed he was most stressed by having to report to a number of people on both the Elphin and Vox Elite sides but also, as he described it, "trying to marry the cultures" of the two companies.[1] Joel described Vox Elite as flexible and Elphin as somewhat rigid—which made sense in light of the fact that Vox Elite, as one of the oldest and most global third-party providers in the world, had grown accustomed to twisting and bending to accommodate the needs of corporate capital, whereas Elphin, a company with a strong brand name and specific corporate culture, was used to doing things its way. As Joel explained, it was by far the biggest project he had handled in his twenty-one years working in human resources, which included working for Coca-Cola and Toyota, both in the Philippines.

Still, Joel was excited about his work and what was happening with the company. "Once you've tasted the adrenaline rush of this job, of working in a call center, it's really difficult to settle for a more comfortable role or routine, where you won't be jumping from one emergency to another." Joel let out a bemused laugh, as he often did when talking about his work. When I asked if he could pinpoint what gave him the adrenaline rush, he cited the novelty of the industry. "The BPO industry is relatively new here in the Philippines," he started. "While in my case you may have a couple decades of HR experience to lean on, there are still so many gray areas, ambiguous scenarios, where you can't rely on experience . . . just nail biting." Joel laughed again and then continued, "The old industries here in the Philippines—manufacturing, banking, pharma[ceuticals] and so forth—you can't always apply what you might know from there. This is just such a new environment." It was the refrain I had been hearing again and again from my research participants: call centers were a world apart, workplaces so different and so particular, with their own social world and cultural practices.

I conducted several long interviews with Joel, who had studied social sciences at an elite university in the country and seemed to take vicarious pleasure in my research. When he suggested that I apply for a call center job at Vox Elite—and generously assisted me in getting the proper approvals for the research—I was eager to get started. As I came to learn over those next several weeks, the sense of call centers as a space apart begins the minute one starts the application process. Most call center companies, Vox Elite included, do not even use the term *application process* but rather *recruitment,* the corporate word of choice when referring to attracting, selecting, and hiring employees. With its military connotation, *recruitment* does not include only choosing appropriate people to enter a call center's highly demanding social and cultural environment. Recruitment also has a pedagogical function: applicants learn about the company or work in question by undergoing a series of evaluations that ostensibly prepare them for the challenges that lie ahead.

Applying and training for a call center job at Vox Elite brought me face-to-face with the contradictions and predicaments of call center work that I have explored in the previous chapters: the highs of competition versus the lows of emotional labor, the tedium of routine tasks versus the privilege of the workspace, and the delights of friends versus the near delirium of working overnight. Most important, during U.S. cultural competency (CC) and Elphin product training—the two main components of Vox Elite's training process—I began to see how Philippine call centers are not just sites of corporate communication about mundane matters like printers and mobile phones but spaces where workers actively construct national identity and the nation-state through a contradictory engagement with, and disavowal of, the United States as both a material entity and an imaginary location. Training sessions in CC and product information were rich sites from which to observe such dynamics because both offered direct engagement with America and Americans: CC in its presentation of the United States as an object of pedagogical significance, and product training through the actual presence of American trainers from Elphin. As a Filipina American participating in and getting to know people in both settings, my presence, too, came to reflect and refract these negotiations. This chapter thus builds on the previous ones by offering a grounded and detailed ethnographic look at how workers negotiate the terms of Philippine postcolonial nationalism through Filipino/American relatability specifically.

Drawing the Line: Vox Elite Recruitment

April 2009. Vox Elite's application center was located on the fourth floor of a shopping mall in one of Metro Manila's densest commercial and public transportation hubs. Although the mall did not officially open until ten-thirty in the morning, Vox Elite applicants could enter the building earlier by signing in with a uniformed armed guard. In the absence of shoppers, store clerks, and music blaring from retail establishments, marching up the mall's frozen escalators to the application office felt somewhat bleak. A whole different scene unfolded, however, on the fourth floor. When I entered the glass doors, a tired-looking administrative assistant asked for my résumé, hurriedly stapled something to it, and then handed me a lengthy application form. As I took my seat among fifteen or so other applicants already diligently filling in the names of their past employers or the schools they had attended, I noticed a small placard reading "English only" and a large flat-screen television flashing Vox Elite corporate media on the wall behind the front desk. Directly behind the wall, through another set of glass doors, were about eight cubicles where the recruitment staff worked pushing papers and checking lists. Industry and IT-related magazines like *Corporate World* were strewn about me in the waiting room.

That call center work entails high-paced productivity and efficiency was apparent from the second I stepped into Vox Elite's main recruitment office that morning at a quarter past nine. Before I had even completed the first of the form's five pages, the administrative assistant called my name and handed me a small piece of paper stating the time for my first period of testing: eleven o'clock. As would later become clear, job seekers had to pass two rounds of computer-based tests before being granted a group interview with a recruiter from Vox Elite's human resources department. If applicants made the cut after the group interview, they moved on to a voice test called Vox Check. While the application process consisted of six parts, it was possible to undergo them all in a single day, as tests and interviews were scheduled at regular intervals and applicants were placed in time slots according to the time they arrive at the recruitment office. As my research participants would later confirm, the pace was unlike that of any other professional line of work in the Philippines, where it might take weeks to learn whether one was being offered a position.

After completing my application form around ten o'clock, I sat and observed the constant flow of applicants into the recruitment office. Fifteen to twenty people entered the office every twenty minutes—almost one person per minute—and only a handful of applicants seemed past their twenties. Each applicant was dressed neatly but casually—no suits, blazers, or dress shoes. By a quarter to eleven, the office could no longer accommodate all of the applicants, so people spilled out into the public space of the shopping mall, which was slowly filling up with patrons. I knew from talking to human resources recruiters from other large call center companies that the number of applicants could reach upward of two hundred in one day, and yet only 5–12 percent would be offered a job at the end of the process, with more than half of the applicants not even making it through the initial rounds of computerized tests. Next to me, a young woman with a Vox Elite employee badge around her neck was helping her nervous-looking friend fill out the part of the application that asked about familiarity with software. After they completed the application, and her friend left to return to her shift, I asked the young woman, whose name was Glenda, whether it was her first time applying to a call center. She answered with a cautiously optimistic "Yes" and then explained that she had just graduated from nursing school and needed money to take the review courses that would prepare her for the nursing board exams. We continued talking until my name was called for the eleven o'clock testing session, and although I did not see Glenda again after that interaction in the lobby, I wondered if, like my cousin, she would forego nursing and stick with call center work if given the opportunity.

The first round of tests took place in a large room situated behind the recruiters' cubicles. The room contained four rows of ten cubicles that each housed a computer monitor and headset—a much smaller version of a typical production floor. As the thirty-seven other applicants and I sat down, a proctor called out our names to determine that we were in fact sitting at our assigned terminals. When two young men realized they had switched seats and began giggling as a result, the proctor admonished them with an authoritative and irritated look, making the situation seem not unlike my experience taking standardized tests in secondary school. With everyone settled, the proctor told us to begin the fifty-five-minute testing session.

Like other call centers, Vox Elite tests job applicants for the qualifications necessary to work on specific types of jobs assigned to the call center by corporate clients such as Verizon or Sony. In a manner typical of flexible labor markets, these clients may contract third-party BPO firms such as Vox Elite to take on their customer service or technical support needs before the BPO firm actually has the people to fill the positions on the account. In other words, the BPO firm often already has a corporate account or two waiting in the wings when evaluating job applicants, and thus the tests administered to applicants are tailored to those specific accounts. When I applied for a job at Vox Elite, the company was looking for people to do customer and technical support for Cobalt, a mobile phone account, and Elphin, a printer account, both of which were U.S.-based companies. Thus, the second, fourth, and fifth tests of that first exam period were related to computer hardware, printers, mobile phones, and some of the technical specificities of the Internet and networking. The questions addressed matters ranging from consumer-oriented knowledge (such as "Which of the following is not a manufacturer of cell phones?") to more technical knowledge, such as what the acronyms *WAP* and *VPN* stand for. Some of the questions even ventured into customer service and technical support territory, using hypothetical scenarios like the following: "A customer calls to complain that she cannot make a call with her phone. Which of the following do you not need to ask?"

In this way, the contradictions and tensions regarding the skill and knowledge involved in call center work began to emerge in the application process itself. Although there was indeed knowledge being tested here, one did not have to be a computer scientist or an engineer to pass these tests. Any type of continued exposure to *IT*—whether as a consumer, a student, or a self-taught person—could prepare applicants for the exams; prior professional experience could help but was not necessary. At the same time, the exams were clearly weighted toward applicants with a high degree of familiarity with consumer electronics, and thus individuals with the means to access such goods, whether through personal ownership or schools with such resources. Although I was stumped by a few of the questions during that first round of tests (I could not confidently identify all the hardware of a desktop computer, for example), an *educated* guess is perhaps all I needed to pass these technical tests, since educated guesses are exactly that—based on education and thus cultural capital. My upbringing in the United States, which included having computers and the Internet in my home since I was fourteen years old, gave me sufficient knowledge to make it to the next round of tests. Since in the Philippines private ownership of these kinds of consumer electronics was at the time of my research mostly limited to affluent and some middle-class people, I assumed that most applicants who passed these tests either had some background in computers or other *IT* or had access to them at home or in well-resourced schools. It was impossible to tell, though, just who was tech savvy and who was not, since the exams also wove together tests of technical knowledge with assessments of applicants' knowledge of English grammar. The first test asked applicants to identify the word or group of words that would correctly complete a sentence written in English, while the third required reading a paragraph-long short story and retelling the story using direct speech. By requiring applicants to switch rapidly between technical acumen and language competency, the test modeled the way that call center work drew on both sets of skills simultaneously.

As suggested by their squeaking chairs and restless movements, most of the applicants finished the assessment about forty-five minutes into the session, although one or two people seated near me worked until our time was up. No more than five minutes after the official end of the test, our proctor called out about fifteen names—a little under 40 percent of the applicants in the room—and asked those people to collect their things and leave. She then congratulated the rest of us, announcing that we would be moving on to the next round of exams. Many people breathed a sigh of relief or uttered, "Yes!," underscoring the competitive but also exciting nature of the testing process. Given that I had stumbled on some of the tech tests, I, too, was relieved to have passed. It was my first taste of how call center work could be challenging but could also leave people with a sense of accomplishment and reward.

The second set of exams proceeded immediately after the rejected candidates left the room, but the tests themselves were shorter. The first test in the second set consisted of a timed scavenger hunt, in which we were asked to scour the Internet for the answers to trivial questions, such as "What is the longest bridge in the world?" This test of comprehension, speed, and resourcefulness was followed by a short essay question that asked applicants to write down "anything about yourself" and then to describe a personal experience of selling something to someone else, and the reasons that we did so. Although I was keen not to be placed on a sales account—owing to my strong aversion to trying to convince people to part with their money—I drew on my experiences as a customer service representative at a bookstore where I worked directly after graduating from college. Once again, at the end of the test, the proctor called out the names of the people who did not pass. At that point, only eleven people—just over 25 percent of the original testing group—were asked to return to the application center at five o'clock that afternoon for the next stage of Vox Elite's application process: the group interview.

Since I had a few hours to spare between the end of the second round of testing and the group interview, I walked to a nearby mall, where I plopped down on a lounge chair in Starbucks, hungry and already tired from the morning's activity. As I ate my lunch and wrote out my field notes, I began to reflect on how the recruitment process worked like a well-oiled and productive machine, turning eager and willing young people into human resources for a large company that would mold and discipline them even further. It was also possible to see how almost every affective aspect of call center life that I had observed for myself or learned about through my research participants was manifest in the recruitment process: the competitive spirit, but also the camaraderie between friends, the regulated environment, and the relief that came from a sense of achievement or the disappointment in not moving on. The need to multitask, to simultaneously engage cognitive and communicative skills, and the fact that nothing went unrecorded—these, too, were elements of call center work that made their way into call center recruiting. I had even already encountered the cultural politics of and social tensions surrounding the English language, when in the lobby I overheard a discussion between a few older applicants who, apparently upset by the way the administrative assistant at the front desk had treated them, declared rather loudly that she "didn't even know how to speak English." However, besides the stress that came with wondering whether one had passed Vox Elite's evaluations, I had not yet seen anything that evoked the psychologically distressing aspects of call center work—that happened in the group interview.

When I returned to the center for my group interview, the place was empty except for applicants waiting for testing or employees processing paperwork. At precisely five o'clock, three other applicants and I were called into a frigid room no more than eight by ten feet in size. In my group were Abby, Janice, and Matt, all recent college graduates in their early twenties. Jeff, our interviewer, walked and talked as though he was a seasoned Vox Elite recruiter, although he too seemed to be in his twenties. Sitting down to face me and the other applicants, Jeff wasted no time getting down to brass tacks. "Okay," he said, looking down at a stack of completed job applications, "let's start with Matt." Matt straightened in his chair and eagerly responded to Jeff's prompt by saying his name and the college he graduated from and listing his work experience. Then Jeff began:

"Okay, Matt, so why do you want to work in a call center?"

Responding with enthusiasm, Matt said, "I believe it is my destiny."

Apparently amused by Matt's answer, Jeff scoffed, "*Destiny!* That's a strong word. Okay . . ."

"Well," Matt continued, "I was going to go into engineering, but I failed the entrance exam to my field, so I think . . . that wasn't my destiny."

Jeff chuckled and then moved on. "Okay. So, Matt, if you could be any superhero in the world, which one would you be?"

Again Matt answered quickly. "I will be Superman."

"Why?"

"So I can move mountains."

"Move mountains? Why would you want to do that?"

"It's an idiom . . ."

With a full laugh, Jeff responded, "*An idiom?!* Okay, so what else would you do?"

"I will help people."

Jeff pushed. "Like who? Who would you help?"

"I will help the beggars."

"Help them do what? Would you rob a bank?!"

Finally, Matt paused. The confidence he had displayed at the beginning of the interview seemed to wane as he sensed, as I think we all did, that Jeff was deliberately trying to frustrate his attempt to fashion an articulate response to the question. Indeed, I suspected that Jeff was performing the role of an antagonistic and pompous customer, whose condescending responses to a nonnative English speaker would be masked by a jocular affect. Matt continued in earnest:

"No, I would take them . . . I would take them . . ."

Jeff's tone radiated with irritation. "*Take* them?! You mean you are going to kidnap them? Where would you take them?"

Matt, unable to conceal his nerves, replied, "I would take them, and . . . I would take them . . . Oh, what is this? [*How do I put it?*] . . . I would take them . . ."

Matt continued in this semifrozen state for a few more seconds before Jeff interjected, "Okay, you would take them somewhere. What else would you do as Superman?"

Clearly eager for this exercise to be over, Matt responded rapidly, "I will fly around because that's what I want. I will see places I have never seen."

At that, Jeff thanked Matt and then moved on to Abby, with whom he used a similar destabilizing tactic.

"Abby, how would you describe the color red to a blind person?"

Abby thought for a few seconds and then replied, "I would say it is the feeling of a rough rock."

Jeff pounced on her response. "I don't understand. How is a rough rock like the color red?"

Nervously turning her hands as if holding a rock, Abby said, "The rough rock . . . a rough rock . . . is like the color red because . . . it is rough and . . ."

With some hostility, Jeff said, "I don't get it."

After a long pause, Abby responded, "The rough rock symbolizes red for me. I would also describe something hot, like *pancit canton* [cooked noodles]." She then smiled a little, apparently pleased with her recovery from the line of questioning.

At that point, Jeff let Abby off the hook and moved on to Janice, who seemed to have a relatively easy time answering Jeff's question about which candidate she favored in the upcoming presidential elections.

As someone who has both witnessed and experienced firsthand the demeaning treatment of service workers in the United States—especially workers of color or those who come across as foreigners—I found the tenor of Jeff's questions immediately recognizable, even if I was a little surprised that he actually chose to test the candidates in that way. Such techniques made clear that recruiters look for applicants with both good speaking skills and the ability to withstand the many pressures of the job, including interacting with hostile, rude, and racist customers over the phone. In other words, like the flight attendants at the center of Arlie Hochschild's canonical study of emotion work, call center workers must be smart but also able to cope with being treated as dumb.[2] In this way, Jeff's orchestration of this emotional exercise speaks to the prevalence of racializing encounters in transnational call center work, a process of racialization that occurs on the terrain of speech and accent. The fact that Jeff refrained from posing such tricky questions to me, a native English speaker and American citizen, underscores this point—although it is worth considering that Jeff was not exactly easygoing with me, either. In response to my description of my master's thesis, which Jeff asked about as part of the interview, he somewhat aggressively stated that he did not understand the point of the study. I suppose I passed his test by calmly and confidently responding to his question and not taking a long time to do so.

The group interview marked the end of my first day undergoing recruitment. Later on that evening, as I was getting ready to see some of the Pyramid Processing employees before their shift started, Jeff called me to say that I would be moving on to the last stage of recruitment, which consisted of the Vox Check, a voice, accent, and comprehension test that I completed first thing the next morning. Alongside me were ten other applicants, one or two of whom I recognized from my testing group. That Vox Check was the last major hurdle in a multistep application process underscores call center work's reliance on English-language communication. The examination required us to don a headset with a microphone and then listen to and answer a series of questions in English. Part 1 of the test asked applicants to repeat aloud sentences they heard through the headset, while part 2 asked applicants to listen to sentence fragments and put them together into a complete sentence. Part 3 involved listening to a short, six-sentence story, answering a series of questions that tested one's comprehension of the story, and then retelling the story in one's own words. Finally, the last two questions asked applicants to speak extemporaneously about two different topics: the importance of family in our lives, and music and art. Once again, only minutes after the test ended, applicants who did not pass the test—two people—were asked to leave. The rest of us completed a typing test and were then told to come back to the recruitment center at three o'clock. At this point, the reason we were being asked to come back was unclear. Would there be another evaluation? Had we passed the final test and were being offered a job? Some of the applicants even asked the guard stationed outside of the main lobby of the recruitment office, but he simply shook his head and said he didn't know.

Back at the office at three o'clock, I was quickly shown into a small room where seven chairs were arranged in a circle. I took a seat among four young men and one woman. Within minutes, a Vox Elite recruiter entered the room holding a bundle of papers. With a big smile, she welcomed us all to Vox Elite and handed us each a piece of paper describing the job we were being offered on the Elphin printer account. About seventy newly hired employees in total were being assigned to this one account alone, she explained. The job offer paper described the main details of our position, the account we would be working for, and our compensation, benefits, health insurance, and "attendance bonus"—additional pay given to employees who did not miss a single day of training. Then the new hires' questions started to fly: Was it possible to be moved to another account? Was it possible to request the morning shift? How soon could someone apply for a higher position in the firm? One young man even explained that he was unhappy with the ₱15,000 per month compensation Vox Elite was offering, quoting ₱20,000 per month as the entry-level pay of his previous technical support job. He then told the recruiter that he would have to think about the offer and left the room before the others in the group were done asking questions. That moment made me realize that despite or perhaps because of the rigorous process of weeding out numerous unqualified applicants, the remaining individuals did not see themselves as supplicants to the firm. Somewhere along the way—most likely through previous call center positions, as suggested by the dissatisfied applicant—they had learned to negotiate the circumstances of their employment and look for ways to move both up and out. Indeed, at this moment I saw quite clearly how young Filipinos struggle to affirm the value of their labor within the structural and psychological constraints of racialized and gendered capitalism.

Orientation, Orientalism, and Capital's Objectives

About two weeks after being offered a job as a technical support representative for the Elphin printer account at Vox Elite, I began the orientation and training process. The time lag between recruitment and training contrasted sharply with the swift and efficient application process, but it, too, reflected something important about outsourcing: its contingency on corporate capital. As I learned from Joel during those two weeks, Vox Elite still needed to find enough suitable employees to fill the seats on Elphin's printer account, which meant that those hired earliest would have to wait the longest to start working. Even the amount of time it takes to train for an account depends both on the complexity of the product that technical support representatives must learn to service and on parameters set by the client, such as how much they are willing to spend on training. Some training sessions can last up to two months, while others can run for as little as two weeks.

For the Elphin printer account—in which we were to service only one type of Elphin printer (the inkjet) for one type of use (personal), with the others being serviced by a different account—the new hires and I were scheduled for one week of training in American culture through a course called U.S. Cultural Competency, or simply CC, and four weeks of product training with Elphin. Like other courses of its kind in call centers across the global south, CC aimed to orient new call center agents to features of American culture and society deemed relevant to customer service and technical support work, including major U.S. holidays and the abbreviations for each state, as well as U.S. history, American English and accents, and American norms of interaction and social behavior. To prepare new employees for the physical rigors and psychological challenges of working in Western time zones, the class started at ten in the evening and ended at seven in the morning.

Vox Elite's orientation and training sessions were held on the eighth floor of a high-rise building not far from their recruitment offices. Compared to other call centers I had visited during my fieldwork, Vox Elite's facilities were unexpectedly bare and cheerless. There was no lobby with brightly colored couches or computer stations where employees could surf the web in their downtime, and smokers made do with the corner of a parking garage, where cigarette butts lingered in pools of oil and dirt on the cement floor. Still, as I settled into a seat in the middle rear of the classroom for orientation, I sensed that the dozens of other trainees were happy to be employed in a place in which computers and air-conditioning were integral features of the working environment, and where our hourly rate—around ₱86 per hour (about $1.80)—included extra pay for working at night and was well above the country's minimum wage.

Waiting for orientation to start, I met Archie, a Philippine citizen who, as an immigrant in the United States, had just spent two years in California working as a call center agent with a major U.S. gaming company but who had gotten tired of the loneliness and expense of living in the United States and wanted to come home to Manila. Then there was Mika, who had worked on an Elphin account before but in sales, which she found stressful. "There were days when I couldn't make extra sales on top of the ones that the customers had called in for, and I felt so stupid," she explained. As the three of us were chatting, orientation began, and it was quick but illuminating. A human resources staff person, whom I recognized as one of the facilitators of the aptitude tests, offered her congratulations and then welcomed us all to the company and the account. She also wasted no time in assuring us that Vox Elite was a top-notch company providing some of the best customer experiences in the world and therefore that we had "made the right decision" in coming to work for the company. Another recruiter then chimed in to convey that there were ample opportunities to move up in the company, and swiftly. Knowing what I did about attrition and job-hopping, I understood these opening remarks in relation to agents' willingness to leave a call center for a better opportunity elsewhere or because of the stress of the work. Capital's struggle for adequate labor thus continued even as employees were being integrated into a firm's culture. To this end, the recruiter ran through the list of amenities and services we could expect to find at Vox Elite, such as sleeping quarters and a free fitness center. When she covered the working hours and the various shifts—the majority of which were of course at night—the recruiter reminded us that "this is the industry you wish to embrace." She then lightly clapped her hands in front of a new hire who had already fallen asleep in his chair, and many laughed.

Following this presentation by human resources, I found myself in a classroom containing twenty two-person desks, with a computer station for each person. A lone window covered with a sheet of peeling dark blue cellophane was set high on the wall in the back of the room, compounding the sense that we had entered a temporal and physical capsule, isolated from the outside world. Still, there was enough nervous energy among my thirty-four fellow trainees—two-thirds of whom were young men—to keep that first night buoyant and engaging. Once we were seated, our CC instructor, Bella Chiu, a fair-skinned young woman who was about my age, led us in our first icebreaker exercise, in which each person was asked to draw a picture that described their personality and then present it to the class. To my surprise, the soft-spoken shy young man sitting at my desk got up to present his drawing and with a dry tone said, "My name is Junior, but you can call me '007'"—a reference to the fictional British secret agent James Bond—which drew laughter from the class. As my fellow trainees presented their drawings and more jokes were made, a relaxed tone began to permeate the room. There was polite silence, however, when I presented my drawing of a bicycle—which I used to describe myself as a "balanced, skilled, and fun" person—as it was the first time that anyone in the class heard my American accent. Indeed, my status as the only person in the class who had been born and raised in the United States set me apart from the others and, as I would soon learn, affected how some of my fellow trainees related to me during the course of our training.

As soon as we were done with our introductions, Bella flipped to a page in a thick spiral-bound training manual and said, "Okay. So, who here knows the meaning of the word *ethnocentrism?*" In response, one of the new hires quickly shouted out that "ethnocentrism means seeing things from your own culture's perspective." Satisfied by this definition, Bella said, "Correct! So, remember this, everyone: On the [production] floor, it will always be the perspective of the Americans that you should be adopting." Bella then showed the class a PowerPoint slide displaying two columns of cultural descriptions, one for Americans and the other for Fili-pinos. Americans, the lists informed us, are task-oriented, individualistic, and egalitarian, while Filipinos are relationship-oriented, collectivist, and hierarchical. Bella further explained that "Americans have 'now or never attitudes,' process information sequentially, and do things in an orderly fashion," whereas Filipinos "often try to process many things at once." Americans' task orientation, moreover, means that they value productiv-ity, unlike Filipinos, who most value social relationships. Last, Bella told us, the United States's egalitarian culture means that Americans regard each other as equals, such that differences in status only signal differences in skill or development, not essential personhood: "Teachers are guides, not gurus, and managers empower employees, rather than demand defer-ence." Bella continued by explaining that we should think of American and Filipino culture as two icebergs that might collide.

Writing all of this down in a small notebook, I was struck though not surprised by the rather blatant Orientalism on display. Before my field-work, I had read much about the way offshore call centers, as transnational spaces of global capital and communication, reproduce colonial dynam-ics of control. The CC training fulfilled this expectation right off the bat, establishing hard-and-fast distinctions between Americans and Filipinos and therefore indexing a legacy of colonial relations through which the West produces knowledge of the East, especially through the realm of cul-ture.[3] According to this catalog of difference, Westerners are rational in both thought and action, while non-Westerners adhere to tradition and nonrational social and kinship bonds. Here, then, was our first major les-son in relatability. Filipinos would have to adopt American ways of being in the world and use their flexibility to cross the imagined chasm of culture to reach Americans on the other side—or, in CC's metaphor, to keep the two icebergs from colliding. But what exactly would it mean for these cultures to clash? What, in other words, was at stake in this cultural negotiation, this pedagogy of relatability? The next part of the lesson made clear that call center work required particular behaviors and affective orientations that were necessary for Vox Elite and its client companies to achieve their bottom lines. "To do [your] jobs well," Bella said, agents needed to develop "cross-cultural skills" that translated into "certain comportments," such as immediately and accurately getting tasks done, speaking descriptively but concisely to customers, working efficiently, practicing a sense of urgency, and being assertive. As agents, Bella elaborated, we would have to think "in a linear" way, give directions clearly and directly, and not "beat around the bush" when explaining things to callers. The latter is considered a passive form of communication that would surely irritate American callers.

The first lesson of CC was therefore a key moment of colonial recall in the service of capital's objectives. Just as Orientalism has historically justified the control of peoples deemed irrational, unruly, and traditional by those considered elevated to modern and civilized status, CC used racial and national difference to further discipline Filipino call center agents into conforming to company standards and to rationalize the behavioral and affective rules to which Vox Elite agents would be subject. That the company's standards were often represented as *customer* needs—rather than capital's demand on both customers and labor—made these expressions of power all the more insidious. This obfuscation of the capital-labor relation reminded me of the many ways that the figure of a generic American consumer who wants cheap goods and fast, efficient service is often evoked in dominant discourse as a justification for the free trade policies that allowed corporations to outsource offshore in the first place. In contrast to this dominant explanation, during my fieldwork I overheard (and heard of) more than a few calls in which customers did not express the sense of urgency that CC implied they would; in fact, the opposite was the case, as customers were often slow or inefficient in their explanations of the problems at hand, had to search for information the agent needed to address the customer's problem, or even deliberately kept the agent on the line to talk about something unrelated to a product or technical problem.[4] This is not to suggest that there were never customers who acted in the ways that the CC lesson described. Passive explanations of problems and excessive apologies indeed irritate many callers. Yet the need for extreme efficiency and obsessive adherence to the labor process is more directly tied to management rather than consumer demands.

Training in CC was therefore about teaching agents to discipline themselves and control customers through various scripts and communicative techniques, such as "call flow" and "active listening." Only through call control, managers argue, can agents meet the long list of demands that corporate clients place on BPO firms, including call-volume quotas, customer satisfaction scores, and new sales. For the Elphin printer account, for example, we would be pressured to achieve "first-call resolution"—meaning completely handling a caller's issue the first time he or she calls about it. At the same time, the imperative for agents to engage in efficient communication and controlled conversations was coupled with the seemingly contradictory demand for polite speech and empathic behavior—that is, to relate to customers in an understanding manner. When customers expressed their issues with agitation or frustration, for example, we were told to mirror their dispositions by saying things like "I understand that you are frustrated" or "I can see how that would be a problem." Agents were also told that it was almost never a good idea to indicate that the customer was the source of the problem about which they were calling. As a result, agents' affective skills are both activated and constrained.

Revising the Script

Despite what I considered the intensity of the messaging in cc, the class itself was relaxed and rather fun, with our lessons broken up by group exercises meant to ease us into a new environment but also instill the camaraderie that was characteristic of call centers. However, although people in the course were generally boisterous and engaged with one another, and although I found the cultural training rather problematic, my fellow trainees seemed to absorb the lessons with relative indifference, as if learning about the United States was uninteresting or perhaps even passé. While Bella talked about American and Filipino cultural differences, for example, most people surfed the web, played online games, watched YouTube videos, visited social networking websites, and chatted with friends via instant messaging.[5] In fact, although Vox Elite had placed Internet-blocking software on all the computers, it proved a minor obstacle for many in the course who knew how to access tunnel websites that bypassed the blocks—the irony being that the very tech savviness that helped trainees qualify for call center work in the first place also allowed them to avoid workplace demands and maneuver around management-imposed barriers. I engaged in such distractions as well, since there were moments when neither the content of the course nor the field I was observing was more than minimally stimulating.[6] Bella, either blithely ignorant of everyone's transgressions or aware of but entirely unconcerned by them, almost never said a word about these activities.

A number of explanations for a lack of interest in cc come to mind. One is the perception of the rather low stakes of training. In fact, to pass CC, the trainees only had to successfully perform a single mock call (in which our instructor Bella played the role of a caller) as well as tests that addressed easily memorable facts like the abbreviations for American states, the names of state capitals, and famous U.S. landmarks. Perhaps most important, new hires could take these tests as many times as needed to pass them. Then there was the fact that, as I learned throughout the week, many people had been previously employed by a call center and therefore were already quite familiar with the communication protocol and accustomed to providing customer service to U.S.-based callers. Such familiarity even allowed trainees to informally critique the official CC training manual, often by exposing the ways that American callers, not Filipino agents, were unruly, combative, or communicated poorly. During lessons on call handling and control, for example, a young man named Arthur explained that customers cause agents stress because "they only want to hear what they want to hear." One woman, Beatrice, drew on her past job experience to make an explicit intervention with regard to the idea that trainees are their own obstacles to good call control. In response to a PowerPoint slide that addressed "what agents need to overcome to ensure total customer satisfaction"— where the bullet-pointed items were "negative emotions," "lack of confidence," "personal beliefs," and "fear of the customer"—Beatrice said to the class, "It's really not necessary to be scared of Americans. They are just really rude, but you don't need to be scared." In other words, Beatrice suggested that American callers, not Filipino agents, were the ones with the problem to overcome.

In some ways, then, the new Vox Elite employees came to the training with an understanding that while there may be differences between Americans and Filipinos, this did not have to signal relations of inequality. Indeed, there were a number of moments during CC in which Bella and the others worked against not only CC's training protocol but the very logic of Filipino/American relatability as a history of inclusionary and exclusionary colonizing and imperial practices. For example, Bella punctuated her introduction of CC by stating that although we would be taking on American perspectives during service calls, "this did not mean upholding Americans as the best people in the world." After she had run through the first set of slides on American and Filipino cultural differences, Bella also cheerfully implored the class, "Remember, we are not Americans, we are Filipinos!"—an exhortation met by nods of agreement from many in the class. Later that week, during an exercise meant to convey the idea of the United States as a melting pot of immigrant cultures and a site of upward mobility, Bella stopped to ask whether people in the room "still believe[d] that America is the land of milk and honey," to which someone emphatically replied, "No, because now we have their [Americans'] jobs!" Such comments signaled not only resistance to the official training script but a decolonizing position anchored in a disavowal of the desire to achieve proximity to American culture. Expressing more than just resistance to Vox Elite's training script, for example, Bella's interjections struck me as subtle but critical revisions of a larger narrative of U.S.-Philippine relations. By *reminding* the class that "we are Filipinos, not Americans" (a statement that did not technically apply to me as a U.S. citizen, and was also problematic in its implication that one could not be both Filipino and American), Bella not only reinforced a distinction between the two identities but also implicitly undermined inclusionary racist narratives that cast Filipinos as part of the American family, either as "little brown brothers" or as part of a redemptive and reciprocal historical relationship between the Philippines and the United States.[7] As I discussed in earlier chapters, such explicit clarification is necessary only in a historically specific ideological setting that would cast Filipinos in the American mold and exalt the latter into positions of superiority in the first place.

One of the most illustrative moments in the negotiation of Filipino/American relatability was during cc's activity concerning immigration history. Upon our return from lunch one day, Bella split the class up into groups and asked each group to do about thirty minutes of web-based research on the history of "early settlers" in the United States. The ostensible goal of the lesson was to discover how the United States became a melting pot of people of various national origins. Yet the only immigrant groups we were asked to research were the English, Italians, Irish (to which my group was assigned), and Chinese. The assignment's complete omission of Native Americans and African slaves, as well as the absence of almost all non-European immigrants, clearly reproduced a narrative of America as a nation of predominantly European origin (while the inclusion of Chinese immigrants perhaps played to a contemporary narrative about Chinese economic prosperity and the size of the Chinese diaspora). The lesson also further invisibilized the history of Filipino migration to the United

States, with which many, if not all, of the people in the class would have been familiar. By eliding this history, CC's lesson on immigration—the only U.S. history to which we were exposed during training—reproduced what scholars have called Philippine amnesia, or the symbolically violent exclusion from U.S. history of the Philippine-American War specifically and the experience of Filipinos as racialized labor more broadly.[8] Moreover, such elision erased the very conditions of the Philippine call center's production—that is, the ongoing appropriation of Filipino labor for U.S. capital and the imperial regime in which that capital is intertwined. In this way, what constituted lessons in American culture were not just holidays and landmarks but ideologically specific ways to know and understand America—as white, as a melting pot, as a land of opportunity—in turn confirming how "'America' is a social relation as well as a set of knowledges," rather than an empirically secure entity.[9]

The next day's training on accent neutralization and American English reinforced these contradictory dynamics of relatability. Again, at the start of the lesson Bella presented us with a list that compared American and Filipino culture, only this time the list consisted of American phrases with their Filipino English counterparts, referred to as "Filipinoisms." Thus, the American "Goodbye" stood in contrast to the Filipino "I'll go ahead," and "I'll pick you up at 10 A.M." appeared alongside "I'll fetch you at 10 A.M." The lesson was clearly designed to alert us to the ways that Filipino English is inadequate for customer service delivery to a U.S. customer base, reinforcing the contradictory recognition of Filipino English as an autonomous version of the language while also marking it as insufficient.[10] Later that same day came a lesson on accents, in which Bella instructed the class to practice articulating the *f* sound and the *p* sound (which many Filipinos use interchangeably), pronouncing words containing long vowel sounds, as well as placing the stress in multisyllabic words. We did this by gathering into groups and reciting English-language poetry before our classmates, with Bella occasionally stopping the speaker to correct his or her pronunciation of a word. The lesson then moved on to a "Guide to the American 'T,'" which enumerated the handful of ways that the letter *t* is or is not pronounced in American English and in various regions of the United States.

Writing about the control of the voice, speech, and accent of Indian call center workers, Raka Shome argues that within call centers "language functions as an apparatus of transnational governmentality through which the voice of the third world subject is literally erased and reconstructed in the servicing of the global economy."[11] Thus, "the Indian agent becomes reconstructed as a 'modern subject' (i.e. able to speak to a 'modern' clientele) by the presence of an impending legal apparatus of a faraway country that monitors her/his speech and language use."[12] Yet accent neutralization is not only about expunging "unwanted cultural particulars" but also about creating and refining a placeless accent—one that cannot be fixed in any regional or national site, thus preventing customers from knowing exactly where their calls are going.[13] Indeed, over and over again in the media and marketing related to the Philippine call center industry, Filipinos are described as having neutral or light accents that are easy to understand, with tacit or sometimes explicit comparison to Indian accents, which U.S.-based customers not only find difficult but also recognize *as* Indian. The value of the Filipino accent therefore lies in its seeming detachment from a particular people or place. While such methods work only if a caller is not familiar with Filipino accents, the attempt at obfuscation is premised on the assumption that Filipinos are largely unknown and imperceptible in the United States—in and of itself an effect of the historical erasure of Filipino bodies, labor, and voices from the dominant U.S. culture. Finally, such language training always already assumes that the customer is a native and/or fluent English speaker—which agents soon learn is not the case—thus reinforcing how the term *American,* despite being the object of pedagogical attention during training, is in actuality an unmarked, undifferentiated category to which racialized Filipino voices register as *other.*

Again, there seemed to be very little enthusiasm for these lessons among my fellow trainees, most likely because the mock-call test would focus on the trainees' ability to engage in the correct call flow rather than on any particulars of grammar, vocabulary, or accent, and perhaps because having already made it through recruitment or having worked in call centers before, many in the class did not want or need additional English-language instruction. In any case, as indicated by the laughter that percolated throughout the room at the time, what seemed to interest the trainees the most was not the list of American English phrases but the list of Filipinoisms. On the following day, Bella asked each person to talk about something they had learned over the previous two days. A popular topic among the trainees was the lesson on Filipino English phrases, which they found particularly funny—a reaction that I understand through the analytic rubric of Filipino/American relatability as a practice of proximity. My sense is that the Filipino English phrases struck the trainees as rather uncanny—that is, both strange and utterly familiar—when seen alongside their American equivalents. Their apparent delight registered recognition of the gap between the "original" American phrases and the Filipino "copy" in a way that is consistent with popular Filipino comedic performances in which one person tries to imitate someone or something else, such as an American person or accent. The popularity of such performances, and indeed their very designation as jokes, suggests the humor in what Rey Chow has described as "a certain advantageous position" of the colonized, who is "much closer to the truth of the mediated and divisive character of all linguistic communication" than the colonizer.[14] This double consciousness—knowing what one sounds like to oneself and to the judging ears of power—is possible only because, for colonized subjects, learning the colonizers' language "became . . . a lesson in none other than the continual, disciplined *objectification* of an intimate part of themselves."[15] The gap between native and nonnative English thus became a source of both anxiety (in the context of the call center labor process, which demands the use of American English) and amusement for many in the class. Filipino/American relatability could thus also open up ways of knowing the many dimensions of the postcolonial experience as well as ideological and ontological struggle.[16]

Throughout CC the story of America, and the lesson in how to relate to it, got revised in subtle ways. While the ostensible goal of the lesson on immigrant groups was to convey that harrowing economic conditions in people's home countries compelled them toward the United States as the land of opportunity, by asking whether anyone in the class "*still* thought the U.S. was the land of milk and honey" Bella also cued us to think about how many immigrants' expectations of upward social mobility were *not* met after they settled in the United States. Such narratives circulated throughout the classroom, as when a young man named Michael introduced himself on the first day of class as someone who wanted to work in a call center so he could provide assistance not to his family in the Philippines but his family in the United States. Later in the week, Michael explained that his father and stepmother owned a small bakery in Las Vegas, but he saw "how difficult it can be to make ends meet" in the United States. When one of the other trainees asked Michael whether he had plans to join them in the

United States, he shook his head and said that he'd rather stay home in the Philippines and work in a call center where, if people said racist things to him, he could at least hang up the phone at the end of his shift, whereas "in the U.S., you have to live with discrimination everywhere, all of the time." The one person who actually answered Bella's question about the perception of the United States as the land of milk and honey—by saying, "No, because now we have their [Americans'] jobs"—highlighted yet another reason that the trainees questioned the narrative of immigrant success in the United States. Although the comment reinforces the misguided characterization of U.S. outsourcing as solely a competition between workers of the first and third worlds (rather than the struggle between global capital and labor), it also suggested that the United States was no longer a place where people, especially middle-class Americans, could find and maintain stable, decent-paying jobs—an idea that the agents and I would directly confront in the figures of the American trainers from Elphin whose classrooms we entered the following week.

As I tried to process the lessons from CC, I also found my attention drawn to the way my own relationships with fellow trainees were playing out. Indeed, the struggle over how to relate to the United States seemed manifest in the very way that particular people in the training course related to me. While the majority of my fellow trainees paid me no particular attention—a fact that suggests that my presence as a Filipina American was somewhat unremarkable—I did become an object of attachment for three individuals who each cathected in me some aspect of the larger relations and imaginaries that I analyze in this book. As mentioned earlier, when CC first started, I chose a seat near the back middle of the room so as to observe the classroom space quite easily; seated next to me on the first day was Junior, the quiet guy with the droll affect. By the second day of class, however, a nineteen-year-old young man named Lester—the young man discovered sleeping during orientation—had displaced Junior as my seatmate. I had taken notice of Lester the day before but not yet spoken directly to him.

I found it curious that of all the people Lester could have chosen to sit next to, he chose me, but it soon became clear that he saw in me a one-woman audience for his seemingly endless stories of his talents and abilities. One day, he insisted on showing me a YouTube video of his performance during a mixed martial arts competition; another day, he explained to me all of the things he had learned about car repair while working with one of his uncles, an auto mechanic, the previous summer. While it could have been that Lester simply wanted relief from the boredom he was experiencing in the class and didn't quite know how else to engage me in conversation, I sensed that his desire to impress me resulted from something more than tedium and social awkwardness. One night when Lester and I were walking together in a food market in search of "lunch," he overheard me speak Tagalog to one of the vendors and in response laughed directly at me for my American accent and imprecise pronunciation. The laughter was neither subtle nor friendly. It had the sting of ridicule, and I calmly let him know that he embarrassed and upset me. Still, I was not surprised that it was on the terrain of language and accent that Lester attempted to achieve some power and cultural superiority over me, for language was precisely the arena in which my own capacity to relate to Filipinoness was quite weak, not to mention the capacity of his that would be tested every night on the job. At that moment I could see more clearly the power struggle in which Lester had been interpellating me as a woman and a Filipina American: constantly seeking my recognition and approval of his many abilities, he seemed to jump at the opportunity to make his powers of judgment and derision felt and known.

The situation could not have been more different with Sammy, a gender-queer man with aspirations of becoming a female supermodel and moving to the United States. I had spoken to Sammy a few times during CC, as he usually joined the circle of smokers who became my primary social group during breaks.[17] By the end of CC, however, Sammy, too, expressed a desire to be my desk mate—although, unlike Lester, Sammy asked me how I would feel about this arrangement beforehand. Sammy was also always eager to engage me in discussion, although the topics always revolved around life and culture in the United States, especially New York City, where I had lived since the late 1990s. Invariably, Sammy would use these conversations as opportunities to rehearse and confirm the cultural capital embedded in his knowledge of America, asking questions such as "Isn't it true that people in New York City have really nice cars?" This grammar of validation, in which Sammy established his psychic proximity to a place he had never visited physically, also allowed him to construct an imaginary space for his glamorous ambitions. One night, for example, Sammy expressed the desire to someday purchase the apartment that his celebrity idol Mariah Carey owned, which led us to a conversation about real estate in New York City. In the last chapter of this book, I consider the ways that my relationship with Sammy was anchored in his desire to share with me his aspirations for gender reassignment and surgical alterations that would allow him to become a supermodel. Here I wish to point out that Sammy's adoration of New York City life and American celebrities reverberated in his treatment of me as someone who he clearly assumed always wanted "the best" of everything, even with regard to things as seemingly trivial as canned foods. One day during a lunch break, after I had removed a can of tuna fish from my bag, Sammy asked whether it was a particular American brand, which he had heard was "the best out there." To Sammy's mild disappointment, I had chosen a common Filipino brand.

The third person in the class who befriended me was Andy, a man my age who had worked aboard a U.S. cruise ship and therefore among Americans and other foreigners for several years. Andy was my neighbor by happenstance; he had simply chosen the seat across the aisle from me on my left. Throughout the training Andy was a constant source of witty remarks and self-deprecating humor; it became clear to me later that while these were natural aspects of his personality, they also helped him cope with the anxiety of being a married father of three young boys who was new to call center work and thus had a lot on the line. While I am tempted to say that my conversations with Andy felt the most organic—that is, as though there were fewer social stakes in the outcome of our interaction for him than for Lester and Sammy—I know that our affinity was preconditioned by the circuits of capital that had placed Andy within English-speaking spaces and thus made him able to converse with and relate to me quite easily.

The affective attachments that bound me to Andy, Sammy, and Lester were each informed by the structure of feeling that binds the Philippines to the United States: enamored of my social and cultural capital, Sammy admired and respected me; Lester saw me through the lenses of pride, rejection, and ridicule; and Andy's seemingly easy rapport with me was made possible by his experience as a transnational labor migrant. In this way, each relationship embodied a configuration of America/Americans in the Philippine imagination in the twenty-first century, a relationship underwritten by capitulation and critique. In the next section, I explore the interactions between the Vox Elite trainees and a different group of Americans—American trainers from the Elphin printer company.

Performing Knowledge Transfer

Elphin product training took place in a similar classroom as cc on the same dark and cool eighth-floor office space. As I entered the classroom that first night of training, the instructor, Tim Wheeler, was busy connecting an Elphin laptop to a digital projector. From a spot in the middle of the room, Sammy waved me over to his desk and then offered me the seat next to his. As soon as I sat down, Sammy anxiously asked me whether I had seen his crush, Paolo, arrive that night. He was worried that Paolo had left Vox Elite for another job, because he had heard Paolo saying something to that effect during the last day of cc. To Sammy's relief, Paolo walked into the room just as class was about to start. "I'll ask him about it later," he whispered wistfully.

Everyone was at attention when Tim, standing nearly six feet tall and wearing denim pants and an untucked short-sleeved button-down shirt, started to speak. Tim introduced himself as a trainer who had been working for Elphin for six and a half years. Some of the trainees nodded affirmatively when Tim described himself as lucky to have weathered the company's recent round of outsourcing and layoffs and confessed that he was "happy to have a job," a comment that marked him as an embodied contradiction of globalization. As one of the last people standing on a corporate path that led to downsizing and unemployment, an American trainer's job is essentially to make himself or herself obsolete by "collud[ing] in the effort to upload the contents of their brain" to offshore employees.[18] As Tim stood at the head of class sharing these details of his life with us, I could not help but note the precarity he so clearly represented and was experiencing. Tim then went on to explain that it was his first time in the Philippines and only his second time outside of the United States; the first was when he conducted Elphin training in Germany two years earlier. Born and raised in Texas, Tim had relocated to Tallahassee, Florida, to work for Elphin; there he met his second wife, with whom he had a two-year-old daughter. There was a loud silence in the room when Tim told the class that he was divorced and had a ten-year-old son with his former wife. His casual proffering of these facts implied that he did not know that divorce is illegal in the Philippines and thus that his status as a remarried divorcé was rather foreign to many in the class.

Once he had finished introducing himself, Tim immediately situated our roles as call center agents within a larger corporate and consumer frame by saying, "You'll be doing tech support for Elphin—yes. But your real job, your overarching goal, is to generate revenue for Elphin. As tech support, you are an extension of sales. People in sales only need to sell a product once, but tech support and customer service people, they sell the product and the company again and again, in how they handle the customers and their issues. This is crucial in a consumer-driven economy." During that first day of product training, Tim spent ample time making the point that as agents we were there to serve consumers, who were "responsible for the company's future, and therefore [our] future, too." He explained that in a world where products were often quite similar, bad customer service would drive consumers to competing companies and that, for better or for worse, we should fear the ways that Americans "love to gripe to others about a bad customer service experience." In this way, there could be no mistaking that we were workers tasked with instilling confidence in consumers about the products and the company, which we not only represented but, according to Tim, were "synonymous" with.

Then Tim launched into some introductory remarks that encapsulated his general approach to training. "Most Americans," Tim declared, "see call centers as the person they have to call to get what they want. They're thinkin,' 'Yes, I know my computer's broken. I know what I need. Just give it to me.' The truth is, you will see more problems in one week than a good IT administrator sees in a month, 'cause a good IT administrator sets things up so they won't break." Tim paused and then added, "I'm the kinda guy who's into immediate gratification. If you're anything like me, helping people makes you feel good." At this point, I was struck by the rhetorical maneuvering in Tim's choice of words. Tim clearly sought to empower us as new agents by elevating our troubleshooting skills above those of IT administrators; the latter might know a lot of things about computers, Tim implied, but we would *fix* problems, which came with a special kind of interpersonal satisfaction. Moreover, Tim's comparison between technical support and IT implied that he understood the hierarchy of the value chain and wanted to neutralize or even subvert it. Right off the bat, then, Tim was helping to manage the ambiguity of skill and value attached to technical support while also continuing to erode the boundary between work and worker, as suggested by his slippery description of call centers as people.

Tim was also clearly doing some relational work. By creating a caricature of American consumers as entitled know-it-alls, Tim seemed intent on diminishing them as a threat to us as future call center agents. He also established a willingness to identify with the trainees ("If you're anything like me") but also the authority to speak on behalf of "most Americans." Throughout the product training that I experienced at Vox Elite, Tim concocted a fluid mix of confidence in the trainees, sarcasm about Americans, and instructional authority. Even in this brief opening monologue, it was clear that Tim could easily shift between the roles of customer, agent, and trainer, often changing his voice, accent, and body language to indicate when he was acting as one or another. This shifting of perspectives was a skill that enhanced his teaching not only by modeling empathy but also by affirming that emotional labor, as a performance, requires acting in a particular role.[19] In this setting, Tim's job was to give us the lines and stage directions appropriate to our roles as call center agents, as well as to teach us what to expect from the other customers in a technical support interaction. No matter what role he performed for us as a trainer, though, Tim always made clear that he related, or was trying to relate, to our challenges as agents. I believe that this disposition earned him fondness and respect among the trainees, much like how my research participants felt about their team leaders and other managers. At the same time, these relational ties always led back to Elphin. For Tim, agents and trainers were in it together on behalf of Elphin, whose identity we should all assume. We were labor for consumers, and thus for capital—not against them.

As we proceeded through training, I filled pages and pages of my notebook with technical information about Elphin printers, although the first week of product training was dedicated to learning about Elphin's entire line of products as well as its particular protocol and script for technical support. We learned how to check on the warranty of a product and what parts of a printer could be easily replaced; we even went over computer hardware, from the chipset in a motherboard to voltage regulator modules. The information was dense and highly detailed, but when I asked others whether they were experiencing information overload or confusion, most just shrugged their shoulders and said some of the information was stuff they already knew, and the rest they could practice during nesting, the period of time when new agents take calls but are supervised and assisted by more senior agents or managers. Indeed, the affect during training sessions was one of boredom and benign mischief, as once again most of us just surfed the web, played games, or chatted with friends online in between the moments when we scribbled down notes from Tim's Power-Point presentations. Perhaps the energy in the class would have changed if we had actual printers to look at and learn from, but these never manifested during my time in training. It seemed we were expected to learn and internalize the information put before us but with nothing material to attach it to. To me, the tedium I experienced cut straight to a contradiction about call center work that I had often sensed but not quite put my finger on until I underwent Elphin's product training. On the one hand, call center work and technical support jobs in particular had a rather hip cachet in the Philippines, linked as they were to technology, youth, and high wages. On the other hand, the things we came to learn, while perhaps exciting to tech aficionados, were relatively uninteresting to most people, in part, I believe, because this knowledge merely helped reproduce the mundane material culture of office life in workplaces far away. The job might have some sparkle, but the products in question were encased in plastic chassis and performed limited and banal functions.

Woven into our daily instruction on processors and toners, however, were more lessons on the United States and relating to Americans. "Knowledge transfer," it seemed, could involve much more than technical information. Throughout product training, the majority of Tim's scripting and stage directions were geared toward assuring agents that they could overcome the challenges of interacting with American customers. To do so, Tim relied heavily on the trope of Americans as unintelligent, a strategy used in other offshore call centers as well.[20] During the second week of product training, for example, Tim explained that there are times when customers are reluctant to troubleshoot a technical problem with a call center agent or even hostile to the idea of doing so. When I asked why that might be, Tim responded, "Well, let's see . . . ignorance, fear, and general stupidity!," which earned big laughs from the class. Tim then parlayed these comments into a discussion of call control. "Every call is a conversation with a goal," Tim told us. "And conversations that have a good goal also need a good leader." Tim emphasized that technical support representatives must see themselves as doctors, since the latter take control of conversations with patients by asking them key questions to diagnose a problem and then chart out a plan of action. Technical support representatives, that is, must adopt an attitude of leadership, in which confidence is key.

Tim's explanation revealed how encouraging agents to think of themselves as doctors with diagnostic authority was foundational to the emotional structures upholding Elphin's bottom line. Agents *had* to take control of conversations with customers; otherwise, valuable service time could be lost, replacement parts sent in error, or actual on-the-ground Elphin workers dispatched to offices unnecessarily. But in thinking of themselves this way, agents were also learning to negotiate the uneven social relations and cultural capital on which offshore call center work was premised. In other words, by learning to think of themselves as experts on even the most esoteric matters, they could redefine what counted as valuable knowledge, thereby resisting their subordination to the almighty customer. Even Tim's discussion of "educated customers" played on the discourse of stupid Americans and of agents as empowered experts. "Some of the people that you speak with will be educated people; they are working in offices, a lot of them. But keep in mind that there are two kinds of educated people: those who are smart enough to know what they don't know, and those who think they know everything." With this comment, Tim expressed his belief that how well Americans recognized their own ignorance was the real measure of their supposedly superior education. No matter what kind of customer an agent was speaking to, however, the agent would ultimately be the party with more knowledge. As I observed Tim use relational labor to help the class build this emotional structure, it became clear why people in the industry would later come to embrace the idea of the call center agent as a subject-matter expert.

Yet there were cracks in the emotional edifice. For one, the discourse of American unintelligence downplayed the material privilege that made customer service and technical support call centers possible in the first place. Many of these material differences manifested in agents' unfamiliarity with the products they would be servicing or with customers' "first-world problems" with those products. Lauren Joy, a fellow Vox Elite trainee who had prior experience working in technical support, explained, "Actually, there would be times that I don't know how to empathize with the customer because I don't know the things that they are asking about. Like problems with DSL [a Digital Subscriber Line]. I don't even have Internet in my house"—which was unfortunate given her interest in web design, an activity she had to pursue in Internet cafés or at the homes of friends or relatives who did have Internet access. Such differences were sometimes lost on Tim. In a passing remark during one of our lessons, he made it clear that he thought everyone in the class had a washing machine and dryer in their homes, which from my experience I knew to be far from true. In another situation he unsuccessfully tried to start a conversation with some trainees about local restaurants—a type of discussion that presumed cosmopolitan knowledge of how to evaluate food as a cultural commodity—apparently unaware that most trainees brought food from home or did not participate in restaurant culture in the way Tim and the other trainers did.

These moments of friction were more than cultural clashes that a little diversity training could prevent. Rather, they pointed straight to the tensions and anxiety over race, nation, labor, and value that I came to see as defining the call center experience for many of my participants. Such moments also revealed how working as an offshore call center agent involved a double class subordination, in which third-world, racialized agents were cast as cheap labor servicing products for people living in a material world that the agents themselves could not readily access. The attempt to see oneself as equally powerful to, or even more powerful than, those one is serving—what Rachel Sherman calls the desire "to construct powerful selves"—thus allows workers to subjectively overcome inequalities of power and privilege while also leaving uneven social relations intact.[21] This is not to suggest that agents' empowerment is *merely* psychological or in their heads. To the extent that agents can harness this affective strength to control calls and perform well on the job in general, empowerment has material value for the company and personal value for the agent. Yet there is no doubt that it is a contradictory form of agency, one that emerges because the political-economic terrain on which call center work is situated is always and already so uneven. While representing Americans as unintelligent might help instill confidence in the new agents, it also often served as an agent's *only* coping mechanism in the face of various types of insults and injuries they would experience during service calls, including customer racism. During one class session, we listened to a recorded call handled by an Elphin call center agent based in Tallahassee. The agent sounded like a young man, and the caller like a middle-aged woman; both sounded like white, native English speakers. After the agent completed the opening part of the call flow, the caller remarked, "Oh, good. It seems like whenever I call Elphin I seem to get a foreigner," a comment the agent did not verbally acknowledge. When Tim heard this portion of the call, he went to the classroom's board and wrote "bigoted Cx [customer]." When the call was over, he said the following: "About talking to people in foreign countries: a lot of Americans are fine with it. You won't get this a lot. But in some areas, like the Rust Belt, people are sensitive to outsourcing. And some, through generations of idiocy, have a very ethnocentric view of the world. In the call we just listened to, the agent did the best thing possible: he ignored the comment. If it's any consolation, people with those attitudes aren't tolerated back home. Please accept my apologies for those calls. My grandmother still refers to African Americans by the *N*-word."

While Tim recognized that historical and regionalized experiences of deindustrialization might instigate a customer's antagonism when speaking with a Filipino agent, he once again evoked the notion of idiocy as a way to frame these challenges. In this way, Tim's response also functioned as a lesson in a worldview that sees individual ignorance and stupidity—rather than white supremacy or structural racism—as the basis of racist actions and beliefs, while also imagining that the worst articulations of racism, while still alive today, are simply old-fashioned or anachronistic. Tim also painted an erroneous picture of a United States in which racism is not only not tolerated but largely nonexistent, except among families or social groups who pass ignorance from generation to generation like a bad but ultimately benign genetic abnormality. Finally, by offering the agents a preemptive apology for the racist encounters he believed they would experience, Tim performed both penitence for American racism and the hope that agents would learn to disavow it. I would later learn about the larger impact of this kind of cultural training when I interviewed a Filipina communication and cultural trainer from Call Control named Vivica in 2013. Referring to callers who insisted on speaking with an American customer service representative, Vivica explained that "we shouldn't generalize or stereotype the Americans based on how they talk to you and respond to you, because the people who are calling in are just a small percentage of Americans." When I asked whether Vivica could pinpoint when and where she learned to think this way, she cited a learning module during her own training experience, leading me to believe that, over time, informal methods like Tim's had come to be institutionalized and reproduced in call center training.

There were times, too, when Tim revealed the boundaries of his political beliefs. When explaining that Elphin had recently revised their warranties to refer to "acts of nature" rather than "acts of God," Tim said in an irritated voice, "PC [political correctness] in the States has gone completely rampant. There are phrases we don't use because they might offend someone's delicate sensibilities." Indeed, the further off-script Tim went, the more his and the other trainers' political inclinations showed. One of the most striking of these moments occurred one night when several training classes were combined, and thus all four American trainers—three white men and one black man, all in their twenties with the exception of Tim—were standing at the head of the class. As everyone was settling into the somewhat cramped new arrangement, the trainers introduced themselves and then offered to answer any questions the trainees had for them. My sense is that the trainers, thinking of themselves as authoritative sources on the first world who could satisfy third-world curiosity, did not expect the first question—which came from Sammy—to be what they thought of "President Barack Obama's economic stimulus package." In response, Tim announced his identity as a libertarian and then opined that TARP, or the Troubled Asset Relief Program, was a bailout "of stupid people" (by which he meant the U.S. banks) who did not deserve to be rescued. Quinn, perhaps the youngest trainer in the group, then added his two cents about the U.S. economic recession in particular. "As someone who looks at things as an outsider," Quinn proudly remarked, "I see people as a bunch of lemmings. So some idiot analyst on Wall Street says we're in a recession, and then everyone stops spending and pulls their money out of the bank." Another trainer, Nick, then chimed in by saying that "the bailout was dumb" because it meant that the United States had to borrow money from other countries, to which Quinn responded that the situation was made all the worse because for years "the U.S. has lent money to third-world countries who never paid us back." Avi, the black trainer, was the only one of the four who did not take part in the conversation.

The exchange demonstrated not only a common misunderstanding or lack of knowledge about the destructive reality of loans and structural adjustment in third-world countries but also the ease with which a discussion of the failure of the U.S. financial system and the volatility of the economy could be rerouted to a vilification of the poor and nonwhite. Moreover, watching this display of white male derision—an affective position predicated on entitlement to some fictional outsider status through which one smugly judges the behavior and intelligence of others—I was struck by how the performance of America that we were witnessing was tied to the particular intersection of class, masculinity, and whiteness that these men occupied. It was not difficult to hear in their comments the same rancor and tone that I heard from aggrieved white men in the United States—men dissatisfied, sometimes dangerously so, with the economic shifts that had dried up blue-collar work and the social changes that were making America increasingly less white. The complex social positioning of the trainers was confirmed one evening during one of our lunch breaks at one in the morning, sometime near the end of the first week of product training. I was standing around with Andy, Lester, and a woman named Ginger as they smoked, when Tim and Nick joined us. Ginger was explaining to the group that she was working in a call center because she had not yet finished college—she was getting a degree in education—and therefore couldn't get another decent-paying job. Upon hearing this, Tim let out a sad laugh and said that because neither he nor Nick had graduated from college, "we'd be screwed here." Nick went on to say that a lot of his friends didn't have college degrees either and that they "worked in factories or military jobs, and so college wasn't something they necessarily considered doing, at least not right away."

Rewriting the Nation

I cannot say for certain whether this discrepancy in education reinforced or undermined Nick's and Tim's sense of accomplishment and value as white American men. What I can say, however, is that seeing these young men in the very place that symbolized the precarity of the American economy, alongside young Filipinos struggling to elevate the Philippines' place on a value chain, brought to light the way that globalization was changing the national narratives and social scripts through which Americans and Filipinos alike derived their identities and sense of purpose. My fieldwork at Vox Elite thus made clear to me that for Filipinos in the twenty-first century, learning to relate to Americans involved much more than understanding the significance of St. Patrick's Day or the meaning of English-language idioms. It also clearly revealed that nations, as imagined entities, are unevenly co-constructed through transnational processes that ascribe meaning to everything from race and geography to speech and accent, and that individualized senses of race, gender, and class identity could be reconfigured through material and symbolic reconfigurations of national economies.

Out of research money and out of time, I left Vox Elite training in June 2009 and returned to the United States just one week shy of the account's nesting period, when agents took live calls for the first time. Back in New York City, I looked for opportunities to interview Americans who had gone to the Philippines to work with or train Filipino call center agents. One such person was Jessica Daly, a white woman my age who was pursuing her undergraduate degree after having worked for nearly a decade in the private sector. I close this chapter with a brief discussion of my interview with Jessica in order to reiterate the transnational racial and class complexities of the Philippines' sunrise industry and thus the fragility of the dominant narratives about global partnership among structurally unequal nations.

In the early 2000s, Jessica was working for a large manufacturer in northeastern Indiana, a part of the Rust Belt, when the company decided to have one of its largest accounts handled by BPO workers in Manila. Jessica was one of a handful of employees asked to travel to the Philippines to train the new hires and oversee the transition, which she recalls was not a popular proposition among her coworkers:

> First things first, people at the company did not want to go train their replacements. The second thing was that they were so ignorant of the Philippines. People were asking, "Do they even have electricity over there?" or saying things like, "It's a third-world country," "You're going to die over there," or "They hate Americans." Some people didn't even know what the Philippines were. Anyhow, I was young, I was twenty-four or twenty-five at the time, and I wanted to go. I had never traveled outside of the U.S., but my father was in the navy, and he had actually been to Manila—Subic Bay—years ago, so I had heard stories about the Philippines and other places.

Jessica's description of her coworkers' attitudes about Filipinos reveals the racist and xenophobic discourses in which offshore outsourcing from the United States has been historically embedded—a backdrop for understanding the possible worlds from which the Elphin trainers themselves might have hailed. Although Jessica levels a critique against her coworkers, it is complicated by her own entanglement in the history of U.S. militarism in the Asian Pacific, which in turn has given rise to new intersections of tourism and capitalism that she as an American trainer represents. Jessica's description of the chance to go to the Philippines as in part a travel opportunity thus echoes Tim's marking of his stay in Manila as just one more addition to his collection of international experiences.[22]

In our interview, Jessica went on to detail the ways her fellow white American trainers and managers talked about Filipino trainees in their private conversations: "You know, white people have no problem talking to another white person and using racial slurs. It's like this hidden society between whites when they feel they can talk shit about other people."

I told Jessica that I had long been aware of the private show of racism among white people. Understanding that she was making a contrast between herself and her former coworkers and managers, I asked Jessica how she dealt with such situations.

It was very hard, because I became friends with a lot of the Filipinos. And some of the Filipinos came here to the U.S. to get a better understanding of the job. So when they were here, I heard my American coworkers saying awful things—and keep in mind people knew that there were layoffs coming and that they had to help with the transition. It was a hostile environment. So you would hear these snide remarks like "They don't wash their hands when they go to the bathroom." Or "They smell." Or "Why do they always walk together?" "They are so weird." "What's wrong with them?" "They share their food." All of these little remarks. "They all look the same." "I don't understand them." "Why can't they speak English?" And of course when it came time for them to sit down with the Filipino trainees, there was none of that. Though I will say that while I didn't say anything like that, I didn't do anything to stop it.

In her description of this experience, Jessica exposes the racism of her former coworkers, locating it in both whiteness in general but also aggrieved whiteness in particular, demonstrating the way white Americans' anger about structural changes in the economy is not just displaced onto the bodies of nonwhite workers but can be linked to, and constitute, a form of racism. Jessica's descriptions also made me shudder to think about the way that Filipino call center agents are trained to ignore customer racism while so much private racism is being maintained around them. Unlike for the majority of her coworkers, however, Jessica's cultural capital and her prospects for class mobility made it possible for her to relate to Filipinos in a more affirmative manner. "I think having traveled all around the U.S. and my father being so cultured, I wanted to get to know them, not ridicule them," she explained. "Also," she said, "I didn't care if I was losing my job. I was young. I knew I could get another good job. It wasn't like I had worked there my whole life. I think that's what ultimately kept me motivated; I didn't feel the same hostility or tension as the other people. And my productivity increased, while theirs went down."

Later in our conversation, Jessica described an American manager from the company named Darren, who had traveled to the Philippines with her and also established a different relationship with Filipino trainees. Jessica described him as "very much engaged and a friendly guy." But what bothered Jessica about Darren was that "he enjoyed flaunting the fact that he had a lot of money." This led to a conversation about the relative value of Darren's salary in the Philippines, and the refractions of class identity that such a salary created for American trainers. "Darren was making maybe $38,000 a year here, maybe a little more," Jessica explained, "which is really nothing. But over there, in the Philippines, you perceive things differently. Because he stayed in a house and had a driver and a lot of cash and could spend anything on dinner, he acted like he was rich, and a lot of the Filipinos treated him like that, too. They really admired him . . . I mean, he *was* really nice, like I said, but I think the fact that he had money had something to do with that [admiration]."

Jessica's description of Darren hints at the way that, for many tourists or businesspeople who travel to developing countries, the racialized economic hierarchies among nations allow middle- or lower-middle-class Americans to feel a greater sense of wealth and superiority than they would in the United States. As Steven Gregory succinctly puts it, for these first-world subjects "hierarchy feels good."[23] In this transnational context of wealth differentials, Filipino/American relatability thus also provides a class framework in which Americans can experience elevated social status relative to Filipinos. Once again, however, these feelings are complicated and potentially destabilized by the realization that one of the sources of Americans' status—corporate jobs—is becoming available to Filipino people who often have relatively higher educational credentials than the trainers themselves. Neither Darren nor Jessica had been to college when they went to the Philippines as trainers, but, as Jessica observed, "every one of the people we were training in the Philippines had a college degree. It's really amazing how many degrees they have."

4

SERVICE WITH A STYLE

Aesthetic Pleasures, Productive Youth,

and the Politics of Consumption

In February 2009 the national newspaper the *Philippine Daily Inquirer* ran a job advertisement for the global BPO firm Convergys (Figure 4.1). "We've expanded our world and have arrived in Makati's shopping district," announced the ad, specifying that Convergys's new office had been integrated into Glorietta 5, the fifth and then most recent addition to the already extensive Glorietta shopping mall in Makati, one of Metro Manila's financial, consumer, and business hubs. The background of the ad depicts a crisp rendering of the modern structure, lit from within at night, with crowds of people and moving cars on the street outside the building. The foreground features a smiling young woman in midstride, carrying a shoulder bag and a mobile phone. Below her, the ad elaborates: "Welcome to a place that marries work and lifestyle. Work for a reputable company in a stylish and ideal workplace, all in one prime location"; below that, it states: "Convergys. Out*thinking*. Out*doing*."[1] Emphasizing the company's location in a shopping area frequented by affluent locals, the business elite, expatriates, and tourists, the ad lends the company a vibrant tone that simultaneously conveys cosmopolitanism, youth, and consumption. The ad further suggests that working in Convergys's modern, air-conditioned building takes on a global style, where "global" appears metonymic for the industrialized north; the woman's dark coat, pants, and scarf are, after all, unrealistic attire for the Philippines' tropical locale, marked by the palm trees lining the sidewalk in the background. Moreover, the ad's emphasis on mobility and ongoing action—walking, thinking, doing, driving—strongly suggests that the world of call centers is a relentlessly produc-

Figure 4.1 A Convergys job advertisement blurs the boundaries between labor and leisure, work and commerce, and global north and global south.

tive one, where workers reap abundant material benefits from burning the midnight oil and therefore propel themselves toward a bright future. By highlighting the consumer lifestyle made possible through call center work, the Convergys job advertisement blurs the boundaries between workplace and marketplace, labor and leisure, and production and consumption, thus epitomizing the ethos of the postindustrial age.

In the everyday contestation over the social and cultural value of call center work, the question of the industry's longevity and professionalizing prospects looms large. From family dinner tables to industry conference rooms, many worry about whether the Philippines will be able to remain a strong link in the global value chain and whether young Filipinos taking up call center jobs are squandering their educations on service work. In this climate of uncertainty, Filipino call center workers' ample earnings and elevated purchasing power also become sites of intense contestation.

Is their surging consumption an illusory sign of success that masks the financial as well as social, physical, and psychological risks the work entails? Or is it a truly meaningful measure of the industry's rewards, including its ability to ensure economic mobility into the middle class? Within these debates, images like the Convergys ad play a significant role in shifting the emphasis away from fatigued bodies, dead ends, and subjugated labor toward a discourse of progress and success measured by cosmopolitan consumerism, modern lifestyles, and hyperproductivity. Consumer culture thus emerges as an important battleground on which the meaning of new forms of work, and the reorganization of capital those forms represent, is debated. Given that one of the primary justifications for globalization is that it can raise the standard of living of those in the developing world, understanding the possibilities and politics within consumer culture becomes paramount.

This chapter interrogates the emerging perception of Filipino call center workers as upwardly mobile consumer subjects and the discourses of productivity, propriety, and class with which this perception is intertwined. I first examine how workers contend with the criticism and disapproval of their conspicuous consumption, and then discuss the social exclusions of call center consumer culture—exclusions hinted at in the Convergys ad's depiction of a Filipina mestiza whose light skin and facial features suggest that call center work is ideally suited for affluent youth whose material privileges and presumed cosmopolitanism already mark them as global subjects, as well as those who aspire to such status. This chapter also continues to explore the affective contradictions of call center work introduced in the first chapter—that is, the stark contrast between the dispiriting elements of call center work, on one hand, and its opportunities for affirmative relations between coworkers, personal fulfillment, and now luxury and glamour, on the other. The chapter asks how an industry characterized by some as a dead end for cheap labor also produces experiences of aesthetic and bodily pleasure, and to what ends. Finally, this chapter also examines how consumer practices and cultures embedded in and linked to call center work contribute to a productivist ethic and thus the cultural construction of call center workers as what I call *productive youth*. In this chapter and chapter 5, I focus specifically on how the social and cultural contradictions of call center work come to bear on workers' bodies and how contestations over call center work's value are directly linked to the aspirations of call center workers for modernity, mobility, and pleasure that are manifested through bodily expression and practice.

"A Product, a Package, a Lifestyle"

It is difficult to miss the signs of consumerism that surround the Philippine call center industry. Every call center that I visited during my fieldwork was surrounded by convenience stores and new restaurants catering to BPO employees, while local resorts or banks would set up tables in BPO office lobbies, looking to capture employees' attention with their special deals and offers. However, few sources displayed the Philippine call center industry's culture of consumption more clearly than *Spiff*, a now-defunct monthly magazine launched in January 2008. As a lifestyle magazine with the tagline "powering up the call center life," *Spiff* centered on the commodity culture and leisure lifestyle surrounding call center workers. Even a cursory glance at a typical table of contents reveals how robust the call center workers' appetite for consumer goods had supposedly become in such a short period of time (see Figure 4.2). Sections of the magazine entitled "Ramp Up," "Tech Squad," and "Rec Room" featured page after page about fashion, the latest in personal electronics, food culture, and travel, while "Release" and "Help Line" were dedicated exclusively to the trials and tribulations of workers, including workplace sexual scandals. For quick reference, the table of contents was also accompanied by images of actual consumer goods, such as a mobile phone and a personal cosmetic item. In turn, this visual logic and language suggest, for example, that the young man with sunglasses, upturned collar, and necklace is in many ways his own product, composed of all the right accessories to complete his look—both the look he has and the one he gives off.

In these ways, *Spiff* magazine could suggest that young Filipino call center workers are not only serving up satisfaction for consumers on the other end of the 1–800 line but harnessing their purchasing power to find satisfaction of their own, especially in and through their bodies—adorning themselves with new clothes and hairstyles, trying new foods and aesthetic goods, and finding new ways to escape the psychological grips of emotional and affective labor. In April 2008 this emphasis on bodies was made literal, as the cover featured windswept "Cleo" pressed against bare-chested "Mitch," both sun-kissed and standing on the beach

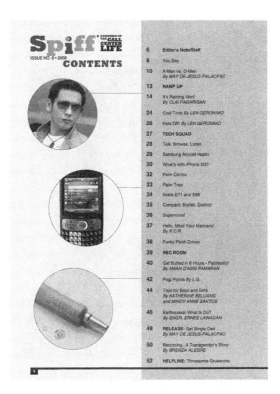

Figure 4.2   A 2008 issue of *Spiff* magazine's table of contents: stimulating and satisfying call center workers' appetites for consumption.

(Figure 4.3). While Mitch's and Cleo's slightly self-conscious facial expressions fall short of the look of professional models—indeed, all the people featured in the magazine were actual call center workers—the image as a whole nonetheless situates call center workers as both subjects and objects of casual leisure and conspicuous consumption, figures who consume and luxuriate before the eyes of others and who are aware of how they appear in the process. The covers and contents of *Spiff* magazine laid bare how call center work could be, and for many had become, a lifestyle—a way of living in which decisions about such things as what to eat, where to shop, or how to spend one's free time abide by an aesthetic logic and/or ethics that often corresponds to, while in some ways masking, specific class orientations or sensibilities, in this case middle-class ideals. In placing call center

Figure 4.3 Cover of *Spiff* magazine for April 2008: emphasizing casual leisure, conspicuous consumption, and bodily pleasure.

workers within a larger assemblage of imagery and products that evoke the spectacle of consumption, *Spiff* did more than simply represent call center workers' newfound lifestyles. Rather, the magazine helped bring that life-style, and the identity attached to it, into being.

In many ways, *Spiff* represented a reality among my research partici-pants, whose personal possessions seemed to multiply on a regular basis, as they bought themselves not only clothes but laptop computers, high-performance digital cameras, or limited-edition brand-name sneakers. The musicians whom I knew from Integral often channeled their money into expensive guitars or accessories, and a number of people I talked to were saving money to buy new cars. Moreover, because participating in the realm of the social—that is, having a social life—requires higher levels of consumption, the opportunity to spend money also opened up an even greater social world for many of the call center workers I encountered; for many of these young people, the elevated purchasing power enabled by call center work feels truly thrilling, as a vast array of alluring goods become available to them for the first time.[2] Reminiscing on her first several paychecks, Mia told me, "I was thinking, 'Oh my God, I can spend so much, I can do anything I want. It's like, for the first time, you see a T-shirt you really like, and you think, 'I can buy this.'" Such descriptions are especially meaningful considering the way consumer spaces allow shoppers to feel a particular version of freedom, not only to control their own resources but to access realms where their imagination and sense of style find expression.[3] Talking to Mia and many of my research participants, I was taken back to my first job during high school (working as a cashier at a drugstore in suburban Florida), remembering the excitement over having my own money and spending it on clothes and music that were part of the alternative style I was going for.

Despite the state-based rhetoric touting call center workers as national heroes, their engagement in conspicuous consumption has opened them up to criticism from onlookers who see in these actions only vice and misplaced priorities. In keeping with the assumption that call center work is merely a high-paying dead-end job, many people see call center workers as chasing decadence and lacking discipline. "You know call center workers when you see them," a friend living in Manila once told me. "They have the clothes, the cell phones, that whole lifestyle. You see them smoking and drinking in droves around shopping malls, with their Starbucks and their credit cards." My friend's amused yet critical description of call center workers reminded me of how members of my own family often expressed disapproval of my young cousin Jocelyn—whose story opened the book—and her supposedly insatiable desire for brand-name shoes, perfume, and apparel, often blaming this desire for her abandonment of nursing and her entry into call center work. The pleasures my cousin found in consumption and consumer goods were thus a site of tension for family members who felt her aesthetic desires were trivial and inappropriate and who thus considered call center work frivolous as well. Yet these moral recriminations elide a number of important things about call center workers, including the social differences among them. As I discussed in chapter 2, the call center industry is unique in the Philippines because it draws people from an array of economic stations and life stages.[4] For college students or recent college graduates who are still significantly reliant on their parents—primarily for housing and other major expenses—call center work is indeed a chance to earn and spend disposable income. Joel Partido, the vice president of human resources for Vox Elite, who had spent years getting to know hundreds and hundreds of call center agents, described this demographic in the following manner:

> You have a call center agent that is just fresh out of college, and they're staying with their parents, they're not paying the rent, et cetera. This is where you have call center agents who have the most disposable income in their hands. They're the most visible, the most flamboyant, the loudest demographic. You know their net take-home pay is something they can dispense with [for] the latest gadgets. You see them driving the family car and not even worrying about gas because their parents still pay for it. They are the ones that you see spending 150 pesos in Starbucks, or just twice or thrice a week doing the new phenomenon in drinking which is called *inumagan*—drinking in the morning after their shifts. They're able to take taxicabs and be on the mass transport system, and [buy] new apparel, clothing, you know, food and entertainment, and even travel. They are the ones who after payroll are looking for the *barkada*-type arrangements [group discounts] going to Boracay or some other popular resorts because I think the travel agencies are packaging it very well for call center workers right now.

In Manila I had come to know many call center employees whom Joel would most likely include in this group, including most members of Calvin and the Talent, the rock-and-roll cover band at Integral, and many at Vox Elite. Yet I also knew a good number of workers whose families—including their parents, siblings, or children—relied solely on their wages.[5] Joel went on to say, "You don't see a lot of those belonging to the other demographics hanging around because they want to maximize every opportunity [to get] overtime and so forth. They are the folks who, despite the invitation of an agent who is very popular and who is probably the informal team leader, who says, 'Hey let's go out after the shift,' ends up saying, 'No, I can't.'"[6]

Before moving on to discuss some of the social exclusions tied to call center work and the experience of less privileged people in the workforce, I want to consider Joel's description of the moment that a shift ends and the chance for socialization begins. As I introduced in chapter 1, the work culture of call centers is directly tied to the demands of the call center labor process; to renew their social and affective capacities, call center workers, isolated from other family members and friends by the temporalities and exigencies of call center work, find numerous ways to bond with one another. Add to this mix of social and cultural dynamics the compensation of call center work, as well as the Filipino affinity for social gatherings more broadly, and the result is a situation in which spending money, especially directly after work, feels to many workers like a necessity. Many of my research participants were quite explicit about this particular point. Joel himself surmised that the vast majority of every call center team (of maybe ten to fifteen people) would spend money at the end of the night as a way to destress, leaving just a few to "go against the grain and say, 'No, I have to go back to my family.'" A former call center agent named Kevin put the matter quite well when he explained, "It's almost like a requirement to go out with your teammates. You're sick of your job, or you're just really tired of those people on the phone, so why not spend a good time with your teammates? That's part of [working in a call center]." Connecting this to consumer culture, Kevin went on to say that "the culture is all about cell phones—high-end cell phones, brand-new cell phones—and [things you] 'must own,' about bragging. Even renting a condo is part of it. The job itself is like a product, a package, a lifestyle." Some call center workers understood these obligations to spend their disposable income as the reason they couldn't save enough money for their longer-term goals or bigger purchases they wished to make.

The conversation with Kevin quoted above in fact started with me asking whether Kevin was able to save money from his call center job. In response, he explained that between the money he needed for personal necessities like rent, transportation, and food, the little bit of money he sent home to his parents, and the money he spent going out, he had not managed to accumulate any savings even after two years. Kevin was not alone in this experience. Pamela, a former employee of Premier Source in Bacolod, explained that "most people cannot save because of the lifestyle, including money spent on team building activities. And, you know, teammates go out drinking, and drinking is expensive. Some don't actually have the money to go out because they have spent their earnings [on] the things they need or given almost all of it to their families, so they would even go so far as to borrow it just so they can [go out with their teammates]." While it may be the case that workers could save more money were it not for the compulsory socializing, these empirical circumstances are also tangled in discourses that filter greater anxieties about shifts in material culture, modes of production, and class identities into a condemnation of young workers' behavior and choices as irresponsible or inappropriate—discourses that have long been used to critique working-class and minority consumers in the United States as well. Such ways of thinking also tend to grossly overestimate the amount and therefore the relevance of the money that can be saved on working- or even middle-class wages. A poor person's ownership of a cell phone, for example, does not prevent them from owning a house, but poor wages do.

Call center workers who choose to save their earnings do, however, learn to manage and stick to a financial budget. Many of my research participants also narrated this part of their financial learning curve to me. For example, Mia admitted that she had been somewhat reckless when she first started earning money as a call center worker, but that was no longer the case. "Once," she explained, "I bought a mobile phone with my whole 30,000 [peso paycheck]. Now, I think about how to buy something without making a huge dent [in my budget], and my savings are really intact. The usual mentality is 'O, *suweldo na!* Withdraw *lahat!*' [Oh, payday! Withdraw everything!]. It depends, though. Some agents are of age, they have families, or they are thinking about the future. Like me, at first I spent a lot. But then I thought, 'I'm twenty-six. I have plans for the future. I might have kids.'" Mia's comments are indicative of the way that a dominant perception of call center workers as young spendthrifts also hides the private domain of social reproduction where more sobering questions of resource management come into play. Mia's matter-of-fact statement about her age, future, and probability of having children illustrates how, for many young agents, the decision to stem their outward cash flow in favor of disciplined money management coincides with the anticipation and acceptance of more familial responsibilities. Philip, one of Mia's coworkers, echoed her logic when he explained to me how he manages his money: "At first, you know, you are excited about your first job. It's the first time you're making money, so you can buy whatever you want, and your parents don't have to buy it for you. But now I'm satisfied, like with the clothes I have [*tugging at his navy blue polo shirt*]. Now I save for the next level."

"What's 'the next level'?" I asked.

"Like my guitar, or a professional camera," Philip responded. "Items that I would say, 'Okay, in four months I should be able to buy this.'"

Curious about whether this budgeting included additional savings, I asked, "And after four months, for example, if you bought the thing you were saving for, would you still have money left over?"

To this, Philip responded, "Of course, yes."

Then I asked, "What's the next level after that, after the camera?"

Philip quickly responded, "A car." But then he qualified his response by explaining, "I'm just lucky because I can stay in my parents' house, and I'm single. But I have a friend . . . his salary is okay, but now he has to think about his wife and kids. He needed to buy a house. Me, I'm free to use my money to buy whatever I want."

It is easy to take for granted the transition from carefree spending to disciplined budgeting as natural shifts that many young people experience in the passage from young to full adulthood. But to do so obscures the social hierarchies, cultural capital, and life stages converging in call center consumer cultures, which Joel Partido's description above alludes to, and Philip's comparison between himself and his friend suggests. In other words, the intersection of class position with life stage (i.e. where an individual is in a cycle of social reproduction) significantly shapes how call center workers experience and understand such seemingly neutral or celebratory terms as *income* and *purchasing power*. So, too, do normative understandings of what family structure and responsibilities look like, as Mia and Philip demonstrate. For workers with spouses and children who are struggling to bring up the next generation—or for those who, as children, must keep their siblings and their parents financially afloat—socializing and spending on new consumer goods were not options. Joel describes the latter as members of "a typical Filipino family" that would be "betting on one of their sons or daughters, expecting them to be their tickets out of poverty." "These folks," Joel went on, "would be toiling a bit harder than other employees or teammates, because for them, if they don't work hard and earn much, they'll not be able to help the other siblings go to college or help out their parents who are nearing retirement." Such agents actively budget their time and money to maximize their chances for social mobility. Andy, the Vox Elite new hire who at the time of my research was living with his wife and three children in his parents' home in Cavite, was slowly saving money to buy his family a modest house of their own. Tess, a collections agent who worked under Mia's supervision, had worked for a car manufacturer in Japan for six months but then moved back to the Philippines when she became pregnant with her second daughter. Her ₱20,000 monthly salary at Global Invest, which she was able to achieve after one year with an impeccable work record, allowed her to place a down payment on a house, also in Cavite, for herself and her two children; her husband, who was unemployed, was looking for work in another major city at the time of our meeting. Tess proudly explained to me that she creates a budget for her family and saves what she doesn't spend; in a practical tone, she explained that she "does not go out after work" because it is a "waste of time" for her, someone with "two kids, a mortgage, and no vices."

Class differences between workers of course create tensions in the workplace, which often manifest themselves through the language of productivity. Two operations managers working at Premier Source in Bacolod, Jake and Cassie, shared with me their assessment of the differences between affluent employees and others. For example, Jake explained, "A majority of the people here [at Premier Source in Bacolod] are working just for the heck of it. So it's actually hard to get them to work. They don't care as much about meeting the metrics or passing their scorecards because they are just in it to be happy, to be with their friends." Cassie chimed in, adding, "Yeah, they don't really need the jobs because their parents can support them so they are working just so they can buy their own things. They are not really going to help their family." Both Jake and Cassie agreed that at least a third of the employees they managed were in this boat, while the other two-thirds were working parents who stayed motivated on account of their economic need. Andy, my neighbor during training at Vox Elite, told me just three days into the course that he was very afraid of losing his job, "not like these rich kids who don't really care." Cassie and Jake thus revealed more of the ironies and contradictions of call center work, including how the people most qualified for the job in terms of education level (and thus English-language skills) are sometimes perceived as the least motivated and least productive individuals. Recruiters had a more nuanced perspective on these matters. Antonio explained to me that he "could see a breakdown by season. Many of the people who apply in a call center just before school gets out, those are the ones who would be really desperate for money, desperate for a job, because they haven't even graduated yet. They say they'll do whatever it takes to get or keep the job. They are like those other applicants who have worked in other call centers but didn't get promoted, so they are willing to start again at lower pay in this company, because they want another chance to move up, to get promoted." Behind all of the conspicuous consumption, we therefore find workers who at the end of the workday must eschew youth-based cultures of consumption for the unglamorous logic of more basic preservation and sustainability. Toiling toward mobility, they face obstacles such as a two- or three-hour commute to work or other forms of marginality and precarity. Rosemarie, an agent working under Mia's supervision, had three young children and a husband with an addiction to gambling; there were times when her husband went missing for days, placing a huge emotional strain on the family and often creating debts that Rosemarie had to pay off.

No matter their social status, all call center workers, it seemed, needed to contend with the cultures of consumption and precarity in which the industry is embedded. Indeed, the more I talked about things like shopping and saving with my research participants, the more I came to see how their initial embrace of call center work's cultures of consumption gave way to ambivalence, self-reflection, and "ethical problematization," a process or state of being in which they considered their own desires and actions as problems in need of resolution.[7] This approach to consumption was tied to the material demands of real or imagined families, as all of these narratives suggest. Believing that being a good spouse, parent, or even person requires financial stability—and thus the ability to purchase a family home and pay for education—my research participants showed measured forethought and self-control, or what Michel Foucault has called technologies or care of the self.[8] Call center workers are thus not part of a monolithic demographic that gets swept up in the flashiness of consumerism, even if it does offer them hope, pleasure, and reward. Rather, their relationships to these material processes are mediated by their class positions and life stages. Given the way that the contestation around call center consumer cultures revolves around their bodies and behavior in public spaces, it is no surprise that my research participants respond to these problems by applying their energies to private life and the domestic space of the family. When public displays of consumption are associated with youth and decadence, individuals wishing to see themselves as respectable middle-class subjects, or to be seen by others as such, will retreat to private space.

Risk, Fortune, and Finance

Like call center work more broadly, the consumer cultures attached to the industry raise questions about the value, risk, and fortune involved in the pursuit of call center work for both individuals and the nation as a whole. Given the range of economic burdens and freedoms that call center workers experience, the question of whether or not call center workers achieve the social mobility with which their work is often associated is difficult to address, but patterns did seem to emerge. For those workers like Mia and Philip who came from economically stable or affluent families, call center work constitutes an opportunity to reproduce their class privilege, albeit in ways distinct from their parents' generation given their wider access to consumer goods and niche markets but also the contradictory dynamics of fast pay raises and precarious work. For workers like Andy, Tess, and Rosemarie, call center work is a possible but also unclear road to economic change that competes or can be combined with labor migration. Both Andy and Tess had spent time working overseas and turned to call center work as an alternative to leaving their young children in the Philippines to be cared for by other family members, a choice that thousands of Filipinos make each year.

The question of call center worker mobility often involves speculation about the ability of call center workers to gain entry into the Philippine middle class or, more specifically, the "new" middle class. While scholars define the old middle class as being drawn from the upper echelons of a long-standing social hierarchy stretching back to the Spanish colonial era, the emergence of a new Philippine middle class is tied to industrialization and the expansion of bureaucracy, which began during the commonwealth era (1935–1946), extended to the post–World War II years, and then continued after the fall of Ferdinand Marcos in 1986.[9] Since the People Power Revolution, the definition of the Philippine middle class has changed considerably, as sources of wealth have increased with the expansion of managerial, administrative, clerical, sales, or semiskilled service work, especially in urban areas.[10] By far the greatest source of this redefinition has been overseas Filipino workers, whose foreign wages translate into homes, cars, clothes, and education for their family members back home. The ability to sustain families in these ways—with the accoutrements of middle-classness—is often upheld as a justification for the hardship of one parent or both going abroad.

Increasingly, however, the question of whether or not call center workers can become part of the Philippine middle class has become more difficult to answer because of the wide definition of what or who constitutes this class stratum. As Michael Pinches writes, "in the Philippines itself, the term 'middle class' is commonly associated with perceived incomes and consumption practices," and "a significant number of people [are] identified as middle class by their occupations and urban lifestyles."[11] The middle classes thus comprise those "who drive cars, own expensive electrical appliances and live in what are known as 'middle class' housing estates."[12] Yet by encompassing *perceived* income, consumption practices, and home-ownership, the term *middle class* conflates disposable consumer goods with assets like property or capital, which represent enduring equity, in turn obscuring the way that those identifying or identified as middle class may or may not have a stable financial base from which to accrue more wealth. In other words, when middle-classness is determined as much (or more) by access to consumer goods that depreciate over time as by assets whose value increases over time, it is difficult to know whose consumption is a sign of material privilege in the form of financial stability and whose is not. As Mia plainly put it, "it's difficult to tell who is middle class anymore." Such uncertainty can destabilize the class identities of more conventionally affluent groups, instigating the kind of anxieties that lead to a moral reproach of fast-money jobs and conspicuous consumption.

Thus, another ambiguity of call center work emerges: if middle-classness is defined by access to high-status goods, then it is possible to say that call center workers, at the time of my research, were becoming members of this group. However, if middle-classness is defined in terms of property ownership, the results appeared more dismal. Although almost all of my research participants were interested in saving for and buying property, only those who had reached upper-level management positions—earning about ₱80,000 per month as an individual (or less if one also had a similarly paid spouse)—had been able to do so. This limitation was corroborated by my research participants, who maintained that a "respectable" home and lot in, for example, a middle-class residential neighborhood of southern Manila—a house in which parents and children have separate bedrooms and there is room for a family car or two—would cost ₱4 to 5 million and would therefore require at the very least an ₱80,000 monthly salary to acquire and sustain. It was costs of living like this that caused one former call center worker I met, a young man named Harold, to quit call center work when he realized his starting salary would be a little less than ₱20,000 a month. With plans to not only propose to his girlfriend but financially support her after they got married, Harold knew the call center money would not be enough for their lifestyle, so he started working in his family's construction business instead.

While Harold would go on to inherit the family business, what about call center workers with less family resources? Could they become entrepreneurs, too? A key part of the celebratory narrative of globalization is that otherwise poor or struggling people would earn enough working for multinational corporations to start their own small businesses using their savings as capital. Yet none of the current and former call center workers I met who had started their own businesses followed this model; some had small and informal moneymaking operations that were not lucrative enough to replace a regular income, while others had businesses that were either inherited from or started with capital lent to them by family members. In other words, no one I met had earned and saved enough money from call center work to start their own business and leave the industry. The closest was a couple, Natalie and Rael, who had put some of their savings into a direct-marketing business for beauty products while continuing with call center work. Eventually Natalie did leave the industry, but it was more because of burnout—she had worked there for eight years—than because of the success of her direct-marketing investment. Rael kept going, choosing to stay in upper-level management while staying involved in the side business of direct-marketing.

One afternoon in Bacolod, Pamela—the former Premier Source employee I interviewed along with her former team leader, Ronnie—and I drove to the edges of the next town over to meet Ismael, who owned a small graphic design shop. I talked with Ismael while he sat behind the main counter of the small but tidy space, whose walls displayed the impressive graphics he and his one employee had created. When I asked Ismael about what compelled him to start his own business, he answered in a way that illuminated many of the social, economic, cultural, and familial dynamics that intersect in call center agents' everyday lives.

"Well," Ismael said, "I wasn't thinking of opening something for myself until my sister and brother-in-law, who have their own business, really talked to me about it. They talked to me about being concerned about my future."

I asked Ismael what his sister and her husband were concerned about specifically, but he did not give me a direct answer. Instead, he started to describe how "the lifestyle working in a call center is so, I don't know. How would you say it, La [Pamela]? It's really *different*. The schedule was so irregular. I had to be at work at 3 A.M. a lot, and my parents and sister really hated that. And I was going out a lot, partying a lot. I was spending on drinking, and my car. I didn't save any money." Perhaps not wanting to reproduce call center workers' reputation for social ruin, Ismael added, "But it was my fault. Those were my choices."

In the end, the capital for Ismael's business had come directly from his sister and brother-in-law. As we were wrapping up our discussion, Ismael said something that reminded me that we were in Negros Occidental, where wage labor still carried the stigma of low social rank: "It's good to open a business," he said, "because you can't work forever."

While Ismael aspired to eventually relieve himself from the burden of having to work for an income—instead building his business up so he could have employees do all the labor—other call center workers started small businesses simply to have another stream of income. A Premier Source employee I met named Mary Ann had, for example, started an Internet-based business called Ann's Attic, in which she sold fashion accessories and novelty items to locals. Mary Ann described working at Premier Source as "a good job" but said that she and her daughter still lived "hand to mouth." Her house and her daughter's educational expenses, she explained, had all been paid for with borrowed money. Even Mia's plans to purchase property kept getting stalled and revised. When I first met Mia in person in 2009, she spoke enthusiastically about her ability to save for an investment property, something her parents would be able to coach her through. Because she was still living with her parents and drove her mother's old car, she calculated that she could have ₱100,000 in savings in three or four months "if I really lived bare bones." But as time passed, Mia had to adjust her expectations, as she realized that living on a few thousand pesos per month was too challenging for her. Mia had options, though, and she knew this. Her mother had a thriving education business teaching children with special needs, and Mia could always quit call center work and take it over. Moreover, her parents had money and property to pass down to her.

In attempting to track the social mobility of my research participants, I am less interested in creating what Stuart Hall might call a static inventory of descriptions in order to stabilize the definition of the middle class than in understanding how the belief in upward mobility seems to rise and fall on questions about the meaning and practice of consumerism as part of the popular culture that call center workers create.[13] The moral disapproval of conspicuous consumption and the hand-wringing over middle-class membership all speak, in my estimation, to the way that call center consumer culture is a site through which a new generation of workers is confronting the increasingly hegemonic terms of neoliberalism, with its valorization of the market and its proliferation of risk.[14] The expansion of consumer credit is a major part of this neoliberal landscape, complicating these class formations and struggles. I first started thinking about the role of credit in call center workers' lives when I was out one night with Mia and Sophia in early 2009. As we ate, we moved through our usual topics of conversation: Mia's week at work, Sophia's progress on her thesis for her master's in business administration (the topic of which was call center training), and my research. When the bill arrived, Mia removed a credit card from her wallet, paid the entire ₱1,300 bill, and kept the cash that Sophia and I owed for our portion of the meal. Mia's use of a credit card at that moment surprised me because although I was aware of the Philippines' nascent credit culture, I knew almost no one who actually had a credit card and used it as a mode of payment in restaurants or stores. In fact, when I first started studying consumer culture in the Philippines in 2006, only the wealthiest people I knew, along with foreigners, carried credit cards at all. When I asked Mia about the cards, she said that she used her credit card a lot and hardly ever carried cash.

The shift from cash-based to credit-based transactions for everyday purchases was a testament to how much the country's credit culture had changed in the first decade of the twentieth century.[15] But it also signaled how credit card companies had begun to market to call center workers specifically and what personal financial risks this new credit culture entailed. Joel touched on this subject as well during one of our many conversations, saying, "So, even banks, they know the hottest commodities right now are call center agents. They know that on the fifteenth or thirtieth of the month these guys would be thrilled if the banks or credit card companies would be seeking them out and waiving those first-year, second-year fees, offering them so much spending power. And [the agents] don't even know that it's a vicious cycle that would probably affect their future lives." Mia's experience with credit card debt is illustrative here. Knowing that Mia did not mind frank questions, I asked her whether she had credit card debt. In a tone that signaled disapproval of the idea, she responded, "No," and then went on to say the following:

> There was one time when I wasn't able to [pay off the whole monthly bill], and that's when I took a vacation to Guam. I think the bill got up to about 60,000. I think I paid it off in two months. I make 45,000 pesos a month now. When I first started as an agent, I made 12,000, then I made 16,000, then 19,000, then 27,500. When I started making 41,000, I thought, "Okay, I think I'll get a credit card now." At first, I was just having fun. I was like swipe, swipe, swipe! You know, you feel so rich. It was just so much fun spending. When I saw the first bill, it was only 5,000 pesos, and I was like, "Hey, that's not that much!" I didn't realize that my billing cycle starts on the fifteenth of the month and ends on the fourteenth. I only started charging on my credit card on the sixth! [*Laughing*] I thought it was [5,000 pesos] for the whole month. So when I saw the *next* bill, I was like, "Oh."

Mia's narration of her transition from financial folly to financial discipline illustrates the two primary avenues for productivity laid out through consumer credit: either one enters into a cycle of continuous debt, which accelerates the accumulation of profits for credit card companies, or one learns to be disciplined with one's finances, in which case access to credit simply aids in the continuous process of consumption on which credit card companies and other corporations more broadly depend for profits.

Mia's description of her initiation into the institution of consumer credit was strikingly similar to Patrick's. Neither Mia nor Patrick had applied for their first credit card until they entered a higher income bracket, and at first neither could seem to resist the kinetic pleasures of plastic. Also, neither Patrick nor Mia completely grasped the terms of repayment or interest accrual for the credit account when they signed up. Patrick told me that he didn't understand that although his first credit card had a 0 percent interest rate, that was temporary and eventually he would be charged interest. In any event, Patrick went on to say, he didn't care about any of that initially since he just "really wanted" the new phone he purchased with his new credit card. Eventually, he acquired four credit cards and maxed out all of the credit limits—about ₱80,000. In contrast to Mia, Patrick thus had a harder time getting out of debt. At the time we met—nearly four years after he first acquired a credit card—he was paying ₱10,000 to credit companies each month, or a little less than a fourth of his monthly salary of ₱44,000. Nor was Patrick's story unique. *Spiff* magazine dedicated a whole issue to the problem of consumer debt among call center workers, and Joel from Vox Elite confirmed that debts were often the reason that many agents requested overtime and extra hours at work.

Work, Play, Spend, and Save:
The Cultural Logic of Productive Youth

Critical ethnographies of globalization have emphasized that in addition to creating consumer goods, global workplaces like maquiladoras or other factories also produce people as particular types of subjects.[16] In attempting to answer one of this book's underlying questions—about what kind of people young Filipinos would become through call center work—I have been drawn over and over again to the hyperproductive nature of the workplace and its cultural contours. As I described in chapter 1, call center employees are immersed in and are internalizing a work culture that revolves around productivity, whether on the phone with customers or in their relationships with coworkers. In this climate the consumer culture of the marketplace, like the corporate culture of the workplace, becomes an important site of productive activity, and thus the call center agent becomes a particular type of youthful productive consumer—that is, one who sees personal pleasure as a right granted by work and who applies to leisure time the same desire for outcomes and efficiency that is pursued in the workplace.

As the retail, entertainment, and tourist markets catering to call center workers continue to grow, the Fordist definition of consumption as a space apart from work is increasingly replaced by the notion of consumption as productive play and personal pleasure that is integral to the experience of work itself.[17] Sitting across from me at a Starbucks in Makati, an insurance claims representative named Jonjie held up his Grande Caramel Frappuccino and described it as a "treat" he gave himself for working hard. "I'm earning money, and I should be enjoying what I'm earning," he declared.[18] Jonjie's words echo the editor's note for an issue of *Spiff* called "Work Hard, Play Hard," which articulates this ethos quite well: "24/7 you burn the lines: closing deals, meeting quotas, fixing IT problems, handling irate clients, or simply giving the utmost customer care. Stressful! . . . You've been working hard, you deserve a break. Play hard, guys!" The editors then detail ways to achieve this renewal of affective energies, through expensive video game systems, local travel, or just cable television and DVDs at home. They underscore the urgency of these pursuits by exclaiming, "What are you waiting for? C'mon! Let's play to the max."[19] The panoply of leisure options available to call center workers suggests that play itself is imbued with a productivist ethic that applies rational planning to enjoyment and invites evaluative assessments of how well one did at relaxing, shopping, or taking in new tourist sites (with photography and social media being indispensable for documenting and analyzing such experiences). Like the places in which call center agents work, the marketplace niches that call their attention demand instant action and maximum output of energy. Consumption thus becomes a site for the reproduction of the call center worker as a highly productive person, and its display an important part of the reproduction of the affective energies and subjective resources used in call center work. This blurring of the boundaries between the realms of work, home, and marketplace was most evident when it came to the practices of fashion, which tap into the glamour and celebrity that call center compensation and culture engender within the workforce. In Figure 4.4 customer service call center workers from the outsourcing firm HTMT enjoy a Hollywood-themed company party. Done up in party dresses and cool suits, these young workers pose before a photographer while standing on replicas of Hollywood Boulevard stars bearing the names of celebrities Ben Affleck and Nicole Kidman. The captions that accompany the photos read like those in a fashion magazine, as editors inform readers of the brand names and cost of each person's apparel and accessories.

In this way, the image reveals that, more than simply the by-products of a growing and lucrative new industry, call center workers' consumption and aesthetics, especially as modes and techniques of bodily practice, emerge out of and feed back into the tensions and contradictions of call center work. In the dialectical relationship between the affective and sub-

Figure 4.4 Call center workers pose for a photo shoot at a Hollywood-themed company party; a May 2008 issue of *Spiff* magazine captures the fashion and glamour.

jective demands of relational labor and the social reproduction of these resources through call center work culture, fashion creates an opportunity for workers to form affective bonds through a mutual appreciation and admiration of aesthetic choices and bodily comportment. Throughout my fieldwork it was not hard to miss the way that clothing and accessories were objects of careful attention and allure for many workers, especially cisgender women and gender-queer individuals like transwomen and *bakla*.[20] On the first payday at Vox Elite, for example, Sammy spent much of the training session looking at brand-name sunglasses on the Internet. Instead of going home when our training session ended at seven in the morning, he was going to wait, he told me, until payroll opened at nine so he could pick up his paycheck and head to the mall to buy the pair of glasses he wanted.[21]

In many ways, the modeling of fashion that occurs on the shop floor of a call center or at a fashionable event like HTMT's party is not unlike that which occurs on runways. As Elizabeth Wissinger has argued, professional models excite interest and inspire attraction "by playing on forces that can consciously be perceived as desire, envy, or a need to belong (through being fashionable or 'in the know')"; in turn, affective flows and even community are activated and renewed.[22] Call center workers are not, of course, professional models—which is part of my point. The clothes that workers select and purchase for themselves help create the social and cultural world within which the youthful call center agent moves and appears, in both the public space of the shopping mall or café and the semiprivate space of the workplace. Glamour, as what Nigel Thrift calls a "technology" that "produces captivation" and an "affective force that is . . . both moved and moving," is an important part of this process.[23] So, too, is "being in the know" about what to wear and where to buy it. In other words, call center workers' cultivation of an image of themselves as fashionable, and thus current and creative, constitutes a performance of productivity as manifested through the aestheticization of the body and self. In this way, fashion and other practices of consumption add to workers' sense of affective attachment to one another, by not only providing workers with shared outlets for their stress and disposable income but also creating arenas in which workers can share in aesthetic pursuits and pleasures. It is not insignificant, in fact, that the vast majority of the fieldwork I did outside of call centers proper—was in shopping malls, restaurants, or coffee shops.

The discourse of productivity attached to call center workers' engagement with fashion in particular and consumption in general expresses a cultural logic consistent with postindustrialism's hyperproductive work cultures and post-Fordist flexible accumulation, in which expanding one's productive capacity is simultaneously understood as both a requirement of neoliberal capital and one of the few means to cope with the incessant demands of the work and the persistent sense of precarity these arrangements of capital and labor entail. Blurring the boundaries between work and worker, call center culture thus compels employees to become their productivity—to internalize it, to perform it, and to measure their lives by it. Attitudes and practices related to finance and money management are an important part of this process as well, both because finance and credit are increasingly important components of cultures of consumption and because they are crucial to the practice of personal responsibility that is the affirmative neoliberal counterpoint to the erosion of social safety nets and job security. In other words, in a setting in which jobs do not come with the same guarantees or expectations of longevity they once did, and consumer credit multiplies the risks in everyday life, personal financial management becomes paramount as a practice and ideology.[24] In turn, individuals able to manage money and its meaning are recognized as good neoliberal subjects, or more specifically, productive youth: young people who are productive for the sake of productivity, are internally motivated, identify with the companies they work for, and see their compensation not as an end goal but as a reward for their individual motivation and action— their "out*thinking*" and "out*doing*."[25]

Talking with me about call center workers and financial culture, Joel Partido articulated this feature of the contemporary Philippines by pointing to generational differences. "You know," Joel started, "we were raised in a generation where concepts of savings, investments, being an entrepreneur, these were not discussed, probably because our parents were just like long-tenured employees of some company who offered lifetime employment. So because of that we don't see the need to see what happens if for some reason employment gets cut off." Although Joel was speaking about middle-age and middle-class or affluent individuals like himself, whose parents had had stable work in major national or multinational industries or the state bureaucracy, his words point to how the fixed production schedules and one-job-for-a-lifetime model that defined Fordism have been replaced by just-in-time production and longer résumés, not only in industrialized countries but in developing countries as well. According to Joel, the current generation of Filipino youth thus had some adjusting to do. Indeed, Joel's overarching point was that the generation coming of age through call center work often "do[es] not know where to start" in terms of personal finance. In response, call center human resources departments sometimes step in to teach this kind of financial discipline through instructional seminars or programs on budgeting, saving, and investing; indeed, almost all the call centers I visited during my fieldwork offered or were planning such sessions. Joel went on to explain the importance of these sessions in the eyes of human resources: "Unless people have the right values, the money in their bank accounts may ultimately destroy their internal balance. Unless people understand that early in life—that they need to be financially responsible—money may just be an instrument that would lead them faster to whatever direction they are going in." That call center management has taken an active role in instilling financial discipline in their employees speaks volumes about the new productive subjectivity and forms of consciousness that emerge through postindustrial workplaces, while also reproducing older discourses about how acquiring too much money too fast can be bad for people unaccustomed to it, leading to vice or ruin. Undoubtedly, human resources departments are attentive to issues of debt because indebted workers are sometimes seen as disruptive to the workplace. Credit card companies call human resources looking for agents, for example, or agents' desperation for overtime or passing scorecards is assumed to contribute to an economy of sexual favors among agents and managers, which in turn intensifies the sexualized stigma of the industry as a whole, which is the subject of the next chapter. However, this intersection of work and personal finance also reveals how human resources departments see workers' satisfaction with the job and their motivation as intimately related to their ability to manage their money: the more employees see themselves as productive individuals in the wider world of money management, the more they work to fulfill that self-image.

The financialization of Filipino call center workers thus constitutes a response to postindustrial precarity and risk, as well as to neoliberalism's conditions of possibility: as more and more people are pressured to manage their own financial burdens, the hypervalorization of individual responsibility is increasingly reinforced, with consumer culture the terrain on which the struggle of these emerging forces takes place. It was not hard to see this financial consciousness and subjectivity emerging among my research participants. It was evident in Mia's literal accounting of her income and credit card bills, and her regular conversations with me about her savings and aspirations for investment; Mia was also one of the Global Invest employees who had purchased stock in the company, and she was keeping an eye on that as well. One of the more memorable moments in which cultures of finance became clear was when I first met Zell, a transgender woman who worked at Premier Source. Our meeting took place just after Zell had come from the bank, where she had gone to purchase a greater quantity of a mutual fund whose price had recently dropped. When I asked how Zell got started with money markets, she explained that for a few years she had been the steward of a financial account for a relative who lived abroad, but that after starting her job in a call center "and learning more about the whole money management thing," she became curious about the content of the financial statements she was receiving on her uncle's behalf. After doing some research on investing, she decided to try it on her own. While financial consciousness of the kind that involves stock options and mutual funds came to flourish among workers like Mia and Zell, other research participants of mine remained engaged in finance not as a way of accessing actually existing financial markets but simply as a way to manage their money for family sustainability and survival. In other words, like the consumer practices that rely on disposable income, financial practices that rely on investment or securities would not be available to all workers. Even as it reinforces the harrowing aspects of postindustrial work culture, productive youth is therefore a privileged subjectivity marked in part by one's financial literacy and acumen.

Finally, there is another, less obvious way in which finance, risk, and speculation have come to shape the environment in which call center workers move. If one looks back at the Convergys ad that opened this chapter, it becomes clear that the urban spaces in which shopping malls, restaurants, condominiums, and office buildings arise are an important part of the story of the contemporary Philippines. Indeed, the expansion of both consumer credit and real estate in the mid-1990s resulted from over $19 billion in foreign investment in Philippine financial institutions, which became eager to lend to a new and growing customer base of local banks and local consumers.[26] This led, in turn, to an explosion of consumer goods, the rapid rise of supermarkets and malls, and increases in the buying power of industrial estates and outlying cities, which led the way to substantial real estate development in the country's National Capital Region.[27] Thus, the very shopping malls where I spent time with call center workers—the staging grounds for their credit-fueled consumption and their scrutiny from others—were in and of themselves sites of financial risk for the nation. As I looked at this larger picture, it was not hard to also see that the moral reproach of call center workers reflects not only individual or shared concerns about tasteful comportment or public propriety—always and already a classed evaluation—but also anxiety about the social risks that call center work as a whole has come to represent for the nation.

QUEERING THE CALL CENTER

Sexual Politics, HIV/AIDS,
and the Crisis of (Re)Production

The late 2000s was an exciting time for BPO companies in the Philippines, as the growth of the offshore industry soared to new heights and the country was on the verge of overtaking India as the world's capital of call centers. In January 2010 this exuberance was tempered when representatives of the Philippine General Hospital (PGH) issued an unsettling report showing that the number of people testing positive for HIV (human immunodeficiency virus) had risen dramatically since March 2009, with call center workers making up a substantial number of the new cases.[1] According to the nation's Department of Health (DOH), "young urban professionals or those of the working sector, particularly call center agents," were now being added to a list of "the kinds of people"—namely, "sex workers, gays and drug addicts"—who had become infected with HIV in the past few years.[2] The DOH report also showed that call center workers were carrying sexually transmitted diseases like gonorrhea and chlamydia in higher numbers than ever before. In its coverage of this news, the national media network ABS-CBN showed neither nuance nor tact, as its headline on January 27 read "HIV Cases Soar among Filipino Yuppies, Call Center Workers; Casual Sex, Orgies Are Seen as Possible Cause of the Problem."[3]

The proposition that young urban professionals accounted for a high percentage of the new cases of HIV in the Philippines cast a shadow on the sunrise industry, building on and strengthening the already existing association between call centers and forms of sexual and gender deviance in the public imagination. Indeed, since its emergence the call center industry in the Philippines has been socially and culturally constructed as a queer site that enables the exploration and expression of nonnormative sexual and gender practices, including recreational, homosexual, and/or premarital relations, cross-dressing and other forms of gender-queer presentation, and sex work. In this context, where call center work was already linked with "at-risk" bodies, the news of rising HIV cases incited a number of alarmist responses by workers, government officials, and industry leaders. Some immediately endorsed greater surveillance within the workplace, demonstrating what Michael Tan has described as the *utak police*, or policing mentality, that has been part of HIV/AIDS prevention campaigns in the Philippines since the late 1980s.[4] A doctor from the PGH's Infectious Disease Treatment Complex, for example, suggested that the Philippine Department of Labor force BPO firms to implement mechanisms to monitor workers' relationships—including the removal of unisex sleeping facilities and the installation of video cameras throughout offices—arguing that a lack of "ethical standards" within call centers could lead to "emotional stress, sexually transmitted diseases and *even* broken marriages."[5] However, the most prevalent response to the news involved a counterdiscourse that distanced the prized industry from the stigma of HIV by asserting that working in a call center has absolutely no relation to acquiring or being at risk for contracting the virus. In the contestation over the social and cultural value of call center work, the rise in HIV cases among call center agents was thus seen as a risk not only to people but to perceptions of the entire industry, as well as the industry's ability to produce value and reproduce the nation-state.

This chapter examines the symbolic threat to the professional and productive image of Philippine call center workers represented by not only the rise in HIV cases but also the queering of call center work. Rather than trying to confirm or deny the medical evidence for HIV/AIDS among call center workers, I trace how this evidence and responses to it shaped the meaning of call center work, and how the bodies, sexual practices, and gender identities of call center workers—especially transwomen, *bakla*, and gay men—were marked as risks to the accumulation of capital, as well as to the reproductive order upheld by the Catholic Church and the heteronormative Filipino family.[6] The chapter thus demonstrates how the moral panic about HIV heightened the already pervasive fear that call center work entails modes of transgression—educational, consumer, sexual—that would lead to a literal and figurative dead end for workers and the nation-state. I argue, then, that the alarm about HIV signaled not only a medical concern but also deep anxiety about call centers as sites where deviant bodies put the nation at economic, cultural, and social risk. The interplay between disease, sexuality, religion, and the economy that I analyze in this chapter thus confirms that modernity is always and already imbricated with gendered and sexualized bodies and desires, which in turn become cultural sites of struggle for the nation, labor, and value.

Queering the Call Center

Perhaps more than any other disease in recent history, the meaning of HIV/ AIDS has far exceeded the boundaries of scientific or medical discourse. Since the widespread perception of AIDS as a gay men's disease emerged in the 1980s, the epidemic has, as Paula Treichler has argued, "produced a parallel epidemic of meanings, definitions, and attributions," which she refers to as an "epidemic of signification."[7] In other words, the study, diagnosis, treatment, and spread of HIV and AIDS around the world have consistently led to an outbreak of meanings (about, for example, homosexuality, drug use, or Africa) and the redrawing of social boundaries around *othered* groups who are labeled as being at high risk for contracting the virus and thus are subsequently subject to intense social stigma and control. In the Philippines such processes began around 1985, when the first case of HIV in the country was reported. While the virus has been most heavily identified with women sex workers, the signifying power of HIV in the Philippines is not limited to a single population or line of work. In the 1980s the dominant discourse around HIV focused on it as an illness that foreigners had brought to the Philippines, while in the 1990s, with the exponential rise in Filipino labor migration, the focus shifted to overseas Filipino workers carrying the virus back into the country. Underlying both of these discourses is an assumed link between exposure to HIV and exposure to the racial and national mixing enabled by globalization's demand for cross-border labor mobility. As Michael Tan points out, the development of export-processing zones and a tourist industry in the central Philippine city of Cebu in the early 1990s instigated intense fears about the spread of AIDS as a result of increasing numbers of sex workers and non-Filipino tourists in the city.[8] Worries about contact between differently racialized individuals in the midst of intense urban change constitute what Robin Root has called an "ethnoetiology" of HIV/AIDS—a cultural reason for the association of HIV risk with particular persons or places.[9]

In the days following the release of the PGH and DOH reports in 2010, the Philippine media and medical establishment put forth the notion that call center workers' generally risky and deviant lifestyles were to blame for their high risk. In subsequent reports and articles, call center workers' risk for contracting HIV/AIDS was linked to having multiple sexual partners, having sex in the absence of romantic commitment, or even engaging in nonsexual vices such as drinking and smoking. One study, conducted by the University of the Philippines, showed that "a significant number of call center workers had contracted [sexually transmitted diseases] through non-romantic but regular sexual engagements known in the industry as FUBU, short for 'F**ked [Fucked] Buddies.'"[10] Paraphrasing Secretary of Health Esperanza Cabral, a *Philippine Daily Inquirer* reporter wrote that "many employees in call centres were young people with unhealthy life-styles that included such risk behaviour [as having multiple sexual part-ners and engaging in unprotected sex] as well as smoking, alcohol drinking and inadequate sleep."[11] Ideas about call center workers' risky behaviors generated by the medical establishment were further inflamed by the pop-ular news media. The national news network ABS-CBN reported that "some of those infected said they got the illness after engaging in casual or group sex, which they discovered through social networking sites on the Inter-net." Quoting simply "a doctor," the same report stated, "There are a lot of sites right now that can organize orgies quickly. A lot of young people believe in casual sex."[12]

The image of the call center industry as a site of sexual deviance was not new in 2010. Previously circulating discourses about the sexual culture of call center workers and their lifestyles in many ways primed the Philippine public for a panic about HIV. The earliest articulations of these discourses made implicit and explicit links between call center work and sex work, both of which necessitate the circulation of young laboring bodies in ur-ban environments late at night. Making a pun on the word *call,* Filipino agents in the early days of the industry would sometimes humorously re-fer to themselves using a local term for sex workers—*call boys* or *call girls.* In this way, call center workers' presence in public space at a time of day when people are normally in private settings, and social activity and labor are thought to cease altogether, instigates anxieties about the convergence of bodies, sexuality, and commerce.[13]

Another articulation of this sexualized discourse linked call center work with the production of Internet pornography. Here, it was the *invisibility* of call center work that exacerbated public anxiety. Call center offices are often highly conspicuous as modern-looking environments in otherwise unkempt urban settings, but their high security and lack of signage tend to cloak these spaces in secrecy, making it possible to imagine that the bodies making up the large, young workforce are providing services of an erotic variety for a primarily non-Filipino audience. Alleged pornographic "cybersex dens," for example, became the target of the Philippines' National Bureau of Investigation, as did individual call center workers like Edwardson Base, who allegedly circulated pornographic images on the web. In July 2010 the Manila Police District arrested Base after he allegedly uploaded to Facebook a video of his ex-girlfriend and him having sex. Although Base was not arrested at work, and the article did not imply that he had made the video at work, the author of the story mentioned his employment as a call center agent—a curious choice that points to the proximity of the call center worker as a social identity to the threat of sexual imagery circulating in public and private space.

Like many forms of discourse, the sexualized imagery attached to the Philippine call center emerges from a complex interaction between powerful imaginaries and actually existing practices. Without extensive investigation of the hundreds of call centers in the Philippines, it is impossible to gauge the extent to which concerns about Filipinos' involvement in the transnational sale of cybersex are based on real Internet pornography businesses, although in 2007 the National Bureau of Investigation did manage to infiltrate one such company, called American Chat Link, that was making and selling pornographic images.[14] However, it is clear that the discourse draws attention to Philippine call centers and to call center workers' assumed vulnerability to what Radha Hegde calls "global exposure"— fears that build on earlier concerns about the exposure of Filipino bodies that cross real and virtual borders for a living.[15] Alongside other stories (such as an article in August 2010 about a local city councilor receiving reports that Internet cafés and call centers in his town had been transformed into "sex cybernets"), these representations of the IT-enabled transnational service world sexualize not only the laboring bodies of call center workers and their workplaces but the entire technological, material, and corporeal assemblage in which the call center is embedded—what Hegde calls "a complex infrastructure connecting the flow of laboring bodies, electricity, roads, and transportation."[16] This discourse raised the question of what, exactly, call center workers are producing: economic value or sexual excess?

After the PGH and DOH reports were made public in 2010, other information and studies detailing the HIV risk factors of certain subsectors of the call center workforce circulated in the media. Some focused exclusively on male call center workers who have sex with other men, gay male call center workers, and workers who engage in casual and/or group sex. Yet it was not the primal fear of deviant sexuality alone that made the PGH and DOH reports newsworthy but the discovery of such deviance and risk within the BPO industry as a "professional" sector. Both the Philippine media and the medical establishment represented the newest upsurge in HIV cases as significant because it challenged the intertwined ideologies of class and sex that suggested that only poor Filipinos were susceptible to the virus. The imagined inverse correlation between class status and deviance was implied in the DOH report quoted at the beginning of this chapter, which implicitly excluded "sex workers, gays and drug addicts" from the category of "young urban professionals or those of the working sector," even as it pointed to how the categories are being brought together under the umbrella of "at-risk." Similarly, a number of reports highlight that many of the people recently diagnosed with HIV/AIDS in the country were "well educated," as if this might surprise readers.[17] While this description counters the belief that only less-educated or uneducated people are susceptible to HIV/AIDS, it also resonates with a description of call center workers as well-educated workers whose potential is limited by dead-end call center work. Such reports therefore suggest that *not only* does call center work devalue a middle- or upper-class education, but it will *also* put the workers at risk for HIV/AIDS.[18]

However, other reports in the Philippine media raised the question of whether call center workers might already be commercial sex workers. One study suggested that up to "twenty percent of male call center workers are commercial sex workers while 14 percent of them give payment in exchange for sex."[19] My research informants spoke to this possible continuum between call center work and sex work as well.[20] My interview with Antoinette, a young single mother and Call Control employee of eight years, began with her recounting a very recent conversation with two of her gay male coworkers about prostitution as an alternative to call center work. Antoinette represented the exchange as facetious although not entirely outlandish: "They said to me, 'Day [*Inday*, or "girl"], I really don't know what I'm going to do if there's no BPO industry here in Bacolod.' Then one of my friends asked me what my job would be if I didn't work in a call center, and I said, 'Well, maybe I'll be a *pok pok* [slang for *prostitute*].' I was kidding! But I did ask myself where would I end up, and I thought maybe I would be jobless or working in a mall or Jollibee or here at McDonald's." When I asked Antoinette how her friends responded to their own question, she commented, "Well, they said that because they are gay, they may end up jobless or booking something for, you know, a gay thingy [commercial exchange]? That's very rampant nowadays here in Bacolod."

The sexualization of call center work is therefore also linked to broader changes in sexual culture among Filipino youth—changes that are apparent among call center workers given that the workforce is primarily composed of young people. As other scholars have noted, both premarital sex and cohabitation are increasing in this demographic, especially among those living in urban settings, with cohabitation replacing the more traditional practice of *tanan*, or elopement, and premarital sex contravening the sexual regulations of the Catholic Church.[21] In this context, the call center, as a gathering place for large numbers of young people in an environment that directly encourages socializing and indirectly enables intimacy, becomes a place to meet potential sexual partners. My informant Stephanie, whom I interviewed along with Enrique, her live-in boyfriend of about six years, explained that it's easier to get romantically involved while working in a call center because most of the employees are "of the same age group, and it's easy to develop a serious relationship with someone because of the proximity. You'll always be together at night, and of course you go out after work, so people basically get closer, and their relationship gets deeper." A comic strip about call center work captures these intimate details of call center life (Figure 5.1).[22] In it, the character Clover—a young, gay call center agent—excitedly alerts his female coworker Cathy to the possibility that their respective chances of finding a new boyfriend will vastly improve because the company they work for is about to hire a new batch of employees. Created by a Filipina call center agent, the cartoon illustrates call center

Figure 5.1 *Callwork* comic strip creator Hazel Manzano illustrates how call centers create opportunities for social, sexual, or romantic encounters between coworkers. (Copyright Hazel Manzano)

employees' perception of their workplace as one where they can seek and find sexual partners with relative ease.

Because of the frequency of intimate relationships between call center employees, many of my research participants spoke of their working environment as a threat to previously monogamous or long-term relationships. Enrique confirmed this: "Actually, there's a reputation about being a BPO [worker] because couples go into side relationships. . . . It's because you're always together, you spend more time with these people that you are working with and you're not spending time with your husband or your wife. Sometimes a lot of relationships get ruined. So that's one reputation that call centers have." In turn, this leads to a social reputation in which call centers are seen as workplaces where people engage in multiple casual relationships. A Call Control employee named Ellie corroborated this by similarly describing how call center work brings together people of the same age who are undergoing the same experience for long stretches of time during the night "when hormones might be higher." Ellie went on to suggest that young women seeking marriage were unlikely to find such a partner in the call center industry, "since it's like the people who work there are looking for casual relationships."

Call Centers and the Culture of Death

When my research participants talked about the challenges that call center work poses to the reproduction of long-term relationships, they used the very same language to describe their relationships as they did for the job itself. Call center work is often understood as a temporary or dead-end job, just as many of the potential relationships forged within the industry are assumed to be; the job is thought of as easy to get, which parallels the supposed availability of sex among call center workers; and the job is considered unstable, just as it presumably destabilizes relationships. Even the figure of the call center hopper—someone who readily quits call center jobs in search of better or different opportunities—signifies a type of promiscuity. Together, these ideas reinforce skepticism about the ability of the industry to socially reproduce the nation: just as call center jobs are thought to be contingent and temporary, so too are the relationships forged within them.

In addition to being associated with sex work, pornography, and casual sex, the call center industry in the Philippines is also increasingly linked to diverse sexual orientations and gender identities, owing in part to the industry's unique policy of not discriminating against gay, lesbian, and cross-dressing workers in recruitment and promotion, which gives the impression that call centers are open environments where gender and sexual diversity is accepted and valorized.[23] In one of many conversations with my fellow Vox Elite trainee Sammy—whose goals were to have male-to-female sexual reassignment surgery with the money he saved from call center work and then move on to a career in professional modeling—he explained why he had left the medical field and started working in a call center, despite being trained as a nurse and having parents who were both doctors.[24] As we were standing together on the second floor of the parking garage where we took our breaks during training, Sammy explained that working in a hospital meant restricting his gender expression; the example Sammy gave was having to keep his hair cut short. "They wanted me to be professional, but it wasn't open," Sammy explained. "But I like it here [at Vox Elite]. It's so *me*. I can be open." Evoking the paradox of professionalism and perversity established by the sexualized and queer discourses surrounding Philippine call centers, Sammy went on to say, "Sometimes being a professional and being open don't match, but here, yes, they do."

I point out the call center industry's nondiscrimination policy and its perceived openness not to celebrate the spread of liberal Western forms of sexual and gender-based rights to the supposedly "backward" global south. Southeast Asian countries have long produced sex/gender systems that are in fact more fluid and complex in their understanding of gender and sexuality than tends to be acknowledged within dominant culture in the West, even as queer groups and/or women in those countries experience oppression and violence that should be condemned. Moreover, despite the recognition of call centers as workplaces welcoming to all people, gay call center agents certainly face violence and hostility from coworkers. An incident that occurred between Sammy and Lester before the start of training at Vox Elite one night made this crystal clear. At the time I was sitting at my desk surfing the web, while others around me were either doing the same or talking with each other. Then Sammy entered the room, visibly upset. He explained aloud that he had taken a cab to work but that the driver had passed the Vox Elite building several times, even though Sammy had instructed him to stop. Lester, who had been sitting behind me the entire time, then asked Sammy, "Why didn't you offer to suck his dick so he would stop the car?," to which Sammy quickly responded, "What do you know about sucking dick?" There was some laughter in the room—mostly from some of the straight men—but for the most part tension took over. Angered by Sammy's retort, Patrick stormed out of the room, muttering, "I'm going to kill all the gays."

Instead of dwelling on the question of how triumphant Western sex/gender systems and politics are in the Philippines, I instead wish to highlight how the call center industry has become a flash point in the changing sexual politics in the Philippines more broadly, in part through these employment policies. The panic over HIV and call center workers, for example, took place in the final years leading up to the passage of the nation's first reproductive rights bill, one of the most formidable challenges to the Catholic Church in Philippine history.[25] In addition to instituting measures to help prevent and manage HIV/AIDS and other sexually transmitted diseases, the Reproductive Health Act made sex education mandatory throughout the country, required government health clinics to provide condoms and other contraceptive devices to the public, and supported a national media campaign about family planning and reproductive health.[26]

It is in the context of the Philippines' shifting sexual culture and politics, which are moving toward more secular approaches to sex and partnership, that we should understand the significance of the call center industry as an ostensibly open environment whose high wages, normalization of sexual and gender diversity, and cosmopolitanism pose a threat to the country's hegemonic socioreligious order. Reflecting the historical relationship between capitalism, family, and sexual identity, a number of my research participants described call center work as allowing them to eschew the normative life that their parents prescribed for them, and the workplace in particular as allowing them to be forthcoming about their sexual identities.[27] Such talk imbues the call center with the power to significantly improve an individual's life, tying together corporate mobility and personal liberation. In a *Spiff* magazine article titled "Becoming: A Transgender's Story," Brenda Alegre weaves together a narrative about discovering her gender identity, taking hormone replacement therapy, and moving up the corporate ladder within the Philippine call center industry. Aside from her description of her first call center job as "not easy," Brenda is positive about the industry, writing that "the environment was cool and young, people were really friendly, and very dynamic. I didn't feel discriminated against, I felt at home."[28] At thirty years of age, Brenda was a human resources manager, had earned a master's degree in psychology, and had plans to pursue a PhD.

A conversation I had with Joel Partido, Vox Elite's vice president of human resources, clearly articulates how the sexual and queer contours of the industry pose a problem for the guardians of conventional morality in the Philippines. During the interview I asked Joel to describe his sense of how the parents of young people who choose to work in a call center feel about call center work and the industry. My question was motivated by my knowledge of how many young people in the Philippines are influenced by their parents' opinions about their work, even early into their careers or at least for their first job after college. Joel responded by explaining that a Philippine call center's success depends on its acceptance in the community:

So, in communities where [Vox Elite is the] first player or so, the first call center in that community or province, let's say, it's harder to break ground, because you have to develop the whole community, and because of that there's a cost involved . . . But of course [there are] a few who would know just enough information to make themselves really [fearful of the industry]. Because sometimes they view—and to some extent there's some truth in it—that we are an industry where people who have loose morals [are running] around and [doing] drugs and alcohol [*laughing*]. So, when your hiring requirements allow a very diverse set of new employees, well, I would say you have a variety of . . . sexual orientations [*laughing*] or preferences, which run from the right to the left . . . [Y]ou put together a very young workforce, hormones kicking at night, you just have the right formula for building a nuclear bomb [*laughing*].

Although I generally found him to be a queer-positive person, Joel's metaphor of a call center as a ticking sexual time bomb echoed the alarmist tone of the ABS-CBN article that cites orgies and casual sex as the cause of HIV transmission among call center workers. Yet Joel's description of call centers as workplaces where individuals seek out and engage in a variety of sexual practices offered a much more complex picture of the call center, its role in the production of sexual identities and practices in the contemporary Philippines, and the social and cultural upheaval this represents. For example, Joel's move from the term *parents* to *community* suggests that the stakes of the call center industry are rooted in questions of social reproduction, both of the family and the nation. Parents don't want their children going into this work, Joel suggests, because the kinds of activities they would be involved in there would violate the sexual and gender order upheld by the Catholic Church, which, in communion with the Filipino family, condemns all forms of sexual identity and sexual practice except heterosexuality and procreation within the context of marriage. Premarital sex, however, is merely one aspect of what the Catholic Church in the Philippines sees as a "culture of death" threatening the sanctity of the Filipino family, where *death* is an acronym denoting divorce, euthanasia, abortion, transsexuality, and homosexuality, or simply anything that "leads to an endemic disregard for the procreative value of the sexual act."[29]

As Brenda's story of her gender transition suggests, it is difficult to separate call centers' openness to workers with nonnormative sexual orientations and gender identities from the broader idea of the call center as a gateway to a life not bound to the conventional organization of social reproduction more broadly. Deirdre, a twenty-year-old agent from the southern Philippines whom I met and observed during her first week taking calls at Pyramid Processing, illustrates this point. On my third or fourth day as an observer on the production floor, I noticed that Deirdre had started answering the phones using the name Myra. When I asked her why, she told me that Myra was the name of her daughter, who had died ten days after she was born. Deirdre had become pregnant with Myra by a man she knew in her hometown. Deirdre's situation was particularly problematic because of her father's position as a high-ranking figure in the Iglesia ni Christo (Church of Christ). After Deirdre gave birth and the baby died, her father was eager to restore the gender and sexual order disrupted by his daughter and insisted that she marry the man she currently called her boyfriend, whom she did not really love. "I came to Manila to get away from my family and boyfriend. I came here for my freedom!" Deirdre exclaimed. By this time, two close friends of Deirdre's had joined the conversation, although it was clear that they had heard the story before. One of them asked, "D, you have to be happy. Will you be happy with him?" "No," Deirdre replied, "I will be happy with you. Let's all get married!" Deirdre's off-the-cuff call for a plural marriage of coworker-friends demonstrates the emotional fulfillment and support she finds among a "family" of coworkers, in contrast to the biological kinship network or the family her father was pushing her to establish.

Given the ideological impact of the Catholic Church in the Philippines, Joel's phrase "loose morals" thus refers to workers' engagement in nonprocreative and/or premarital sexual activities that destabilize the rigid sexual control exercised by religious and familial authority figures. The advice column for the call center industry's now-defunct lifestyle magazine *Spiff* speaks indirectly to these shifts, as it featured regular stories about unmarried heterosexual couples, extramarital affairs, and same-sex relationships among call center workers. In one, a young man who is engaged to a woman finds that he is attracted to another man and then has sex with him; in another, a young woman has sex with a married male coworker and becomes pregnant by the man, who then refuses to acknowledge her and the child. Yet another worker asks for advice about what to do when her romantic relationship with a male coworker is threatened by a female coworker's dangerous infatuation with her. While it is impossible to determine the veracity of these undeniably sensationalized stories, *as stories* they narrate and thus provide evidence of the various social locations of workers who engage in queer intimacies, nonmonogamous relationships, or nonprocreative sex outside the confines of marriage.[30]

A particularly memorable interview with Lucy, a former call center worker who was pregnant with her first child during our meeting, also spoke to this sexual culture. Lucy started the interview by asking me whether I would be posing any personal questions because, as she went on to explain, "there are a lot of those kinds of questions when it comes to call centers. You know, call center workers are perceived as being very sexually . . . active." Lucy elaborated on her statement by describing how, within the first few days of training for the call center job she had in Manila, her eyes were opened to same-sex and recreational opposite-sex relationships, neither of which she had been exposed to in Bacolod. Like a lot of companies, the one that Lucy worked for took the new hires on an overnight retreat to a local resort. As the first day of the trip drew to a close and the organized bonding activities ended, Lucy noticed people pairing off for sex and other forms of physical intimacy. Lucy also described her experience of call center work as making her aware of gender nonconformity: "In Manila," she explained, "it's a lot more open. . . . There would be girls who look like boys, and boys that look like girls, but with same-sex partners. And you can't tell that . . . that they are the same [sex]."

It is particularly telling that Deirdre's story, as both she and her friends understand and articulate it, juxtaposes concepts such as *love, freedom, happiness,* and *mobility* to familial obligation and marriage. The conflict that many workers experience between their bids for freedom in general, and same-sex relations in particular, and the sanctions their parents place on that freedom is evidence of the contradictory status of the family within capitalism. As an economic system that compels individuals to sell their labor, capitalism can free people from the confines of the family as a unit of production, making it possible for individuals to construct lives, and thus identities, outside of heterosexual norms.[31] Call centers are precisely the kinds of workplaces that allow some young people to achieve a measure of financial and thus affective autonomy from their families. However, as the tension in each of the stories above suggests, organizing one's life around love and affection for other people, or around one's own individual happiness, rather than familial duty, is not easy. Despite the ways in which capitalist relations weaken the material foundation of family life, the family has been and continues to be elevated to a position of ideological privilege.

Visible and Invisible Bodies

Fears that call centers were breeding grounds for HIV built on and rein-forced the already existing anxiety that call centers were dens of vice, sex-ual transgression, and disease that destabilized the heteronormative order of Philippine society even as they allegedly stabilized the economic well-being of individual households and the national economy more broadly. The paradox of the call center industry's economic value and professional-ism and its perceived underlying perversion revolved in particular around male call center workers who have sex with other men.[32] While attention to the latter may have been justified epidemiologically, it is striking that such attention arose at a time when support for nonheteronormative sex-ual practices and identities was gaining ground in the Philippines' sexual culture and politics.[33] Just as a diverse range of people found unparalleled social and economic opportunities within an industry considered vital to the national economy, the industry became stigmatized by its association with a growing epidemic. As a result, the emergence of HIV-related con-cerns around male call center workers who have sex with men amplified the already heightened visibility of gay men in general in the call center en-vironment. In a manner that echoes how gay men in the United States have been characterized as especially good at tasks that utilize aesthetic acumen (such as interior decorating or fashion and apparel design), young gay men, transwomen, and bakla in the Philippines are perceived as uniquely gifted at call center work. This perception revolves around the notion that such individuals are particularly good at relating to other people: "They are good at building relationships with the customer," says Charlene, a former operations manager of eight years. "Gays are quite chatty. It's easy for them to make the customer warm up, even if initially the customer was really irate." Mel, an agent who identifies as gay, saw his sexuality as giving him a particular benefit over others: "Well, I think for my personal experience, being 'gay' in this industry, you are more at an advantage because when you are gay you can more easily adapt to the environment, because you are flexible, you have an open mind in how you deal with things, and maybe intellect-wise, maybe gays, maybe not all but most of them are intellectu-ally much better compared to straight girls or guys." Antoinette, whose remarks about sex work were quoted above, described how she and her coworkers called gays "performers," because "they know how to manage their metrics." This echoed comments made by Gary, a Call Control team leader for a sales-based account, about the gay agents he had worked with over the years: "Most of the time, with gays in the team, it's fun. Because they keep the team motivated. Since they are very loud and perky, as a team leader, you can use it to your advantage. Gays like to compete. They really want to be on top, they want to prove themselves." Such comments point to a process of sexual segregation and division of labor within the Philippine call center industry in which transwomen in particular constitute a "purple-collar" segment of the workforce that is "often expected to produce queer value through their performance of a specifically Filipino queerness, a lightheartedness that yields comfort among workplace teams."[34] Charlene also made it a point to say, "It's actually more fun to work with gay people. . . . They can be particularly loud. That's one of the stress relievers we have on the job." Araceli Manchavez, another call center manager, echoed Charlene's comments. "We love cross-dressers," she explained. "They are fun because of the colorful language they use."

In citing these moments from my fieldwork, I am less interested in determining the empirical value of these statements—that is, whether or not gay male call center agents actually achieve better scorecards than their coworkers—than I am in understanding the conditions that make it possible for gay male identity to be more visible and receive increased attention vis-à-vis call center work and, ultimately, how this relates to the perception of their risk for HIV. Known or seen for their performances on the job, but also for the cultivation of conviviality, a hyperengagement in social relations (a.k.a. "dramatics"), and a tendency to be job-hoppers, gay, trans, or bakla workers are all the more present and visible in the workplace. One way of understanding the hypervisibility of gay men in the call center world is by considering how, as I previously described, Philippine call centers constitute social factories with liberal hiring policies and therefore encourage (although not always) the expression of individual personalities and identities. "The environment really encourages people to come out with what's real," Charlene added, following up on her comments about gay men's supposed talent for customer service. Sharon, a lesbian who had particularly laudatory things to say about Call Control's diversity policies, described call centers as "the only corporate world in which I worked wherein you can be who you are."[35] There is, however, an important irony to this claim that call centers encourage expressions of greater authenticity.

Authenticity is a particularly slippery concept within the call center context. As a type of service work that demands emotional labor, call centers require what Arlie Hochschild, using the language of theater, identifies as "deep acting," which is geared toward the production of ostensibly authentic feelings.[36] While Hochschild's work points to the particularly troublesome repercussions of deep acting for the participants at the center of her study, I found something of the opposite among the people I observed and interviewed: the invisibility of call center agents and their relatively short interactions with customers often translate into a greater freedom to "be whoever you want"; they therefore experience some aspects of the acting requirement as enjoyable. When I asked Mel whether he felt his identity would be as accepted in other kinds of workplaces, he responded, "I think the BPO [industry] is more likely the safest field that you can work in, especially if you have gender issues." I asked him to elaborate on the word *safe,* to which he replied, "I would explain it as there is not much discrimination, compared to other fields. Let's say you are a nurse, and you have a patient which is a guy, and what if he [finds] out that you are a gay then maybe he will be conscious of you assisting him . . . or dressing him. But in the BPO industry, when you are talking to a person over the phone, maybe you sound like a girl but you are a guy, but it doesn't really matter, as long as you can resolve their issue and you are nice to them. I mean, they don't really care." Indeed, it is striking that Mel's example of a workplace where his sexuality might not be accepted is one that requires intense physical contact between people. Visibility and invisibility are thus contradictory conditions informing the experience of gay call center agents, who are perceived as both pillars of service and potential carriers of disease. For gay, bakla, trans, and cross-dressing Filipino men, who have been socialized in some ways to cultivate what Fenella Cannell has described as the imitative skills of bakla, anonymity presents a vital opportunity, not to be real, but to act.[37] Charlene explained this as gay agents having a "flamboyance that they wouldn't be able to [use] with normal Filipinos, like if you're just talking with your friend . . . you have a different persona when you're on the phone," while another person simply described it as a proclivity to imitate. Thus, while the corporate culture and hiring policies seem to offer the opportunity to present an authentic self among one's coworkers, the anonymity of the voice-based interaction provides the opportunity to be not inauthentic, but perhaps an authentic version of another self.

Queer Confessions

Returning now to the question of HIV risk, we can see how issues of visibility and invisibility played out in agents' responses to the panic. If the AIDS epidemic constitutes a crisis of signification, it also instigates an epistemological crisis.[38] Coupled with the information about rising numbers of HIV cases, the national news coverage reproduced intense uncertainty, on the part of call center workers, public officials, the media, and members of the public, about how to understand the ostensible links, if any, among call centers, sex, and HIV/AIDS. In such a climate, what had already been characterized as call center workers' morally questionable lifestyles became much more strongly associated with disease and death, both biological and religious. Furthermore, the Philippine media coverage of the DOH and PGH reports demonstrates how the construction of call center workers as a possible new high-risk category hinges on hegemonic associations of the transmission of disease with sexual transgression and social vice in general rather than the particular modes of sexual contact that are likely to transmit the virus between people. Nowhere in the picture of workers rushing to have "orgies" does the ABS-CBN article refer to protected or unprotected sex—at least not until the very end of the article, and even there the phrase *unsafe sex* is not clearly defined. In this way, the Philippine media and medical establishment did nothing to significantly alter the way the public understood the physical transmission of HIV.[39]

As mentioned in this chapter's introduction, the most immediate response by call center workers and industry leaders to the news of rising HIV rates was to swing the pendulum in the other direction by denying any link between call centers and HIV. An op-ed column by longtime HIV/AIDS activist Bong Austero of the *Manila Standard Today* illustrates the difficulty and irony inherent in such attempts.[40] In the column Austero describes how, following the release of the DOH statistics, his colleagues in the call center industry called him to inquire about the "veracity" of the information. "As in the past," Austero writes, "my friends were in full defense mode citing all kinds of possible explanations for the glitch in the statistics." Austero writes:

> My friends wanted to know if there was a possibility that more call center agents tested positive for HIV because the call center industry

happened to be the industry with the most number of employees whose demographic profile fit the global profile of those most vulnerable for HIV infection: Young (between the ages of 15–39), sexually active, productive (i.e. with money to spend). . . . My friends also theorized that the call center industry's liberal recruitment and hiring policies . . . probably account for the high incidence of HIV infections among call center agents. Call centers are supposedly more open to hiring candidates who are more outgoing, more sexually active, more open-minded and prone to experimentation. In short, my friends were saying that the [HIV] phenomenon is not really borne out of factors that are inherent to the call center industry—it's just that the industry hosts people who are probably more vulnerable to HIV infection.

Ironically, in arguing that there is nothing inherent to call center work that exposes workers to HIV risk, Austero's interlocutors describe many of the social factors that allow for the correlation between call centers and the rising number of HIV cases among young Filipino people. For his part, Austero argues that in refusing to link HIV with the workplace in any respect, his critical colleagues also implicitly reject programs that "address the distinct needs of people living with HIV/AIDS at work." Austero elaborates, "It is unfortunate that . . . the call center industry seems to have been singled out as a breeding ground for HIV/AIDS. . . . At any rate, the challenge now is putting in place effective HIV/AIDS prevention and education programs. This includes HIV/AIDS in the workplace programs because whether we like it or not, we'll have to start learning to manage a workplace that has become a little more challenging than ever before."

Austero's op-ed piece points to the difficulty in addressing a highly stigmatized epidemic as it intersects with an industry seen as both economically promising and morally threatening. Such a struggle was perhaps most apparent through the figure of "Joseph Ryan." In February 2010 a video of a young Filipino call center worker confessing his HIV-positive status was uploaded to YouTube by the workers' activist group AKMA-PTM (Aksyon Magsasaka Partido Tinig ng Masa, or Farmers' Movement—Voice of the Masses). The twenty-year-old, referring to himself by the pseudonym "Joseph Ryan," appears in complete disguise: a dark baseball cap shields his eyes, while a cloth and a hospital mask cover the rest of his face and his ears. Ryan speaks, however, with a clear, ostensibly unaltered voice. Expressing himself in Taglish, he says the following:

Ako po si Joseph Ryan. I am a call center agent, and I am . . . I am HIV positive. I have decided to come out in public to clarify the rumor that working at a call center leads to acquiring HIV. *Nakuha ko po ang aking sakit sa isang tao na nakilala ko sa isang* street party *sa* Quezon City. *Hindi po siya taga-*call center. [Audible sobbing.] *Siya po'y nagtatrabaho sa isang* hospital *sa may Bulacan.* I acquired HIV because I did not practice safe sex. I thought since I was young and healthy, *hindi ako tatalaban ng kahit na anong sakit. And dahil din siguro ito sa aking* carelessness. I wish to apologize to my parents, my friends *at sa mga* teammates *ko sa* call center. *Patawarin nyo po sana ako. Ako ay nananawagan sa mga tao o sa publiko, huwag nyo po sana kaming husgahan sa pagiging* call center agents just because you see us smoking and hanging around Ortigas. *Alam ba ninyong* we are a huge contributor *sa* Philippine economy. And there are already 500,000 agents today. I am now undergoing treatment. Once I regain my strength, I will try to live a normal life again so that I can support my family. And to my fellow call center agents, please, please, be protected and please practice safe sex. *Maraming salamat po.*[41]

I am Joseph Ryan. I am a call center agent, and I am . . . I am HIV positive. I have decided to come out in public to clarify the rumor that working at a call center leads to acquiring HIV. I contracted the disease from someone I met at a street party in Quezon City. This person is not from a call center. [*Audible sobbing.*] This person works in a hospital in Bulacan. I acquired HIV because I did not practice safe sex. I thought since I was young and healthy, I would be immune to any kind of disease. I suppose this is also due to my carelessness. I wish to apologize to my parents, my friends, and my teammates at the call center. Please forgive me. I would like to appeal to the public: please do not judge us for being call center agents, just because you see us smoking and hanging around Ortigas. Please know that we are huge contributors to the Philippine economy. And there are already 500,000 agents today. I am now undergoing treatment. Once I regain my strength, I will try to live a normal life again so that I can support my family. And to my fellow call center agents, please, please, be protected and please practice safe sex. Thank you very much.[42]

As is the case for call center workers in the Philippines more generally, Ryan's appearance takes on a conspicuous invisibility, alerting viewers to how young Filipino bodies are at the center of public concerns about the culture of the call center industry in the Philippines. Ryan's reference to call center workers "smoking and hanging around Ortigas"—a commercial and entertainment hub where young people congregate at night and on weekends—speaks implicitly to this discourse. Indeed, we might read Ryan's plea for the public to suspend their judgment of call center agents hanging around Ortigas as pointing not only to the visibility of sexualized, queer, or otherwise nonnormative bodies within urban space, and thus their vulnerability to censure, but to an expansive discourse of call centers as sites of social and sexual transgression. Ryan's formidable attempts to obscure his own body underscore the context and significance of his plea.

However, despite his shame, Ryan's "coming out in public" is key to dispelling misinformation about call centers and HIV. Ryan transmits this message by implicitly disentangling the proliferating perceptions of the social identities of call center workers as well as the vague information disseminated about how one contracts HIV. As the media and medical reports suggest, the cultural construction of call center workers as a possible new high-risk category hinged on associations linking the transmission of disease with social and sexual transgression in general rather than unprotected sex in particular. The comments posted about the Ryan video, although not many, more than underscored the strength and persistence of these misperceptions, as well as the public's vitriol. Over a year later, one viewer wrote, "Fuck off! *basta may* AIDS *ka, dahil katangahan at kalandian mo kaya ganyan!!!!* (Fuck off! If you have AIDS, it's because of stupidity and promiscuity!!!!)" Around the same time, another commenter expressed skepticism about Ryan's story and spoke explicitly about his or her beliefs about Filipino call center workers:

> How did he know *na dun sa* nurse *n naka-sex nya nanggaling yun* AIDS *nya? namatay nb sa* AIDS *yung* nurse? *o sinabi n sa kanya n me* AIDS *cya? naku kailangan msagot yang tanung ko n yan* or else *ang* stigma *sa mga* call agents *ay ganun p rin sa isipan ko* . . .

How did he know that the nurse he had sexual relations with was the source of his HIV/AIDS? Did that nurse already die of AIDS? Or did that nurse inform him that he has AIDS? These questions need to be answered, or else I won't change my mind about the stigma about call center agents . . .

Ryan's public address differs from previous responses by the media by distinguishing call center agents' identities as workers from their sexual practices and identities. Ryan makes clear that he acquired HIV by having unsafe, unprotected sex (although he, too, stops short of explicitly defining the terms *safe* and *protected*). Furthermore, by not stating the gender of the person or persons with whom he had unprotected sex, Ryan avoids any associations among his acquisition of HIV, his sexual activity, and his sexual identity. Describing the "someone" (*isang tao*) he met at a street party, Ryan explains that "*this* person is not from a call center" and that "*this* person works in a hospital." Thus, Ryan's use of gender-neutral language (which is in part inevitable given the lack of gendered pronouns in Filipino languages, but is also due to his seemingly deliberate word choice) performs three acts: distancing HIV/AIDS from sexual identity, distancing nonnormative sexual identity from call centers, and distancing his own identity from sexual-object choice. Such efforts are redoubled in Ryan's figurative mapping of his exposure to HIV. Ryan first explains that he acquired the virus from someone he met at a party in Quezon City, not at work, and that the person was not a call center agent but someone who worked at a hospital in Bulacan, a province outside of Manila. Ryan's mapping thus figuratively distances the person from whom he acquired HIV from Manila as the epicenter of the Philippine call center industry, a configuration consistent with his desire to distance HIV risk from call center work and to locate it in unprotected sex. Ryan's mapping of his sexual activity also mirrors that of another HIV-positive call center agent named Humphrey. In an interview with ABS-CBN, Humphrey explained, "The activities that would give me the virus . . . is personal activities. . . . I do them outside work, outside the house, I do them . . . on my personal time"—that is, not during time spent in sleeping quarters or behind other closed doors at the call center where he works.[43]

Although Ryan's testimony opens up the possibility of understanding HIV transmission in ways that demystify nonnormative Filipino bodies, it walks the line between a commitment to warning his viewers about the perils of unsafe sex and a desire to clear the call center industry of its sexualized stigma. In its form, the video illustrates the contradiction in which Ryan seems to be caught. How does one justify the visibility of bodies and practices that seem to disrupt a heteronormative religious order and the hyperproductive operations of the global marketplace? Ryan demands that his body be seen as working for the nation, while the dishonor he associates with HIV demands his disguise. Indeed, Ryan's confession is as much about his HIV-positive status as it is about the impossibility of being a worker whose identity is culturally constructed as both an agent of Philippine modernity and the literal embodiment of the industry's supposed disorder and disease. It is important, then, that Ryan locates the unsafe sex and the virus with a hospital worker and thus in the medical field. This detail of Ryan's confession is especially meaningful when viewed within the locally and culturally constructed framework in which Filipino labor in medicine—especially nursing—is more highly valued than Filipino labor in outsourcing, as I discussed in chapter 1. By reminding his viewers that people employed by hospitals can also be carriers of HIV, Ryan challenges the superlative value attached to nursing work and attempts to recuperate the lost symbolic value of call center labor vis-à-vis rising HIV rates.

By using his confession to remind listeners of call center workers' economic contributions to the Philippine economy, Ryan addresses these national and transnational predicaments through his affect in particular. Ryan expresses shame and dishonor; literally cries out to parents, friends, coworkers, and the public; and issues an apology, yet he never makes clear what his anonymous apology is for, allowing the form of the confession to stand in for content. Instead, he contrasts his unhealthy and weakened body with the economic health of the nation that his labor helps secure, suggesting that the virus he carries, along with his "careless" actions, disgrace the nation as a whole. Indeed, Ryan's use of Taglish suggests that despite the potential global reach of YouTube, the video is primarily intended for Filipino audiences. If we read the nonnormativity of Ryan's body and his sexual transgressions as that which are *other* to the nation, then his anonymity does not diminish the strength of the apology but reinforces it. Having transformed the confession into a space of abjection, Ryan then seeks the possibility of redemption by sermonizing on the economic strength of the global workforce of which he is a part, and which he vows to rejoin once he regains his strength.

I want to offer a final reading of Ryan's confession as evoking and forging familial bonds between call center workers. In Ryan's message he specifically lists his teammates alongside his parents and friends as the targets of his pathos and regret, while he links his intention to rejoin the workforce to becoming once again an economically viable member of his family. Ryan thus constructs a continuum between his cultivation of familial relationships at home and at work, relationships that he sees as ruptured by his transgressions and repaired by his medical treatment. Coupled with the desire to distance HIV risk from the call center industry, the discourse of the family as the site of redemption and healing suggests that the call center family—workers with affective ties to one another—absorbs and resolves the nationalist anxieties regarding the contradiction of an industry that produces profit and supposed perversity. Ryan's confession thus succeeds in absolving the call center industry and the Philippine state from connections to queer identities and the supposed problems these identities entail—an act that preserves the image of the call center industry as the nation's savior. Ryan's video thus attempts to resolve the contradictions between professionalism and perversity posed by the link between HIV and call centers, by implying that although individual workers and their "families" will bear the shame, it is worth it for the economic contribution they make to the nation.

CONCLUSION

October 2013. It was exactly nine in the morning when I passed through the revolving doors of an upscale business hotel about a mile from the White House and the National Mall in Washington, D.C. I had been invited there by a member of the Philippine consulate to attend a small breakfast forum to market the Philippines as a top-notch site for outsourcing back-office medical work, such as processing medical claims or providing human resource services. Organized in conjunction with the Philippine Board of Investments, the forum was attended by thirty-five to forty health care administrators and other professionals interested in outsourcing jobs from one of the newer niches on the global services chain—health information management—to the Philippines. Alongside scrambled eggs and Danish pastry, the audience was treated to a high-production promotional video that in modern graphics and bright colors told the story of the new Philippines—a story of robust economic growth and investment-grade status that in turn conveyed the promise of foreign capital's security in the rehabilitated economy. The marketing presentations also emphasized more intangible forms of safety offered by the Filipino workers who might be tasked with handling not only private information about health care recipients in the United States but, in the case of actual phone contact with ill patients, sensitive interpersonal interactions as well. To this end, an American doctor and businessman who had successfully outsourced health care management to the Philippines testified to Filipinos' "passion to engage" health care recipients and their entire families. Citing Filipinos' ostensibly natural compassion, the speaker echoed earlier comments by a Philippine government official who had claimed that Filipino call center agents know "how to smile when talking to you on the phone" and that such hospitable qualities define "what Filipinos are as a race."

Roughly six years had passed since I set out to understand the intricacies of offshore outsourcing to the Philippines, which at the time of the forum was still holding steady as the world's capital of call centers and still aspiring to move up the global value chain. I therefore immediately recognized the language of investment and partnership, as well as the discourse of Philippine exceptionalism and Filipino relatability, which circulated throughout the presentation. Indeed, more than any other public representation of the Philippine call center industry I had seen during my fieldwork, the message at the health information management event was the firmest in its declarations of the country's newfound economic prowess, epitomized materially and symbolically in its first-time investment-grade rating. I sensed two kinds of hope swelling in that meeting. The first was for business deals that would bring more jobs to the Philippines and lower costs for U.S. companies, a hope affirmed in handshakes and the exchange of business cards between attendees. The second was less obvious but no less powerful: the hope that an ascending Philippines would give new meaning to the nation, its people, and their place in history. It was a yearning for particular forms of recognition by the United States and the world, of wanting to be seen not only as human but as human capital, and not only as friends in fellowship but as partners in business. Filipinos, the forum tried to make clear, were valuable investments, not cheap labor. It was the belief in a global economy that could move beyond the old colonial structures of power, the racial hierarchies, and the gendered systems of signification that had stifled Philippine growth and sullied the country's reputation in the past. That this gathering took place in the U.S. national capital—the source of the imperial imprimatur—added urgency to this desire and amplified the audacity of the new narrative.

A Nation on the Line has endeavored to understand the risks, burdens, and fortunes attached to this narrative and aspiration, the new meanings to which they give rise, and the contradictions, tensions, and anxieties that emerge as the national story is retold. Following call center agents at work, at leisure, and within their relationships with family and one another, I have uncovered how these struggles manifest themselves as crises of social and cultural value, inciting anxiety and tension over the skills of Filipino citizens, their consumption, and their gender and sexual identities and practices. The book has also been carefully attuned to the ways workers symbolically, ideologically, and materially negotiate this complex postindustrial and postcolonial terrain and in so doing challenge the representation of third-world workers as utterly supplicant to the forces of global capital. As my experience applying for an entry-level position at Vox Elite showed me, workers who received job offers pushed back against the terms of their employment as they asked for higher pay, better shifts, and the possibility of moving to different accounts. Moments such as these—along with my research participants' persistent hopes to resume their original career plans, as well as their off-script critiques of U.S. hegemony and American culture—undermine the assumption that the receivers of so-called American jobs are incapable of reflecting critically on the power relations and uneven material conditions that shape their lives. I encountered such assumptions many times throughout my fieldwork, even among call center industry leaders themselves, one of whom told me quite plainly "that Filipinos are happy to have any job as long as it provides for their family." While I do not doubt the dedication to family that this statement suggests, I was struck by the way it obscured and excused the inequalities of globalization, casting Filipinos as responsive only to economic calculations and framing any job as a good job. In contrast to such superficial assessments of globalization, most of my research participants expressed a much more nuanced affective relation to their line of work: they were thankful for the industry while simultaneously preoccupied with their pasts and futures.

The complexities of my research participants' understandings and experiences of call center work also shed light on the many obstacles to union organizing in the Philippine call center industry, a subject I have saved until last in part because, unfortunately, so little has been achieved in this regard. While challenges to unionization and collective organizing can of course be traced to companies that actively discourage or outright ban such activity among workers—which describes most if not all BPO firms I knew of—they are also linked to the kinds of contradictions, tensions, and ambiguities I have detailed throughout the book. For one, the transient nature of call center employment undermines the long-term efforts and solidarity building that a strong and effective union requires; as a problem manifest in sectors all over the world, worker transience reveals how postindustrial work patterns are not only antithetical to unionization but embraced by management precisely because of the way short-term work contracts and contingent labor undermine and prevent union efforts. Second, the affective attachment and camaraderie among workers had, at least at the time of my research, only strengthened workers' identification with corporate culture, rather than leading to large-scale resistance against capital; add to this the hyperproductivity, emphasis on individual performance, and opportunities for personal discovery and development that are part of call center culture, and it is not difficult to see that, as two researchers have noted with regard to the lack of labor organizing in Philippine call centers, "the internalization of discourses of rule within individual life strategies . . . is preventing the establishment of unions and other collective action structures" in the nation.[1] Finally, for many workers, the class character of call center work—while ambiguous and unstable, as I have pointed out throughout the book—makes unionization and its various activities, such as striking and picketing, seem inappropriate to their status as professionals and not workers. In fact, many call center employees reserve the latter term for those working in agriculture or blue-collar jobs. By using the term *call center worker* throughout this book, I am in many ways challenging this perception in the hopes that a specifically worker consciousness among Filipinos might be enhanced.

Instead of unionization, efforts have been made to address call center workers' issues and protect their rights through nongovernmental organizations, such as the BPO Workers' Organization, formed in 2012. Focused on the physical repercussions of call center work (especially damage to workers' vocal and auditory systems, the health complications associated with overnight work, and HIV risk), the organization's efforts make abundantly clear that the labor on which postindustrial work increasingly relies is never completely virtual or immaterial but always and already embodied. As the last two chapters of the book highlighted, postindustrial work cultures have introduced new ways in which the risks and fortunes of globalization are rendered in and through the body, via the aesthetic pleasures of fashion and consumption, on one hand, and the visibility and intimacy of queer bodies, on the other. Moreover, as waking and sleeping along with the rising and setting of the sun becomes yet another privilege denied people in the developing world, it is clear that any attempt to address working conditions in the twenty-first century must critique how the subsumption of labor and capital accumulation are increasingly organized to exploit the human body's temporal and biological systems, and thus not just labor alone but whole systems for sustaining life.[2]

In the future, advocates, activists, and scholars alike may also find that the affective demands and psychological repercussions of offshore work have intensified in ways that require more attention to capital's colonization of the human psyche. In the last few years, we have already seen how the maintenance of the Internet as a safe space requires the arduous labor of monitoring websites for violent and offensive images, such as depictions of beheadings and bestiality (work that Sarah Roberts dubs "commercial content moderation"), and thus has deleterious emotional effects on the thousands of Filipino workers who do it.[3] The emergence of such work is just the beginning of a potential seismic shift in the global landscape of back-office and customer service, in which more and more of the basic tasks currently handled by the likes of Filipino call center agents are automated, leaving the more complex communicative and relational tasks to people (although such tasks are undergoing automation, as well). With this ever-finer breakdown and relegation of service labor to machines, new hierarchies of affective labor will certainly emerge to mark the distinction between high-quality, high-value jobs that preserve human well-being—such as the offshore medical consultation alluded to at the beginning of the chapter—and those that push the limits of workers' humanity.[4] If the present is any indication, the more harrowing labor will remain and proliferate in the Philippines, while industry leaders and the state work to pull the country up the affective value chain.

By placing the contradictions of labor, culture, and value at the forefront of the analysis, A Nation on the Line has also revealed how Filipino call center agents embody the predicaments of the postcolonial Philippines, and thus how the boundaries between their struggles and those of the nation-state are often blurred. The possibility that offshore outsourcing and neoliberal globalization might lead only to short-term prosperity rather than long-term development was manifest in the disparagement of call center workers for their attraction to so-called easy money, casual relationships, and conspicuous consumption. In needing to assert the value of their relational skills while also presenting themselves as capable of more cognitive labor, call center agents enact the nation's struggle to both revalorize feminized Filipino affective labor and attain masculinized economic prowess and technological advancement, thereby affirming the latter as having the highest status and value. Just as an agent finds newfound autonomy, possessions, and productivity a source of both exhilaration and anxiety, the national feeling of frenzy and hope about call centers is coupled with fear and apprehension about what the future holds for the nation. Drawing out and interrogating this meaning-making process is important for understanding how identities—who people are as citizens, children, parents, partners, and workers—are shaped by new national narratives and a shifting symbolic economy. What struck me about the health information management forum in Washington, D.C., was not only the refrain about Philippine ascendancy but also the suggestion that compassion and care are key components of the nation as a brand. This begs the questions: What are the responsibilities and entitlements of citizens in conforming to the Philippines' brand name? What becomes of national belonging when measured against "staying on" or "adding value" to the brand? And what happens to those who, like many poor and indigenous people, cannot add value in the ways defined by the global marketplace? These are more than speculative questions. The neoliberal corporate restructuring that, along with state support, led to the transfer of knowledge and jobs to the Philippines also strengthened economic processes that distribute wealth upward, producing a crisis of inequality that only exacerbates the already wide gulf between the privileged and the poor in the country. Striving to be on the winning side of this divide, young Filipinos have embraced the ethos of productivity and entrepreneurialism and the discourses of global partnership and human capital. Yet, as I discussed in chapter 4, while call center work may offer opportunities for mobility for those on the margins of the middle class, the call center industry as a whole has always been tipped in favor of those workers with already existing social, cultural, and financial capital. Of the four dozen or so call center employees I directly interviewed for this project, only seven—those with the most elite educational backgrounds and greatest material resources—have left the call center industry to successfully pursue professional careers of their choice. The rest have either remained in the industry—able to partake in its spoils but still unable to move to firmer economic ground—or resigned from call center companies and taken up home-based IT-related jobs, such as cleaning up marketing data, which they find through online labor markets and which pay at hourly or piecemeal rates. As in the nineteenth century, homework in the twenty-first century has become an increasingly popular choice among women, for whom the jobs offer the chance to earn income, care for a family, and attend to domestic work, in turn confirming that homework has not receded with economic restructuring but proceeds alongside or in conjunction with it.[5] The story of the Philippines 2.0, it seems, cannot totally overwrite the past.

Finally, understanding the everyday experiences of call center workers in the Philippines also demonstrates how, for many, work is not just a means to a material end. In creating and sustaining modes of consciousness, identities, and cultures of everyday life, work can also constitute a way of knowing the self, understanding the nation, and envisioning the future; as work changes, is destabilized, or disappears, people and politics change as well. Of course, the stakes of these matters are not limited to Filipinos alone. Writing this conclusion just one month after Donald Trump's confirmation as the forty-fifth president of the United States, I am powerfully reminded of how neoliberal globalization has undermined the American narrative in which whiteness, citizenship, education, and hard work lead easily to good jobs, class mobility, and a sense of security and superiority. Having derived their identities and life meanings from work and the narratives attached it, many who feel betrayed by the shifting story have turned to a defense of nativism and a public reinvigoration of white nationalism to recuperate the narrative of white America's greatness.[6] Such circumstances force us to ask, not how one fulfills the national dream or how we can bring back the story of the past, but who such national narratives of progress and growth were written for, what living up to these narratives means, and what consequences we face when the story changes, ends, or receives a dangerous new narrator.

Indeed, just eight months after the election of Philippine president Rodrigo Duterte—a man whose "radical informality" and offensive bravado have been likened to Trump's—the story of the Philippine nation-state has already shifted toward what Julio Teehankee identifies as a *masa* (of-the-people) nationalist narrative based simultaneously on a repudiation of U.S. hegemony on the international scene and a brutal crackdown on drug dealers and users at home in the domestic arena.[7] Echoing the revival of nationalist sentiments throughout Asia—which perhaps cannot be separated from the region's increasing global economic power—Duterte in October 2016 announced his "separation" from the United States and his ideological realignment with China, demonstrating that his brand of nationalism continues to evoke the gendered and familial narrative that defined U.S.-Philippine relations for much of the twentieth century. Moreover, in what could be perceived as an acknowledgment of the frustrations of call center workers forced to talk to American consumers night after night, Duterte in that same speech publicly described Americans as "loud, sometimes rowdy," their voices as "not adjusted to civility."[8] Bringing into sharp relief some of the primary themes of this book, Duterte's use of the term *separation* and his critique of the quality of American speech made evident the way postcolonial structures of power are understood in affective and relational terms, even as they are being boldly revised.

Observers also note that despite his of-the-people platform, Duterte's support has come overwhelmingly from the middle and elite classes—the same classes who have benefited from the Philippine call center industry's ties to U.S. capital. Thus, while Duterte's expressions of resentment toward and rejection of the United States incited some fears that the industry would weaken or be dismantled altogether, it is more likely that the president's nationalist fervor, like the nationalist sentiments among call center industry leaders, will remain comfortably nested within a neoliberal economic frame, delivering profits and bragging rights to the Philippine elite. After all, Duterte announced a separation, not a divorce, from the United States. Thus while call centers are already a flash point for the nation's postcolonial struggles of labor, culture, and value, in the near future they may become an even more sensitive litmus test of the Philippines' postcolonial predicaments, inviting new narratives to make sense of the country's struggles—narratives that will remind us that the postcolonial nation, as an unfinished discussion about the meaning of freedom and progress, is always on the line.

NOTES

Introduction

1 Vikas Bajaj, "A New Capital of Call Centers," *New York Times*, November 25, 2011.

2 Chrisee Dela Paz, "Philippines' Back Office Shines in 2015, Exceeds Target," *Rappler*, February 3, 2016; Sicat, "'Successes' and Adjustment"; Camille Bersola, "26 Interesting Facts about Call Centers and the BPO Industry," *Philippine Star*, July 29, 2012; "2012–2016 Philippine Information Technology and Business Process Management (IT-BPM) Road Map," Information Technology Business Process Association of the Philippines (IBPAP); and Lee C. Chipongian, "OFW Remittances Reach $25.8B in 2015," *Manila Bulletin*, February 19, 2016. For a brief scholarly account of call centers in the Philippines prior to 2010, and the human resource and cultural questions they raised, see Hechanova-Alampay, *1-800-Philippines*.

3 Outsourced work falls into various categories: *health information management*, for example, refers to work that supports the health care industry, while *business process management* refers to work that supports businesses broadly. *Global in-house call centers* refers specifically to call centers that are still maintained by a parent company, and thus not outsourced but moved offshore. *Knowledge process outsourcing* refers to work that supports knowledge-oriented businesses specifically.

4 Batalla, "Divided Politics"; "PHL Now a Creditor Nation, Helps Troubled Europe Cope with Debts—BPL," Money, GMA *News*, February 21, 2012, http:// www.gmanetwork.com/news/. money/personalfinance/248866/phl-now-a -creditor-nation-helps-troubled-europe-cope-with-debt-bsp/story/; Richard Jevad Heydarian, "The Philippines: The Next Asian Tiger Economy?," *Al Jazeera*, June 14, 2014; Cris Larano, "As Economy Soars, Philippines No Longer 'Sick Man of Asia,'" *Wall Street Journal*, August 24, 2014; and Danessa Rivera, "PHL Is Asia's Second Fastest-Growing Economy with 6.4-Percent Growth in Q2," GMA *News*, August 28, 2014, http://www.gmanetwork.com/news /money/economy/376831/phl-is-asia-s-second-fastest-growing-economy -with-6-4-percent-growth-in-q2/story/. Heydarian goes on to make the vital point that such economic growth did not benefit the majority of the population.

5   Hoang, *Dealing in Desire*, 7.

6   As the term suggests, *sunrise industry* refers to an economic sector that is new but growing rapidly.

7   My use of the term *postcolonial* is similar to that of Dylan Rodríguez in *Suspended Apocalypse: White Supremacy, Genocide, and the Filipino Condition*. Rodríguez deploys the term from a critical perspective in which the Philippines has not quite escaped the colonial condition vis-à-vis the United States. The *post* in *postcolonial* thus refers not to the nation's transcendence of colonial structures of power but to Filipinos' persistent and urgent attempts to define and enact Philippine independence from within those structures.

8   See Heller, "Commodification of Language"; and Hoang, *Dealing in Desire*. More broadly, however, this book also builds on a body of scholarship that has examined how the shift toward neoliberalism has reshaped social relations, cultural practices, and subjectivities outside of the west. See Rofel, *Desiring Subjects*; Ferguson, *Global Shadows*; Gregory, *Devil behind the Mirror*; and Ong, *Neoliberalism as Exception*.

9   Heller, "Commodification of Language," 103. See Tadiar, *Fantasy-Production*; and Gershon and Alexy, "Introduction."

10 Chow, *Not Like a Native Speaker*, 31. See Heller, "Commodification of Language."

11 The canonical text in this vein is Carla Freeman's *High Tech and High Heels in the Global Economy: Women, Work, and Pink-Collar Identities in the Caribbean*. More recently, attention has been paid to India's rise in the global knowledge economy through outsourced work in IT, as well as the material and ideological role of English in Slovakia's turn toward the knowledge economy. See Radhakrishnan, *Appropriately Indian*; and Prendergast, *Buying into English*.

12 Brophy, "Language Put to Work," 411–13.

13 See Brophy, "The Subterranean Stream"; and Frenkel et al., "Beyond Bureaucracy?"

14 On no-collar work, see Ross, *No-Collar*; on Theory Y management, see McGregor, *Human Side of Enterprise*; on the extended workday and work-life balance, see Ciulla, *Working Life*; on presence bleed, see Gregg, *Work's Intimacy*.

15 Similar works in this vein include Patel, *Working the Night Shift*; Hegde, "Spaces of Exception"; Rivas, *Salvadoran Imaginaries*; and Pal and Buzzanell, "Indian Call Center Experience."

16 Although *postindustrial* is a term typically reserved for the areas of the world presumed to have moved beyond manufacturing and into services as a major driver of wealth and national growth, I use it to describe the social and cultural conditions that gave rise to offshore outsourcing in the Philippines precisely because Filipino workers are increasingly integrated into the service operations that support U.S. and other foreign corporations. If, as Michael

Hardt has noted, industrial production, agriculture, and the service industry can now "mix and coexist" within nondominant countries in the world economy—that is, if countries like the Philippines can participate in the growing global services industry while never having fully industrialized to the level of more dominant nations—then the terms and theories that explain postindustrial society must also answer to the areas of the world where "our" service work is carried out. See Hardt, "Affective Labor," 92.

17 See Aneesh, *Neutral Accent*; Mankekar, *Unsettling India*; Mirchandani, *Phone Clones*; Pal and Buzzanell, "Indian Call Center Experience"; Patel, *Working the Night Shift*; Poster, "Who's on the Line?"; Raghuram, "Identities on Call"; Rowe, Malhotra, and Pérez, *Answer the Call*; Russell, *Smiling Down the Line* (which also examines call centers in Australia); Shome, "Thinking through Diaspora."

18 Mirchandani, *Phone Clones*, 3.

19 My understanding and use of the term *affect* are derived from and build on the definition of the term in cultural studies, where affect has been predominantly treated as a state of feeling distinct from but still linked to emotions. In this literature, *affect* names a psychic as well as bodily orientation or attitude toward something and is thus a highly relational aspect of individual and collective life. In turn, various affects, affective registers, or affective relations have the power to create and shape moods and motivations in the realm of everyday social life and politics. See Berlant, *Cruel Optimism*; Gregg and Seigworth, *Affect Theory Reader*; Staiger, Cvetkovich, and Reynolds, *Political Emotions*; and Stewart, *Ordinary Affects*. My understanding and use of *affective labor* has been shaped by feminist sociology and neo-Marxist philosophy that identify the term (along with *emotional labor* or *emotion work*) as the labor that produces particular affective states in other people (such as family members or coworkers) or in a particular place (such as an office or restaurant). See Emma Dowling, Rodrigo Nunes, and Ben Trott's special issue of the journal *Ephemera* (*Ephemera* 7); Hardt, "Affective Labor"; and Hochschild, *Managed Heart*.

20 See also Tadiar, *Things Fall Away*, 12. For work that takes the approach outlined here, see Dowling, "Producing the Dining Experience"; Nakano Glenn, "From Servitude to Service Work"; Vora, *Life Support*; and Ramos-Zayas, *Street Therapists*. For a study of Filipino affects in particular, see Manalansan, "Servicing the World."

21 Long and Moore, "Introduction: Sociality's New Directions," 9.

22 On U.S. empire and militarism in the Philippines, see Baldoz, *Third Asiatic Invasion*; Campomanes, "Casualty Figures"; Go, *American Empire*; Gonzalez, *Securing Paradise*; Isaac, *American Tropics*; Kramer, "Race, Empire"; Mendoza, *Metroimperial Intimacies*; Rafael, *White Love*; D. Rodríguez, *Suspended Apocalypse*; and Shaw and Francia, *Vestiges of War*. On the Filipino diaspora, labor, and labor migration, see D. Aguilar, "Imperialism"; D. Aguilar, "Ques-

tionable Claims"; F. Aguilar, *Filipinos in Global Migration*; F. Aguilar, *Migration Revolutions*; Choy, *Empire of Care*; Constable, *Maid to Order*; Espiritu, *Home Bound*; Fajardo, *Filipino Crosscurrents*; Francisco-Menchavez, *The Labor of Care*; Guevarra, *Marketing Dreams, Manufacturing Heroes*; Manalansan, *Global Divas*; Parreñas, *Servants of Globalization*; R. Rodriguez, *Migrants for Export*; and Tadiar, *Fantasy-Production*. On Filipino subjectivities and imaginaries, see Benedicto, *Under Bright Lights*; Cruz, *Transpacific Femininities*; Galam, *Promise of the Nation*; Hau, *Subject of the Nation*; Tadiar, *Things Fall Away*; Raymundo, "Womb of the Global Economy"; and Tolentino, *National/Transnational*.

23 My attention to the Philippine political economy and culture at the national scale resonates with scholarship of a similar scope in anthropology, sociology, and literature. See Bello, *Anti-development State*; Cannell, *Power and Intimacy*; McKay, *Satanic Mills*; and Tadiar, *Things Fall Away*.

24 Fabros, "Global Economy," 346 and 351.

25 Circulating in scholarship, politics, and the popular imagination today, the notion of a special relationship between the United States and the Philippines rests on the idea of the United States as a munificent imperial power that gifted the Philippines with democratic institutions, American education, and the English language, with the relationship culminating with Filipino and American troops joining forces against a common enemy in World War II. Like other scholars in the field, I am interested in the affective underpinning of this narrative. See Ileto, *Payson and Revolution*; Gonzalez, *Securing Paradise*; and Rafael, *White Love*.

26 Poster, "Who's on the Line?," 271.

27 William McKinley, "Benevolent Assimilation Proclamation," Washington, DC, 1898.

28 McKinley, "Benevolent Assimilation Proclamation," Washington, DC, 1898.

29 We might further characterize this as the power of the colonizer's desire to materialize, through visual or aural means, their power in the *other*—what Homi K. Bhabha refers to as the discourse of mimicry. Bhabha, *Location of Culture*.

30 Quoted in Gamalinda, "English," 48.

31 In *American Tropics: Articulating Filipino America*, Allan Punzalan Isaac draws on the work of Diana Fuss to describe these dynamics of difference. Fuss writes that within the operations of empire "it therefore becomes necessary for the colonizer to subject the colonial other to a double command: be like me, don't be like me; be mimetically identical, be totally other." Quoted in Isaac, *American Tropics*, 10.

32 D. Rodríguez, *Suspended Apocalypse*, 102.

33 D. Rodríguez, *Suspended Apocalypse*, 102.

34 Choy, *Empire of Care*; Guevarra, *Marketing Dreams, Manufacturing Heroes*; Parreñas, *Servants of Globalization*; and R. Rodriguez, *Migrants for Export*. The language of labor brokerage comes from Rodriguez, *Migrants for Export*.

35 Tadiar, *Fantasy-Production*, 19. See Gonzalez, *Securing Paradise*, 37–39.

36 Bello, *Anti-development State*, 13.

37 Balisacan and Hill, *Dynamics of Regional Development*; Bello, *Anti-development State*; and "Philippines: Asia's Knowledge Center."

38 "Philippines: Asia's Knowledge Center"; see Saloma-Akpedonu, *Possible Worlds*, 3.

39 Tadiar, *Fantasy-Production*, 43; and Tadiar, "If Not Mere Metaphor." On the metaphor of penetration and its shifting meaning, see Tadiar, *Fantasy-Production*, 74.

40 R. Rodriguez, *Migrants for Export*, xix.

41 Tadiar, "If Not Mere Metaphor." See also Caroline Hau, who writes that "power relations among countries are asymmetrical, and the hierarchy of nation-states is perceived, comprehended, organized, and managed through the logic and practice of gender inequality." *Subject of the Nation*, 191.

42 R. Rodriguez, *Migrants for Export*, xix.

43 In 2008–9, for example, an entry-level agent in a Philippine call center might earn anywhere from ₱10,000 to ₱15,000 per month—about $1.20 to $1.86 per hour—while an entry-level agent in the United States might earn an hourly wage of $10.00 to $12.00.

44 Yellin, *Your Call*, 27.

45 Palm, "Phoning It In," 28–29.

46 Cohen, *Consumer's Republic*, 285.

47 Cohen, *Consumer's Republic*; and Green, *Race on the Line*. According to Venus Green, Ma Bell was deeply invested in cultivating a "white-lady" image of the telephone operator, an image that drew on contemporary racial ideology and racial exclusivity that maintained that "only white women could be 'ladies,' and the telephone company hired 'ladies' as telephone operators." The status of the white-lady image diminished with increased automation of Bell Systems, and was completely dissolved with the integration of the workforce in the 1960s. *Race on the Line*, 53.

48 Green, *Race on the Line*, 53.

49 David Rohde, "GE Uses PassageWay for CTI," *Network World*, March 25, 1996, 19.

50 Nadjii Tehrani, "A Tribute to the Distinguished Women of Our Industry," *Telemarketing and Call Center Solutions*, January 1996, 2; Tamsen Tillson, "Call Moll," *Canadian Business*, September 1996, 56–57.

51 For example, the catalog center of the major retailer J. C. Penney reported that nearly 80 percent of its workforce was composed of women. Meanwhile, at Pioneer about 50 percent of the workforce was composed of women and 50 percent of black and Hispanic workers. Kim Tyson, "Dialing for Dollars . . . Austin's Attributes Lure National Telemarketers," *Austin American-Statesman*, June 1989, 12.

52 Brenda Read, "Call Center Cool," *Facilities Design and Management*, October 1998, 54–58.

53 Morini, "Feminization of Labor," 43. For Cristina Morini, contemporary capitalism makes "social precariousness," and thus "the baggage of female experience," a "general paradigm irrespective of gender."

54 Brenda Read, "Call Center Cool," *Facilities Design and Management*, October 1998, 54–58. Computer telephone integration allows a telephone system (increasingly an Internet-based system) to connect to an agent's computer, such that when a customer phones a call center, their telephone number automatically brings up their information in the customer database. Customer relationship management tools are the databases themselves, programs that companies use to store and recall customer data, as well as to record the details of customer service calls.

55 "How One Teleservices Agency Successfully Manages Growth: An Interview with Daniel Julian," *Call Center Solutions*, August 1999, 116.

56 For evidence of early outsourcing to countries of the global south, see Martin Conboy, "Call Centers in Asia: A Question of Comparative Advantage?," *Telecom Asia*, November 1997, 82; Julekha Dash, "Customer Support Moves Overseas," *Computerworld*, March 19, 2001, 18; Vivian A. Sun, "Global Access Wireless World Opens New Opportunities to RP Firms," *BusinessWorld* (Manila), June 29, 2000, 1; Mukesh Sundaram, "Outsourcing in the Telecommunications Industry," *Call Center CRM Solutions*, September 2000, 92; Karene S. Witcher, "Asia Isn't Immune to Rash of Hot Jobs—Surveys Indicate Many Types of Employers Have Hiring on Their Minds," *Asian Wall Street Journal*, February 23, 1999.

57 See Roediger and Esch, *Production of Differences*.

58 Radhakrishnan, *Appropriately Indian*, 36–37.

59 Radhakrishnan, *Appropriately Indian*, 36–37.

60 Ong, *Neoliberalism as Exception*, 169.

61 Bello et al., *State of Fragmentation*, https://focusweb.org/content/state-fragmentation-philippines-transition.

62 Blyton and Jenkins, *Key Concepts in Work*, 118. The authors go on to say that "what at first sight may appear to be highly routine activities are often in practice significantly enhanced by the knowledge and experience that the individual workers bring to the job—be that serving meals in an old person's home, tending the garden in the local park or answering queries in the tourist information office."

63 Blyton and Jenkins, *Key Concepts in Work*, 118.

64 Heller, "Commodification of Language," 109.

65 Saloma-Akpedonu, *Possible Worlds*, 3.

66 Radhakrishnan, *Appropriately Indian*, 36.

67 On studying up, see Nader, "Up the Anthropologist"; and Dávila, *Latinos, Inc.*

68 Marcus, *Fieldwork*, 1.

69 de Genova, *Working the Boundaries*, 18.

70 Rosenbaum, "Longing and Belonging."

71 On decolonizing ethnography, anthropology, and the study of minority populations, see Allen and Jobson, "The Decolonizing Generation"; Harrison, *Decolonizing Anthropology*; Smith, *Decolonizing Methodologies*. On feminist pedagogy, see hooks, *Teaching Critical Thinking*. For a discussion of mastery in feminist pedagogy, see Maher and Tetreault, *The Feminist Classroom*.

72 Jackson, *Real Black*, 22–23.

73 Gupta and Ferguson, "Beyond 'Culture.'"

74 I conducted the bulk of the ethnographic observations and interviews from October 2008 to June 2009, as well as from May to June 2013. In between these fieldwork trips, I kept up with research participants through social media and e-mail, collected and analyzed relevant primary-source documents on the call center industry, and conducted interviews and fieldwork in and from the United States. As a result, I have met and observed several dozen call center agents and a handful of industry actors and government officials, and I conducted a total of fifty-five extensive one-on-one or small-group interviews. I also took tours of and observed operations in five different call centers in Manila and Bacolod combined. All the individuals mentioned in the book have been given pseudonyms, as have the various companies I discuss. Many of the company names that I use are, however, shared by real companies operating in completely different industries (e.g., Vox Elite, Premier Source), thus there is no connection between the call centers I portray here and the real companies bearing the same names. I also changed all proper nouns, such as the titles of training courses or customer service evaluation tools, to prevent them from being traced back to particular companies. The only organization whose name has not been changed is the Information Technology Business Process Outsourcing Association of the Philippines (IBPAP) because of the inherently public nature of their mission; however, I have changed the names of all the IBPAP executives that I interviewed.

75 This process occurred over an approximately three-month period.

76 R. Rodriguez, *Migrants for Export*; Guevarra, *Marketing Dreams, Manufacturing Heroes*.

77 The term *bakla* refers to Filipino men who, instead of identifying with a static marker of sexuality like *gay*, understand themselves as situated within what Martin Manalansan describes as "a system of generative practices" that is more transitional and fluid than U.S.-based sex and gender traditions, while also "inflect[ing] gender, class, race, and ethnicity through dramaturgical or theatric idioms." Manalansan, *Global Divas*, x.

78 For accounts of transnationalism within American studies, see Briggs, McCormick, and Way, "Transnationalism" and Fishkin, "Crossroads of Culture," 2005. For transnational in Asian American studies, see Duong, "Transnationalism"; for transnationalism as a standpoint of critique of the nation-state, see de Genova, *Working the Boundaries*, 4.

Chapter 1: Listening between the Lines

1 This dichotomy is perhaps best understood as the contrast between those who, taking up critical theory, see the application of psychology to the workplace primarily as a form of domination, and those who, adopting neo-Marxist philosophy, see the proliferation of social relations and communication among workers as a major step toward worker emancipation and true pluralistic democracy. The latter idea has been associated with the work of *Multitude*, by Michael Hardt and Antonio Negri. For a discussion of the former, see Illouz, *Cold Intimacies*, 17.

2 Hochschild, *Managed Heart*, 83–90.

3 Hochschild describes relational work as "recalibrations of the emotional climate" that flight attendants achieve by paying attention to each other's moods and attempting to adjust them through encouraging talk and light banter (*Managed Heart*, 114–115). These efforts, she argues, sustain the attendants' willingness to treat customers as welcomed guests, rather than nuisances, on a flight. My notion of relational labor builds on this definition by seeing in it a much more expansive and more rationalized set of techniques that management not only encourages but requires. My definition of relational labor thus overlaps with but differs from the notion of relational practice, which names the labor associated with interactive workplaces such as those found in nursing, social work, and education. Whereas these approaches emphasize the interactive work that occurs between a worker and a patient or client, my emphasis is on the way that managing relationships in call center work is part of the burden placed on workers by capital as well. On relational practices, see Fletcher, *Disappearing Acts*; and Holmes and Marra, "Relational Practice."

4 Knights and McCabe, "Governing through Teamwork," 1602.

5 Manalansan, "Servicing the World," 222. Manalansan uses the term *disaffection* to describe a state in which workers feel "antipathy and emotional distance," which "allow them to have the energy to go on, despite the onslaught of material and psychic forces from the outside" (225).

6 For a more robust discussion of subsumption, see Dyer-Witheford, *Cyber-Marx*. Although the term *subsumption* comes directly from Karl Marx, my discussion and ensuing analysis lean firmly on the ideas of autonomist Marxist theorists, especially the concepts of the socialized worker and the social factory. The socialized worker is one who draws not from a particular set of skills learned in job training but from those developed in other areas of social life, such as the home, the consumer realm, or mass media—that is, "the entire social and territorial network within which a person moves." Morini, "Feminization of Labor," 45. The term *social factory* points to the reorganization of social relations to better facilitate capitalist accumulation through intangible human capacities, including emotion, affect, desire, and attention. Writing about the role of social reproductive labor within capitalism, feminist

Marxists Maria dalla Costa and Selma James made clear that the social factory did not mean that the household was like a factory but that the capitalist system relies on "sites of extraction 'beyond the factory,'" in what they called "the community" or simply society itself. *Power of Women*, 121.

7 Vora, *Life Support*.

8 Originating with Douglas McGregor's *The Human Side of Enterprise*, published in 1960, Theory Y management is anchored in the idea that people can find pleasure and personal fulfillment in work and thus that managers should encourage participation and openness among workers so as to fully unleash this positive potential. Y-style managers are contrasted with X-style managers—those with authoritarian methods who discipline and control workers through more punitive means, and who believe that people naturally lack a strong inclination toward work.

9 On disconnection, isolation, and call center work, see Aneesh, *Neutral Accent*; and Rowe, Malhotra, and Pérez, *Answer the Call*.

10 Writing about similar dynamics in the U.S. context, Melissa Gregg argues that workplace activities "bear relation to, even if they do not fully mask, a culture of long working hours that often prevent workers from establishing more traditional friendship and community networks beyond the compulsory sociality of the office." *Work's Intimacy*, 253.

11 In his work on call center workers in the Philippines, Emmanuel David argues that transwomen in particular are expected to perform these socially reproductive roles. "Purple-Collar Labor," 188. I discuss this further in chapter 6.

12 My impression of Global Invest thus lined up with Andrew Ross's observations about call centers in India, which were promoted as "ultramodern, dotcommish funhouses, buzzing with clever hipsters." Ross, *Fast Boat to China*, 143.

13 Weeks, *Problem with Work*, 13, 60.

14 Weeks, *Problem with Work*, 60.

15 I am adapting Michel Foucault's notion of biopower—a form of state power that regulates populations through bodies—to corporate settings, where services, as commodities for the market (exchange value) and for profit (surplus value), are produced. See Foucault, *History of Sexuality*, 140–141. As Hardt and Negri further explain, biopower is "a form of power that regulates social life from its interior, following it, interpreting it, absorbing it." *Empire*, 24.

16 Knights and McCabe, "Governing through Teamwork," 1588.

17 Lazzarato, "Immaterial Labor," 135.

18 For the kind of approach that frames Western-style management and Filipino culture as a clash, see Hechanova and Franco, *Way We Work*. This is not to say that my research participants did not feel a contrast between American and Filipino communicative styles. For example, agents sometimes explained

to me that the need to be direct with customers and coworkers, especially with demands or criticism, conflicted with their desire for harmony and to respond to others in the affirmative that, they felt, defined Filipino relational norms.

19 Cannell, *Power and Intimacy*. In her explanation of the concept, Cannell, building on the canonical work of Raymond Ileto (*Payson and Revolution*) and Vicente Rafael (*Contracting Colonialism*)—argues that unlike the way it has been represented in American social science literature, that is, as a social debt between two parties that spells and hardens their distance and inequality, *utang na loob* does not represent a fixed state of unequal power distribution but one that can be negotiated through proximity (10–11), or what she refers to as intimacy (230). Cannell thus rejects the interpretive framework of exchange and instead develops the language of an "emotional economy" that "represents the experiences of such encounters through terms meaning 'shame,' 'oppression,' 'enslavement,' blending and 'becoming used to,' and especially love and 'pity'" (231). See also Fajardo, *Filipino Crosscurrents*, 87–90.

20 Marla Gonzalez, "Leadership with a Heart," *Breakthroughs! The Philippine Business Process Outsourcing Newsletter*, July–September 2011: 9.

21 Mitchell, *Rule of Experts*, 303.

22 My discussion of the way particular Filipino cultural traits are made compatible with global systems of production resonates with Smitha Radhakrishnan's notion of the "cultural streamlining" she observed among Indian IT professionals. Radhakrishnan, *Appropriately Indian*, 5.

23 See, *Decolonized Eye*, 91.

24 This willingness to work on one's own emotions to achieve a state of agreement with the emotions of others—what Hochschild, writing about gender and emotion work, calls "shadow labor"—tends to be invisible, giving the doer the appearance of a natural passivity or making the behavior seem "automatic." *Managed Heart*, 167.

Chapter 2: Contesting Skill and Value

1 At the time of my research, ₱10,000–15,000 equaled approximately $215–$321.

2 The standard pro-globalization argument here is that although corporations don't pay offshore workers the same wages as workers onshore in the United States or other advanced industrial nations, wages for offshore work are still higher than those that can be found in other nonglobalized sectors of the economy—that is, that something is better than nothing and that people in poor countries are just happy to have a job. Yet the fact that call center wages are considerably higher than what other workers could demand elsewhere in the Philippines, and thus the standard of living may be rising among call center workers, does not change the structural relations in any fundamental

way; it only makes the asymmetry harder to see. Also, it is simply untrue that workers in poor countries are *just* happy to have a job. I address this point at the end of the chapter.

3 Developed by market researchers, these categories are used in everyday conversation among Filipinos, and definitions of them can be readily found on the web. I thus reproduce them here, although with caution. Roughly speaking, classes A, B, and C might be called affluent, middle class, and lower-middle class, respectively, while AB might be referred to as upper-middle class. Like the concept of class generally, the distinctions in the Philippine context revolve around property ownership, family wealth, education, income, occupation, and, more recently, access to status-oriented consumer goods. Class A individuals, like my research participant named Mia Mendez, have been educated in elite institutions, have significant family wealth that can be passed on to children (*mana*), and live in large homes or compounds. Like their counterparts in other classes, class B individuals have finished or are enrolled in college, yet their family income and wealth—property, savings, and so on—are quite modest compared to those of class A, the educational institutions they attended are respectable but not necessarily elite, and they have minimal personal possessions (e.g., cars, personal electronics). Compared to class C individuals, however, class B, or middle-class Filipinos, have relatively consistent access to not simply the means of survival (food, housing, clothing) but some material comforts. Classes D and E are considered the poor and uneducated who lack assets of any kind, and they are not well represented in the call center industry. See PinoyMoneyTalk, "Socioeconomic Classes (SEC) ABCDE Explained," October 12, 2012, http://www .pinoymoneytalk.com/sec-abcde-percentage-population/.

4 When I returned to Bacolod for follow-up research in 2013, this problem had taken a different form. Although it had become more socially acceptable for members of the privileged classes to go into call center work, they were just there, as one manager I interviewed put it, "for something to do" and thus were not as motivated to perform as those who were working out of economic necessity. To a certain extent, then, it was perhaps just a matter of time before would-be employees and their parents gained knowledge of and confidence in the industry. But the point remains that local configurations of class structures, status, and identity matter to the labor market and the experience of young people within it.

5 Andrew Ross notes a similar mentality on the part of Chinese workers in offshore technology jobs. See *Fast Boat to China*.

6 It is important to note that these attitudes on the part of agents did not go unnoticed by management, which, in some call centers that I knew of, adopted the kinds of institutionalized diversity training seen in the United States. I discuss the pitfalls of such training in the following chapter.

7 My research participants' way of relating to me as a possible representative of

their experiences to a specifically American audience demonstrates the extent to which I as an ethnographer was interpellated into the ongoing tacit debate about the meaning and value of their work and thus shows how research "subjects" never simply see themselves as subservient to the researcher or research process but actively involve themselves in it.

8 Luz, "A Time to Celebrate."

9 Juan Miguel Luz, "Statement Poorly Expressed, Speaker Offers His Apologies," *Philippine Daily Inquirer,* April 9, 2013.

10 Mirchandani, *Phone Clones,* 160n4. Mirchandani cites Goldberg, *The Threat of Race.*

11 Mirchandani, *Phone Clones,* 14.

12 This is not to suggest that all applicants hired by a call center speak flawless English in the eyes of corporate management, trainers, and customers. As Cecilia Maribal Rivas has shown in the case of call center workers in El Salvador, the ideal English speaker does not simply exist; he or she must be produced through training and discipline in the workplace. See Rivas, *Salvadoran Imaginaries.*

13 Palatino, quoted in Carl Marc Ramota, "Economic Woes Drive Bright Graduates to Call Centers," *Bulatlat* 5, no. 7 (March 20–26, 2005).

14 *Effort* refers to the exertion required by the specific job task, while *intensity* refers to the conditions under which the effort is made. See Blyton and Jenkins, *Key Concepts in Work,* 58–64.

15 Bello et al., *State of Fragmentation.*

16 Sarah Raymundo describes the state as the primary promoter of transnational discourses that "normalize and naturalize the exploitative conditions of neoliberal globalization." "Womb of the Global Economy," 551–552. Furthermore, Caroline Hau argues that "telling the nation's 'life story' is an intrinsic aspect of constituting the nation as a form of community." *Subject of the Nation,* 9.

17 Bennet Dahl, "BPO Roadmap Plots Philippines Direction for 2010," *Breakthroughs! The Philippine Business Process Outsourcing Newsletter,* May–June 2007: 2.

18 Michael Alan Hamlin, "The Tempered Enthusiasm of the IT-BPO Industry," *Breakthroughs! The Philippine Business Process Outsourcing Newsletter,* April–June 2011: 4.

19 As Kalindi Vora demonstrates, biocapital is value created through "investment in human energy in other bodies," including gestational surrogacy and organ transplant but also "'noninnovative' knowledge work" or customer care. *Life Support,* 1.

20 One of the first of these talent-development initiatives was the Technical Education and Skills Development Authority's Training for Work Scholarship Program. Begun under the Arroyo administration, the program subsidizes the cost of training call center applicants so they can successfully apply for

call center work. "Hiring Rate in Contact Centers Expected to Rise," *Break-throughs! The Philippine Business Process Outsourcing Newsletter*, July-August 2008: 12. Similarly, a program called ADEPT (Advanced English Proficiency Training) was developed in response to the low passing rate of 5 percent for college graduates who apply to work for IT-BPO companies, with language skills being the main reason for not meeting recruitment standards. Marla Silayan-Gonzalez, "ADEPT Program to Further Develop BPO Workforce's English Proficiency Skills," *Breakthroughs! The Philippine Business Process Outsourcing Newsletter*, April–June 2009: 1–4.

21 Penny Bongato, "BPAP National Competency Test (BNCT) Identifies Critical Competences Needed by Industry," *Breakthroughs! The Philippine Business Process Outsourcing Newsletter*, April–June 2011: 15; Abigail Ho, "More BPO Assessment Tests Set," Business/Headlines, Inquirer.net, October 31, 2011, http://business.inquirer.net/27573/more-bpo-assessment-tests-set.

22 Penny Bongato, "Talent Development Initiatives for Globally Competitive Professionals," *Breakthroughs! The Philippine Business Process Outsourcing Newsletter*, July-September, 2011: 6.

23 "BPAP Announces Name Change to IBPAP," *Breakthroughs! The Philippine Business Process Outsourcing Newsletter*, April 2013: 2.

24 Penny Bongato, "Talent Development Initiatives for Globally Competitive Professionals," *Breakthroughs! The Philippine Business Process Outsourcing Newsletter*, July–September, 2011: 6.

25 Martin Crisostomo, "IT-BPO Means Bringing Purpose to Outsourcing," *Breakthroughs! The Philippine Business Process Outsourcing Newsletter*, July–September 2011: 6.

26 Martin Crisostomo, "It's Time for Heroes to Come Home," *Breakthroughs! The Philippine Business Process Outsourcing Newsletter*, October 2010–January 2011: 8.

27 Martin Crisostomo, "IT-BPO Means Bringing Purpose to Outsourcing," *Breakthroughs! The Philippine Business Process Outsourcing Newsletter 5*, July–September, 2011: 6.

28 Crisostomo, "IT-BPO Means Bringing Purpose to Outsourcing."

29 Salvador Bubbles, "Everyday Heroes," *Breakthroughs! The Philippine Business Process Outsourcing Newsletter*, January 2015: 1.

30 In 2011 the corridor housed seventy-five thousand call centers and BPO firms, which were being served by a high-bandwidth fiber backbone and digital network. *The Report: Philippines 2010*, Oxford Business Group, December 16, 2009: 141.

31 Tadiar, *Fantasy-Production*.

32 Philippine Institute for Development Studies, "Services: Today's Most Prolific Industry," *Development Research News* 23, no. 5 (September–October 2005): 8.

33 "Investor Primer 2012," Business Process Outsourcing Association of the Philippines, 14–15.

34 Anna Romina Guevarra, for example, writes about the ways that the reification of care as a distinctly feminine capacity, coupled with the idea that Filipinos possess a "pleasing and comforting nature," constructs Filipino women as ideal nurses, while Kale Bantigue Fajardo reveals how the Philippine state cites Filipinos' labor in the Spanish galleon trade as making them particularly skilled at seafaring work. See Guevarra, *Marketing Dreams, Manufacturing Heroes*, 133–34; and Fajardo, *Filipino Crosscurrents*, 42.

35 The notion of a postconquest identity comes from D. Rodríguez, *Suspended Apocalypse*, 4–5.

36 I refer to the organization as BPAP rather than IBPAP because these interviews took place in 2009, before its name change in 2013.

37 On cost cutting, see Ross, *Fast Boat to China*, 144. See also Aneesh, *Neutral Accent*, 57.

38 See Aneesh, *Neutral Accent*.

39 Aneesh, *Neutral Accent*, 3.

40 Tsing, "Supply Chains," 157.

41 McKinley, "Benevolent Assimilation Proclamation."

42 Rodríguez, *Suspended Apocalypse*, 102.

43 Jonathan de Luzuriaga, "Filipino Qualities as Competitive Edge in This Crisis," *Breakthroughs! The Philippine Business Process Outsourcing Newsletter*, January–March 2009: 5.

44 Jonathan de Luzuriaga, "Filipino Qualities as Competitive Edge in This Crisis."

45 From the Philippine perspective, the key points of comparison between the two countries have been primarily cultural: while India may have the infrastructure and experience to handle the type of work being outsourced there, Filipinos are said to possess many more of the intangible qualities, or soft skills (such as a caring attitude and comprehensible accents), needed to secure the confidence of Western customers. Thus, a discourse of Filipinos as *more human* than Indians ensues.

46 Although the Philippines does not meet the official criteria for an emerging economy, I would argue that we can extend the spirit of this label to the country in this context, since the discourse of emergence evokes the notion of economic partnership and participation between historically strong and growing nations.

47 The language of "nested ideologies" was shared with me by Sumanth Gopinath, who heard and commented on a portion of this chapter at the American Studies Association's annual meeting in 2013.

48 Rafael, *White Love*, 199.

49 Culpeper, *History of English*, 82–83.

50 Smith, "Global English," 57.
51 With the boom in outsourcing, Eric Friginal writes, "it is clear that fluency, accent reduction, and the acquisition of high-level English"—all of which are associated with American English rather than English as an international language—"have gained the upper hand in setting the direction of language planning and shaping of popular opinion." Published in 2009, Friginal's book goes on to foreshadow how offshore outsourcing may affect the debate over language policy in the Philippines: "As a key growth industry currently providing jobs and revenues to the country, the government and the education sectors are ready to respond to the language needs of call centers . . . Highlighting the importance of fluency in English following the typical American variety could define the nature of macro and micro language policies in the Philippines." *Language of Outsourced Call Centers*, 32.
52 Prendergast, *Buying into English*.
53 Chow, *Not Like a Native Speaker*, 31.
54 Rafael, *White Love*, 198–199.
55 Here I take up a critique articulated by Monica Heller, who has argued that the celebration of English as the language of global capitalism erases "the problem of who defines the value of linguistic commodities or, more broadly, of who regulates the market." "Commodification of Language," 103.

Chapter 3: Inside Vox Elite

1 This disconnection between the two companies is what A. Aneesh refers to as a divergence between organizational spaces, which is one of three main challenges to communication in call centers. See Aneesh, *Neutral Accent*.
2 Hochschild, *Managed Heart*, 96.
3 Said, *Orientalism*.
4 For an illuminating study of the way capital disciplines both customers and labor in service work, see Leidner, *Fast Food, Fast Talk*.
5 In this way, the class illustrated rather perfectly what Nick Dyer-Witheford describes as "the increasing popular capacity to reappropriate communication technologies" for personal or political ends. *Cyber-Marx*, 71.
6 Although it is often not discussed in ethnographic analysis, boredom during fieldwork is a common experience. It is sometimes addressed in lessons on ethnographic methodology. See Blommart et al., *Ethnographic Fieldwork*, 37; Pollard, "Field of Screams"; and van der Berg, "Boredom and Lethargy."
7 There is a large literature that examines these dynamics of inclusion. See Espiritu, *Home Bound*; Isaac, *American Tropics*; Manalansan and Espiritu, *Filipino Studies*; Tiongson, Gutierrez, and Gutierrez, *Positively No Filipinos Allowed*; and Shaw and Francia, *Vestiges of War*. For a critique of the idea of

a historical symbiosis between the Philippines and the United States, see D. Rodríguez, *Suspended Apocalypse*. On the politics and language of "inclusionary racism," see Espiritu, *Home Bound*; and Kramer, "Race, Empire."

8 On Philippine amnesia, see Shaw and Francia, *Vestiges of War*; and Tiongson, Gutierrez, and Gutierrez, *Positively No Filipinos Allowed*.

9 Isaac, *American Tropics*, 11.

10 Kiran Mirchandani discusses the characterization of Indian English as "deficient" in *Phone Clones*, 36. In cc, Bella also went on to explain that agents would receive low marks on their QA evaluations if their construction of a sentence in the English language sounded too much like the syntax of Tagalog (or another native Filipino language). This protocol is designed, she explained, to prevent agents from "thinking in Tagalog but speaking in English."

11 Shome, "Thinking through Diaspora," 110.

12 Shome, "Thinking through Diaspora," 111–112.

13 Aneesh, *Neutral Accent*, 7–8.

14 Chow, *Not Like a Native Speaker*, 42.

15 Chow, *Not Like a Native Speaker*, 45; emphasis in original.

16 It is also worth remembering here that, as Fenella Cannell has argued in *Power and Intimacy in the Christian Philippines* with regard to Filipino culture, imitation is a practice in intimacy, which in turn constitutes the practice of negotiating unequal power relations. Thus, Filipino call center agents are not simply imitating American voices and accents but, in speaking the language of those in power, are also constantly mediating the power differential.

17 At the time of my research, "he" and "his" were the pronouns that Sammy was using, at least in the workplace, where we primarily met and interacted.

18 Ross, *Fast Boat to China*, 22.

19 As Hochschild argues, emotional labor requires "deep acting" (*Managed Heart*, 38), or the use of the "trained imagination" (36) to actually feel the feelings that one is displaying—or at least to close as much as possible the gap between what one feels and what one displays.

20 See Mirchandani, "Practices of Global Capital," 362–363.

21 Sherman, *Class Acts*, 19.

22 For an authoritative account of the mutual imbrication of militarism and tourism in the Philippines, see Gonzalez, *Securing Paradise*.

23 Gregory sees this racialized structure of feeling as an important affective component of what he calls "imperial masculinity." *Devil behind the Mirror*, 133.

Chapter 4: Service with a Style

1 Emphasis in original.

2 Chin, *Purchasing Power*, 125.

3 In her study of consumer culture, inequality, and black children in New Haven, Connecticut, Elizabeth Chin describes how "going to the mall alone is

a thrilling experience" that allows her ten-year-old informants to "be playful in ways that are impossible at home and in the neighborhood." *Purchasing Power*, 107.

4 I use the term *life stages* to denote not age but relation to family life—that is, whether my research participants lived with and were supported by, or were supporting, their parents; whether they were married; whether they had children of their own; and so on. All of these situations can be the case for Filipinos, especially those in their twenties.

5 Although it is often difficult to track the many factors that go into constructing the notion of class in the Philippines, I often found that it was not an individual's income alone but the extent to which an individual could rely on the incomes or resources of other family members that was crucial in these constructions. For example, a working single mother whose parents contribute to her budget may have more economic resources than a two-parent family with no other source of income than their own wages. Hence, I focus on individuals whose families rely on their call center income alone.

6 In her study of call center workers in India, Reena Patel discovers class differences among workers similar to those in the Philippines. *Working the Night Shift*, 124.

7 For Clive Barnett, Nick Clarke, Paul Cloke, and Alice Malpass, ethical problematization names the way that people "make a 'project' out of various aspects of their lives." Quoting Ian Hodges (2004, 457), the authors explain that "the concept of ethical problematization directs analytical attention to investigating the conditions 'for individuals to recognize themselves as particular kinds of person and to reflect upon their own conduct—to problematize it—such that they may work upon and transform themselves in certain ways and toward particular goals.'" "Elusive Subjects of Neo-Liberalism," 641.

8 Foucault, *Foucault Reader*, 340–372.

9 See Kimura, "Middle Classes," 266–268; and Pinches, "The Philippines' New Rich," 109.

10 In addition, the Aquino era (1986–1992) saw a rise in the international price for agricultural exports, the state's funding of labor-intensive infrastructure projects, and a 20 percent increase in the state's number of employees—all of which expanded the consumer economy.

11 Pinches, "The Philippines' New Rich," 123.

12 Pinches, "The Philippines' New Rich," 123.

13 Hall, "Deconstructing 'the Popular.'"

14 Cultural studies scholar Randy Martin theorized risk, a central feature of neoliberalism, as a movement marked by the "risk-driven accumulation of finance" by the investor. For Martin, "the investor would become the holiest figure in the trinity of personhood completed by citizen and consumer." *Financialization of Daily Life*, 22.

15 In 2005 the credit card receivables of universal, commercial, and thrift banks

in the Philippines were valued at about ₱70 billion ($1.5 billion). By December 2007 they were valued at around ₱117 billion ($2.5 billion). In 2008 consumer loans made up about 10 percent of total bank lending. See W. Tan, "Consumer Credit."

16 See Salzinger, *Genders in Production;* and Wright, *Disposable Women.*

17 Recent heightened attention to consumer culture in relation to postindustrialism, late capitalism, and neoliberalism has highlighted that the Fordist idea and experience of consumption as a mirror of production—that is, a process reflective of but experientially separate from the productive realm of work—has shifted, such that consumption itself is a productive process. As Nick Dyer-Witheford explains, in the era of the Fordist factory, "capitalist organization . . . requires the synchronization of the factory, where surplus value is pumped out on the assembly line, with the household, where the punishing force of such work is repaired, displaced, and hidden, and the pay packet translated into purchases of standardized domestic goods." *Cyber-Marx,* 74.

18 On the way that commodity culture ushers into a consumer-based society the notion of the right to personal pleasure, see Liechty, *Suitably Modern,* 98–99.

19 "Editor's Note," *Spiff,* May 2008, 6.

20 For a definition of *bakla,* see the introduction, n. 77.

21 In her canonical work on offshore informatics women workers in Barbados, *High Tech in High Heels in the Global Economy: Women, Work, and Pink-Collar Identities in the Caribbean,* Carla Freeman examines the sartorial practices of her Afro-Barbadian informants, arguing that their engagement in fashion is crucial to their construction of professional identities as well as being a source of shared pleasure.

22 Wissinger, "Modelling," 258.

23 Thrift, "Material Practices of Glamour," 292, 297.

24 Martin has referred to this shift as "the financialization of daily life," in his book by that title.

25 I use the term *youth* not only because most people in call centers are in their twenties or thirties but also because, in the Philippine context, workers in this demographic are increasingly the subject and object of the productivist-consumerist ethos—in part because the median age in the country as of 2010 was less than twenty-four years old. "The Age and Sex Structure of the Philippine Population (Facts from the 2010 Census)," Philippine Statistical Authority, August 30, 2012, https://psa.gov.ph/content/age-and-sex-structure-philippine-population-facts-2010-census. Moreover, my definition of productive youth overlaps thematically with Leslie Salzinger's analysis of "productive femininity." *Genders in Production,* 51.

26 Bello, *Anti-development State,* 102.

27 "Marketing in Manila," *Business Asia,* January 18, 1993, 7–8.

Chapter 5: Queering the Call Center

1 "HIV Cases Soar among Filipino Yuppies, Call Center Workers," *ABS-CBN News*, January 27, 2010, http://news.abs-cbn.com/lifestyle/01/27/10/hiv-cases -soar-among-filipino-yuppies-call-center-workers; and "Cabral Vows to In- tensify Gov't Info Drive against HIV/AIDS," Nationwide International News, *Philippine News Agency*, January 29, 2010. The Philippine National AIDS/HIV Registry reported that the number of new HIV cases recorded for all of 2009 stood at 835 (already the highest in twenty-five years) and that in the first ten months of 2010 alone, the number of cases had shot up to 1,305—representing a 56 percent increase over the previous year. The Philippine National AIDS/ HIV Registry also reported that 4,567 Filipinos total were infected with HIV, although a more realistic estimate put that figure around 9,000. Johanna D. Poblete, "AIDS Advisory Body to Lobby for Stronger Law," *Business World*, January 10, 2011; and Johanna D. Poblete, "HIV-AIDS: The Frightening Real- ity," *Business World*, March 12, 2010. Of course, these numbers are remarkably low compared to HIV rates in countries similar in size to the Philippines—an issue that has puzzled epidemiologists and public health officials since the first case of AIDS in the Philippines was recorded in the mid-1980s. Seth Mydans, "Low Rate of AIDS Virus in Philippines Is a Puzzle," *New York Times*, April 20, 2003.

2 "Cabral Vows to Intensify Gov't Info Drive against HIV/AIDS," Nationwide International News, *Philippine News Agency*, January 29, 2010.

3 "HIV Cases Soar among Filipino Yuppies, Call Center Workers; Casual Sex, Orgies Are Seen as Possible Cause of the Problem," *ABS-CBN News*, January 27, 2010, http://news.abs-cbn.com/lifestyle/01/27/10/hiv-cases-soar-among -filipino-yuppies-call-center-workers.

4 M. Tan, "AIDS," 153.

5 Antonio Figueroa, "Rise in HIV/AIDS Cases in Philippines Alarming," *Digital Journal*, January 30, 2010, http://www.digitaljournal.com/article/286683; em- phasis added.

6 My approach is grounded in an understanding of HIV/AIDS as inciting moral panics; in the Philippines, this panic points as much to the assumed social de- viance and symbolic threat of call center workers as at-risk bodies as they do to an epidemiological crisis. See Boellstorff, "Nuri's Testimony"; Crimp and Rolston, *AIDS Demo Graphics*; Glick Schiller, "What's Wrong"; Root, "'Mixing' as an Ethnoetiology"; Patton, *Inventing AIDS*; Sangaramoorthy, "We All Have AIDS"; M. Tan, "AIDS"; and Treichler, *How to Have Theory*.

7 Treichler, *How to Have Theory*, 1.

8 M. Tan, "AIDS," 163.

9 Root, "'Mixing' as an Ethnoetiology."

10 Antonio Figueroa, "Rise in HIV/AIDS Cases in Philippines Alarming," *Digital Journal*, January 30, 2010, http://www.digitaljournal.com/article/286683.

11 Rey M. Nasol, "Steady Rise in HIV Cases Noted in the Philippines; BPOs as Hi-risk Denied," *Philippine Daily Inquirer*, February 5, 2010, https://www.press reader.com/philippines/philippine-daily-inquirer/20100205/282806417452073.

12 "HIV Cases Soar among Filipino Yuppies, Call Center Workers," *ABS-CBN News*, January 27, 2010, http://news.abs-cbn.com/lifestyle/01/27/10/hiv-cases -soar-among-filipino-yuppies-call-center-workers.

13 For such dynamics in relation to India, see Hegde, "Spaces of Exception"; and Patel, *Working the Night Shift*.

14 "NBI Seizes 155 Computers in Cyber Pornography," Nationwide International News, *Philippine News Agency*, December 7, 2007.

15 Hegde, "Spaces of Exception," 183.

16 Hegde, "Spaces of Exception," 184. For the story on Internet cafés and call centers as "sex cybernets," see "Laoag Dad Calls for Regulation of Internet Cafes," Nationwide International News, *Philippine News Agency*, August 12, 2010.

17 "HIV Cases Soar among Filipino Yuppies, Call Center Workers," *ABS-CBN News*, January 27, 2010, http://news.abs-cbn.com/lifestyle/01/27/10/hiv-cases -soar-among-filipino-yuppies-call-center-workers; and Figueroa, "Rise in HIV/AIDS Cases in Philippines Alarming," *Digital Journal*, January 30, 2010, http://www.digitaljournal.com/article/286683.

18 As Michael Tan writes, "HIV has, unfortunately, reinforced class discrimination and pooled prejudicial images: on one hand, the healthy wealthy; on the other, the diseased poor—now overlapping with images of the promiscuous. I will never forget asking, in a central Philippine city, one gay professional if we could conduct HIV prevention workshops for gay men in his area. He looked at me and said, 'Not for professionals. We don't need it. We should do it for the low-class ones. They're the ones with the risky behavior.'" "AIDS," 159.

19 Marjun A. Baguio, "According to Study: Call Center Agents Prone to HIV-AIDS," *The Philippine Star*, January 30, 2010, http://www.philstar.com/cebu -news/544838/according-study-call-center-agents-prone-hiv-aids.

20 In her ethnography of migrant working women in Mumbai, *Street Corner Secrets: Sex, Work, and Migration in the City of Mumbai*, Svati Shah demonstrates that far from being an exceptional realm of work experienced as outside more legitimate sources of income, sex commerce and bartering are best understood on a continuum of survival strategies used by women in the city.

21 Xenos and Kabamalan, "Emerging Forms."

22 Manzano, *Callwork*, "Interview."

23 In "Identity, Mobility, and Urban Place-Making: Exploring Gay Life in Manila," Dana Collins discusses how a discourse of openness is also used to describe places in Manila where people—mostly men—can be public about their sexual orientation toward others of the same sex.

24 As explained in chapter 3, Sammy used the pronouns "he" and "him" at the time of my research.

25 As Julius Bautista reminds his readers, even though church and state are officially separate in the Philippines, the former continues to exert influence on extraconstitutional and legislative processes. Population growth and reproductive health are issues where the church has such influence. Bautista, "Church and State."

26 A majority of Filipinos supported the passage of the bill, which is not to suggest that the bill was unequivocally accepted by its supporters. Like other reproductive health bills, the Philippines' bill was in part framed in terms of population control, which members of the Philippine Left and activists within the national democratic movement reject.

27 See d'Emilio, "Capitalism and Gay Identity."

28 Brenda Alegre, "Becoming: A Transgender's Story," *Spiff* 1, no. 6 (2008): 51.

29 Bautista, "Church and State," 37. The term *culture of death* was first used by Bishop Karol Wojtyla (who became Pope John Paul II) in 1960 in his book *Love and Responsibility*, a philosophical and ethical treatise that states the Catholic Church's position on the "full meaning of erotic love within the context of married life." Wojtlya, *Love and Responsibility*.

30 On the ability of stories to narrate social location, see Duggan, "Trials of Alice Mitchell."

31 As John d'Emilio puts it, "in divesting the household of its economic independence and fostering the separation of sexuality from procreation, capitalism has created conditions that allow some men and women to organize a personal life around their erotic/emotional attraction to their own sex." "Capitalism and Gay Identity," 185.

32 For example, a study conducted by the PGH using rapid HIV tests targeted men only, while the ABS-CBN news article about the study pointed out that, of the 406-person sample, 130 were male call center agents who have sex with men. Other men in the sample were men who have sex with men but who are not call center workers, bisexual males, and male sex workers. This information is followed by a quote from an internal medicine intern at the PGH: "The data we are seeing now, the one that alarms us, is just focused on this small subset of call center agents. So these are the vulnerable call center agents . . . men having sex with men, gays or bisexuals engaging in high-risk behavior." "No Link between Call Centers and HIV Spread?," *ABS-CBN News*, February 10, 2010, http://news.abs-cbn.com/lifestyle/02/09/10/no-link-between-call-centers-and-hiv-spread. This shift in attention alone signifies something important in the public perception of the disease. Michael Tan has argued that in contrast to the way the AIDS epidemic in the United States has been linked quite closely with male homosexuality, such associations have not dominated media representations in the Philippines. This has meant that although homosexual and bisexual men accounted for 20 percent of all reported HIV cases in the Philippines at the end of the twentieth century, their visibility to the public has been disproportionately low by comparison. The link between

HIV and call centers forged a decade later thus shows a different dynamic at play. Tan, "AIDS," 148–149.

33 This situation echoes what Gayle Rubin has written about the United States in the 1980s: "Just when homosexuals have had some success in throwing off the taint of mental disease, gay people find themselves metaphorically welded to an image of lethal physical deterioration. The syndrome, its peculiar qualities, and its transmissibility are being used to reinforce old fears that sexual activity, homosexuality, and promiscuity lead to disease and death." "Thinking Sex," 26.

34 David, "Purple-Collar Labor," 188.

35 Despite the call centers' diversity policy with regard to hiring gay men and women, lesbians are hardly, if ever, explicitly mentioned by informants as a significant demographic within the workforce.

36 Hochschild, *Managed Heart.*

37 Cannell, *Power and Intimacy.*

38 Writing within the Indonesian context, Tom Boellstorff has argued that "HIV/ AIDS is powerfully linked to questions of knowledge" (351), such as knowing the origins of AIDS, knowing about HIV as a virus, knowing who has HIV and knowing why they became infected, knowing how not to become infected with HIV, and knowing how to treat or someday cure HIV infection (358). Boellstorff's emphasis on knowledge does not, however, recapitulate the information deficit model, with its problematic assumption that information is effective as such and thus leads directly to behavioral changes. Rather, Boellstorff focuses on how knowledge of HIV/AIDS shapes how his Indonesian *waria* ("roughly, male transvestite," 351) informant Nuri experiences and talks about HIV, and thus how Nuri produces herself as an ODHA (*Oran Dengan HIV/AIDS*), or "Person With HIV/AIDS" (358). "Nuri's Testimony."

39 Drawing connections among lifestyle, HIV risk, and a particular category of person, doctors, journalists, and state officials drew on and conflated the two dominant categories through which a person's risk for HIV is assessed within the medical establishment: who a person is and what acts and relationships the person engages in. The latter are often understood as part of a lifestyle or culture marked as *other*, which can produce and proliferate ideas about a particular group but not necessarily a better understanding of the cause of contracting and transmitting HIV. See Glick Schiller, "What's Wrong," 243–249.

40 Bong Austero, "HIV/AIDS in the Workplace," Opinion, *Manila Standard Today*, February 1, 2010.

41 Joseph Ryan /AKMA-PTM, "HIV Infected Call Center Agent," YouTube video, 2:15, February 28, 2010, http://www.youtube.com/watch?v=lcaPPMo7TEM.

42 Translation by Agnes (Bing) Magtoto.

43 ABS-CBN News, "Lifestyle, Not Job, Increases HIV Risk, Says Agent," *YouTube. com*, January 29, 2010, http://www.youtube.com/watch?v=ClJyBFEt5EM.

Conclusion

1 Reese and Soco-Carreon, "No Call for Action?," 157. In addition to the two I named here, the authors point to a number of other reasons that unionization has not occurred in the Philippine call center industry: workers' lack of understanding as to the source of their grievances, the perception that grievance procedures are merely token or symbolic gestures, call center hopping, the normalization of working conditions, the stigma attached to unions, and workers' underestimation of their market power. I would qualify the latter by adding that while I believe that workers understand their level of power in the market, they channel this understanding into uplifting the nation rather than attempting to disrupt the power of capital.

2 Here I echo A. Aneesh's question as to why there has been no collective struggle against the night shift, given its intensified use around the world. *Neutral Accent*, 127.

3 Roberts, "Commercial Content Moderation." On Filipinos as commercial content moderators, see Adrian Chen, "The Laborers Who Keep Dick Pics and Beheadings Out of Your Facebook Feed," *Wired*, October 23, 2014.

4 Some of the changes that I am referring to are indeed already taking place. Basic tasks such as retrieving customer data or making changes to a mobile phone account are already being done by software systems, which are becoming increasingly sophisticated. As a result, some predict that in the future humans will be tasked only with jobs that require more complex language skills, such as sales or medical consultation. The trend I want to highlight here, however, is that with these changes there may be an ever-widening gap between the affective quality and intensity of such work—that is, a gap between work one finds fulfilling (such as health care) and that which is directly damaging (such as handling the most irate customers whose demands cannot be met by an automated system). See "The End of the Line," *Economist*, February 6, 2016, https://www.economist.com/news/international/21690041-call-centres-have-created-millions-good-jobs-emerging-world-technology-threatens.

5 See Fernández-Kelly and García, "Underground Economy."

6 On the betrayal of the narrative of American entitlement to knowledge-economy jobs for college-educated men specifically, see Ong, *Neoliberalism as Exception*, 157–160. On the relationship to Trump, see Hochschild, *Strangers*; and Amanda Taub, "Behind 2016's Turmoil, a Crisis of White Identity," *New York Times*, November 1, 2016.

7 Teehankee, "Duterte's Resurgent Nationalism," 79; on comparisons between Duterte and Trump, see Thompson, "Introduction," 4.

8 Trisha Macas, "In China, Duterte Draws Cheers by Saying Americans 'Loud, Rowdy, Not Adjusted to Civility,'" *GMA News Online*, October 20, 2016, http://www.gmanetwork.com/news/story/585826/news/nation/in-china-duterte-draws-cheers-by-saying-americans-loud-rowdy-not-adjusted-to-civility.

BIBLIOGRAPHY

Aguilar, Delia. "Imperialism, Female Diaspora, and Feminism." *The Red Critique: Marxist Theory and Critique of the Contemporary*, no. 6 (2002).

Aguilar, Delia. "Questionable Claims: Colonialism Redux, Feminist Style." In *Women and Globalization*, edited by Anne E. Lacsaman and Delia D. Aguilar, 404–421. Amherst, MA: Humanity Books, 2004.

Aguilar, Filomeno V., ed. *Filipinos in Global Migration: At Home in the World?* Quezon City, Philippines: Philippines Migration Network and Philippine Social Science Council, 2002.

Aguilar, Filomeno V., ed. *Migration Revolutions: Philippine Nationhood and Class Relations in a Globalized Age*. Singapore: National University of Singapore Press; Quezon City, Philippines: Ateneo de Manila University Press, 2014.

Allen, Jafari Sinclaire, and Ryan Cecil Jobson. "The Decolonizing Generation: (Race and) Theory in Anthropology since the Eighties." *Current Anthropology* 57, no. 2 (2016): 129–148.

Aneesh, A. *Neutral Accent: How Language, Labor, and Life Become Global*. Durham, NC: Duke University Press, 2015.

Baldoz, Rick. *The Third Asiatic Invasion: Migration and Empire in Filipino America, 1898–1946*. New York: New York University Press, 2011.

Balisacan, Arsenio M., and Hal Hill, eds. *The Dynamics of Regional Development: The Philippines in East Asia*. Quezon City, Philippines: Ateneo de Manila University Press, 2003.

Barnett, Clive, Nick Clarke, Paul Cloke, and Alice Malpass. "The Elusive Subjects of Neo-liberalism." *Cultural Studies* 22, no. 5 (2008): 624–653.

Batalla, Eric Vincent C. "Divided Politics and Economic Growth in the Philippines." *Journal of Current Southeast Asian Affairs* 35, no. 3 (2016): 161–186.

Bautista, Julius. "Church and State in the Philippines: Tackling Life Issues in a 'Culture of Death.'" *Journal of Social Issues in Southeast Asia* 25, no. 1 (2010): 29–53.

Bello, Walden. *The Anti-development State: The Political Economy of Permanent Crisis in the Philippines*. Quezon City, Philippines: Focus on the Global South and the University of the Philippines Sociology Department, 2004.

Bello, Walden, Kenneth Cardenas, Jerome Patrick Cruz, Alinaya Fabros, Mary Ann Manahan, Clarissa Militante, Joseph Purugganan, and Jenina Joy Chavez. *State of Fragmentation: The Philippines in Transition.* Quezon City, Philippines: Focus on the Global South; Pasig City, Philippines: Friedrich-Ebert-Stiftung, 2014.

Benedicto, Bobby. *Under Bright Lights: Gay Manila and the Global Scene.* Minneapolis: University of Minnesota Press, 2014.

Berlant, Lauren. *Cruel Optimism.* Durham, NC: Duke University Press, 2011.

Bhabha, Homi K. *The Location of Culture.* New York: Routledge, 1994.

Blommaert, Jan, and Dong Jie. *Ethnographic Fieldwork: A Beginner's Guide.* Bristol, UK: Multilingual Matters, 2010.

Blyton, Paul, and Jean Jenkins. *Key Concepts in Work.* London: Sage, 2007.

Boellstorff, Tom. "Nuri's Testimony: HIV/AIDS in Indonesia and Bare Knowledge." *American Ethnologist* 36, no. 2 (1999): 351–363.

Briggs, Laura, Gladys McCormick, and J. T. Way. "Transnationalism: A Category of Analysis." *American Quarterly* 60, no. 3 (2008): 625–648.

Brophy, Enda. "Language Put to Work: Cognitive Capitalism, Call Center Labor, and Worker Inquiry." *Journal of Communication Inquiry* 35, no. 4 (2011): 410–416.

Brophy, Enda. "The Subterranean Stream: Communicative Capitalism and Call Centre Labour." *Ephemera: Theory and Politics in Organization* 10, nos. 3/4 (2010): 470–483.

Campomanes, Oscar. "Casualty Figures of American Soldiers and the Other: Post-1898 Allegories of Imperial Nation-Building as 'Love and War.'" In *Vestiges of War: The Philippine-American War and the Aftermath of an Imperial Dream, 1899–1999,* edited by Angel Velasco Shaw and Luis Francia, 134–162. New York: New York University Press, 2002.

Cannell, Fenella. *Power and Intimacy in the Christian Philippines.* Cambridge: Cambridge University Press, 1999.

Chin, Elizabeth. *Purchasing Power: Black Kids and American Consumer Culture.* Minneapolis: University of Minnesota Press, 2001.

Chow, Rey. *Not Like a Native Speaker: On Languaging as a Postcolonial Experience.* New York: Columbia University Press, 2014.

Choy, Catherine Ceniza. *Empire of Care: Nursing and Migration in Filipino American History.* Durham, NC: Duke University Press, 2003.

Ciulla, Joanne. *The Working Life: The Promise and Betrayal of Modern Work.* New York: Three Rivers, 2000.

Cohen, Lizbeth. *A Consumer's Republic: The Politics of Mass Consumption in Postwar America.* New York: Vintage, 2003.

Collins, Dana. "Identity, Mobility, and Urban Place-Making: Exploring Gay Life in Manila." *Gender and Society* 19, no. 2 (2005): 180–198.

Constable, Nicole. *Maid to Order in Hong Kong: Stories of Filipina Workers.* Ithaca, NY: Cornell University Press, 1997.

Crimp, Douglas, and Adam Rolston. *AIDS Demo Graphics*. Seattle, WA: Bay Press, 1990.

Cruz, Denise. *Transpacific Femininities: The Making of the Modern Filipina*. Durham, NC: Duke University Press, 2012.

Culpeper, Jonathan. *History of English*. New York: Routledge, 1999.

dalla Costa, Maria, and Selma James. *The Power of Women and the Subversion of the Community*. Bristol, UK: Falling Wall, 1972.

David, Emmanuel. "Purple-Collar Labor: Transgender Workers and Queer Value at Global Call Centers in the Philippines." *Gender and Society* 29, no. 2 (2015): 169–194.

Dávila, Arlene. *Latinos, Inc.: The Marketing and the Making of a People*. Berkeley: University of California Press, 2001.

de Genova, Nicholas. *Working the Boundaries: Race, Space, and "Illegality" in Mexican Chicago*. Durham, NC: Duke University Press, 2005.

d'Emilio, John. "Capitalism and Gay Identity." In *Powers of Desire: The Politics of Sexuality*, edited by Ann Snitow, Christine Stansell, and Sharon Thompson, 183–189. New York: Monthly Review Press, 1983.

Dowling, Emma. "Producing the Dining Experience: Measure, Subjectivity, and the Affective Worker." *Ephemera: Theory and Politics in Organization* 7, no. 1 (2007): 117–132.

Dowling, Emma, Rodrigo Nunes, and Ben Trott. *Ephemera: Theory and Politics in Organization* 7, no. 1 (2007).

Duggan, Lisa. "The Trials of Alice Mitchell: Sensationalism, Sexology, and the Lesbian Subject in Turn-of-the-Century America." *Signs* 18, no. 4 (1993): 791–814.

Duong, Lan P. "Transnationalism." In *Keywords for Asian American Studies*, edited by Cathy J. Schlund-Vials, Linda Trinh Võ, and K. Scott Wong. New York: New York University Press, 2015.

Dyer-Witheford, Nick. *Cyber-Marx: Cycles and Circuits of Struggle in High Technology Capitalism*. Chicago: University of Illinois Press, 1999.

Espiritu, Yen Le. *Home Bound: Filipino Lives across Culture, Communities and Countries*. Berkeley: University of California Press, 2003.

Fabros, Alinaya Sybilla L. "Global Economy of Signs and Selves: A View of Work Regimes in Call Centers in the Philippines." *Sociologie du travail* 51 (2009): 343–360.

Fajardo, Kale Bantigue. *Filipino Crosscurrents: Oceanographies of Seafaring, Masculinities, and Globalization*. Minneapolis: University of Minnesota Press, 2011.

Ferguson, James. *Global Shadows: Africa in the Neoliberal World Order*. Durham, NC: Duke University Press, 2006.

Fernández-Kelly, Patricia, and Anna García. "The Making of an Underground Economy: Hispanic Women, Home Work, and the Advanced Capitalist State." *Urban Anthropology and Studies of Cultural Systems of World Economic Development* 14, nos. 1–3 (1985): 59–90.

Fletcher, Joyce K. *Disappearing Acts: Gender, Power, and Relational Practice at Work*. Cambridge, MA: MIT Press, 2001.

Fishkin, Shelley Fisher. "Crossroads of Cultures: The Transnational Turn in American Studies—Presidential Address to the American Studies Association, November 12, 2004." *American Quarterly* 57 (2005): 17–57.

Foucault, Michel. *The Foucault Reader*, edited by Paul Rabinow. New York: Pantheon Books, 1984.

Foucault, Michel. *The History of Sexuality, Vol. 1*. New York: Vintage, 1978.

Francisco-Menchavez, Valerie. *The Labor of Care: Filipina Migrants and Transnational Families in the Digital Age*. Chicago: University of Illinois Press, 2018.

Freeman, Carla. *High Tech and High Heels in the Global Economy: Women, Work, and Pink-Collar Identities in the Caribbean*. Durham, NC: Duke University Press, 2000.

Frenkel, Stephen J., May Tam, Marek Korczynski, and Karen Shire. "Beyond Bureaucracy? Work Organization in Call Centres." *International Journal of Resource Management* 9, no. 6 (1998): 957–979.

Friginal, Eric. *The Language of Outsourced Call Centers: A Corpus-Based Study of Cross-cultural Interaction*. Philadelphia: John Benjamins, 2009.

Galam, Roderick. *The Promise of the Nation: Gender, History, and Nationalism in Contemporary Ilokano Literature*. Quezon City, Philippines: Ateneo de Manila University Press, 2008.

Gamalinda, Eric. "English Is Your Mother Tongue/Ang Ingles ay ang Tongue ng Ina Mo." In *Vestiges of War: The Philippine-American War and the Aftermath of an Imperial Dream, 1899–1999*, edited by Angel Velasco Shaw and Luis Francia, 247–259. New York: New York University Press, 2002.

Gershon, Ilana, and Allison Alexy. "Introduction: The Ethics of Disconnection in a Neoliberal Age." Special issue, edited by Ilana Gershon and Allison Alexy. *Anthropological Quarterly* 84, no. 4 (2011): 799–808.

Glick Schiller, Nina. "What's Wrong with This Picture? The Hegemonic Construction of Culture in AIDS Research in the United States." *Medical Anthropology Quarterly* 6, no. 3 (1992): 237–254.

Go, Julian. *American Empire and the Politics of Meaning: Elite Political Cultures in the Philippines and Puerto Rico during U.S. Colonialism*. Durham, NC: Duke University Press, 2008.

Goldberg, David Theo. *The Threat of Race: Reflections on Racial Neoliberalism*. Malden, MA: Wiley-Blackwell, 2009.

Gonzalez, Vernadette Vicuña. *Securing Paradise: Tourism and Militarism in Hawai'i and the Philippines*. Durham, NC: Duke University Press, 2013.

Green, Venus. *Race on the Line: Gender, Labor, and Technology in the Bell System, 1880–1980*. Durham, NC: Duke University Press, 2001.

Gregg, Melissa. *Work's Intimacy*. New York: Polity, 2011.

Gregg, Melissa, and Gregory J. Seigworth, eds. *The Affect Theory Reader.* Durham, NC: Duke University Press, 2010.

Gregory, Steven. *The Devil behind the Mirror: Globalization and Politics in the Dominican Republic.* Berkeley: University of California Press, 2007.

Guevarra, Anna Romina. *Marketing Dreams, Manufacturing Heroes: The Transnational Labor Brokering of Filipino Workers.* New Brunswick, NJ: Rutgers University Press, 2010.

Gupta, Akhil, and James Ferguson. "Beyond 'Culture': Space, Identity, and the Politics of Difference." *Cultural Anthropology* 7, no. 1 (1992): 6–23.

Hall, Stuart. "Notes on Deconstructing 'the Popular.'" In *Cultural Theory and Popular Culture,* edited by John Storey, 442–453. Upper Saddle River, NJ: Prentice Hall, 1998.

Hardt, Michael. "Affective Labor." *boundary 2* 26, no. 2 (1999): 89–100.

Hardt, Michael, and Antonio Negri. *Empire.* Cambridge, MA: Harvard University Press, 2000.

Hardt, Michael, and Antonio Negri. *Multitude: War and Democracy in the Age of Empire.* New York: Penguin, 2004.

Harrison, Faye. *Decolonizing Anthropology: Moving Further Toward an Anthropology of Liberation.* Arlington, VA: American Anthropological Association, 1997.

Hau, Caroline. *On the Subject of the Nation: Filipino Writings from the Margins, 1981–2004.* Quezon City, Philippines: Ateneo de Manila University Press, 2004.

Hechanova, Regina, and Edna Franco. *The Way We Work: Research and Best Practices in Philippine Organizations.* Quezon City, Philippines: Ateneo de Manila University Press, 2006.

Hechanova-Alampay, Ma. Regina. *1-800-Philippines: Understanding and Managing the Filipino Call Center Worker.* Quezon City, Philippines: Institute of Philippine Culture, 2010.

Hegde, Radha. "Spaces of Exception: Violence, Technology, and the Transgressive Gendered Body in India's Global Call Centers." In *Circuits of Visibility: Gender and Transnational Media Culture,* edited by Radha S. Hegde, 178–195. New York: New York University Press, 2011.

Heller, Monica. "The Commodification of Language." *Annual Review of Anthropology* 39 (2010): 101–114.

Hoang, Kimberly. *Dealing in Desire: Asian Ascendancy, Western Decline, and the Hidden Currencies of Global Sex Work.* Berkeley: University of California Press, 2015.

Hochschild, Arlie. *The Managed Heart: The Commercialization of Human Feeling.* Berkeley: University of California Press, 2012.

Hochschild, Arlie. *Strangers in Their Own Land: Anger and Mourning on the American Right.* New York: New Press, 2016.

Hodges, Ian. "Moving Beyond Words: Therapeutic Discourse and Ethical Problematization." *Discourse Studies* 4, no. 4 (2002): 455–479.

Holmes, Janet, and Meredith Marra. "Relational Practice in the Workplace:
Women's Talk or Gendered Discourse?" *Language in Society* 33 (2004):
377–398.

hooks, bell. *Teaching Critical Thinking: Practical Wisdom.* New York: Routledge,
2010.

Ileto, Reynaldo. *Payson and Revolution: Popular Movements in the Philippines,
1840–1910.* Quezon City, Philippines: Ateneo de Manila University Press,
1979.

Ileto, Reynaldo. "The Philippine-American War: Friendship and Forgetting." In
*Vestiges of War: The Philippine-American War and the Aftermath of an Im-
perial Dream, 1899–1999,* edited by Angel Velasco Shaw and Luis Francia,
3–21. New York: New York University Press, 2002.

Illouz, Eva. *Cold Intimacies: The Making of Emotional Capitalism.* New York:
Polity, 2007.

Isaac, Allan Punzalan. *American Tropics: Articulating Filipino America.* Minneapolis: University of Minnesota Press, 2006.

Jackson, John. *Real Black: Adventures in Racial Sincerity.* Chicago: University of
Chicago Press, 2005.

Kimura, Masataka. "The Emergence of the Middle Classes and Political Change
in the Philippines." *The Developing Economies* 41, no. 2 (2003): 264–284.

Knights, David, and Darren McCabe. "Governing through Teamwork: Recon-
stituting Subjectivity in a Call Centre." *Journal of Management Studies* 40,
no. 7 (2003): 1587–1619.

Kramer, Paul. "Race, Empire, and Transnational History." In *Colonial Crucible:
Empire in the Making of the Modern American State,* edited by Alfred Mc-
Coy and Francisco Scarano, 199–209. Madison: University of Wisconsin
Press, 2009.

Lazzarato, Maurizio. "Immaterial Labor." In *Radical Thought in Italy: A Potential Politics,* edited by Paolo Virno and Michael Hardt, 133–147. Minneapolis: University of Minnesota Press, 1996.

Leidner, Robin. *Fast Food, Fast Talk: Service Work and the Routinization of Everyday Life.* Berkeley: University of California Press, 1993.

Liechty, Mark. *Suitably Modern: Making Middle-Class Culture in a New Consumer Society.* Princeton, NJ: Princeton University Press, 2001.

Long, Nicholas J., and Henrietta L. Moore. "Introduction: Sociality's New Directions." In *Sociality: New Directions,* edited by Nicholas J. Long and
Henrietta L. Moore. New York: Berghahn Books, 2013.

Lumba, Allan. "Monetary Authorities: Market Knowledge and Imperial Government in the Colonial Philippines, 1892–1942." PhD diss., University of
Washington, 2013.

Luz, Juan Miguel. "A Time to Celebrate, a Time to Take on Challenges." University of Saint La Salle, Bacolod, Philippines, March 24, 2013.

Maher, Frances A., and Mary Kay Thompson Tetreault. *The Feminist Classroom: Dynamics of Gender, Race, and Privilege*. New York: Rowman and Littlefield, 2001.

Manalansan, Martin. *Global Divas: Filipino Gay Men in the Diaspora*. Durham, NC: Duke University Press, 2003.

Manalansan, Martin. "Servicing the World: Flexible Filipinos and the Unsecured Life." In *Political Emotions: New Agendas in Communication*, edited by Janet Staiger, Ann Cvetkovich, and Ann Reynolds, 215–228. New York: Routledge, 2010.

Manalansan, Martin, and Augusto Espiritu, eds. *Filipino Studies: Palimpsests of Nation and Diaspora*. New York: New York University Press, 2015.

Mankekar, Purnima. *Unsettling India: Affect, Temporality, Transnationality*. Durham, NC: Duke University Press, 2015.

Manzano, Hazel. *Callwork: A Call Center Life*. Metro Manila, Philippines: Callwork, 2008.

Marcus, George E. "Introduction: Notes toward an Ethnographic Memoir of Supervising Graduate Research through Anthropology's Decades of Transformation." In *Fieldwork Is Not What It Used to Be: Learning Anthropology's Method in a Time of Transition*, edited by James D. Faubion and George E. Marcus. Ithaca, NY: Cornell University Press, 2009.

Martin, Randy. *The Financialization of Daily Life*. Philadelphia: Temple University Press, 2002.

McGregor, Douglas. *The Human Side of Enterprise*. New York: McGraw-Hill, 1960.

McKay, Steven. *Satanic Mills or Silicon Islands? The Politics of High-Tech Production in the Philippines*. Ithaca, NY: Cornell University Press, 2006.

McKinley, William. "Benevolent Assimilation Proclamation." December 21, 1898.

Mendoza, Victor Román. *Metroimperial Intimacies: Fantasy, Racial-Sexual Governance, and the Philippines in U.S. Imperialism, 1899–1913*. Durham, NC: Duke University Press, 2015.

Mirchandani, Kiran. *Phone Clones: Authenticity Work in the Transnational Service Economy*. Ithaca, NY: Cornell University Press, 2012.

Mirchandani, Kiran. "Practices of Global Capital: Gaps, Cracks, and Ironies in Transnational India." *Global Networks* 4, no. 4 (2004): 334–373.

Mitchell, Timothy. *Rule of Experts: Egypt, Techno-politics, Modernity*. Berkeley: University of California Press, 2002.

Morini, Cristina. "The Feminization of Labor in Cognitive Capitalism." *Feminist Review* 87 (2007): 40–59.

Nader, Laura. "Up the Anthropologist—Perspectives Gained from Studying

Up." In *Reinventing Anthropology*, edited by Dell H. Hymes, 284–311. New York: Pantheon, 1972.

Nakano Glenn, Evelyn. "From Servitude to Service Work: Historical Continuities in the Racial Division of Paid Reproductive Labor." *Signs* 18, no. 1 (1992): 1–43.

Ong, Aihwa. *Neoliberalism as Exception: Mutations in Citizenship and Sovereignty.* Durham, NC: Duke University Press, 2006.

Pal, Mahuya, and Patrice Buzzanell. "The Indian Call Center Experience: A Case Study in Changing Discourses of Identity, Identification, and Career in a Global Context." *Journal of Business Communication* 45, no. 31 (2008): 31–60.

Palm, Michael. "Phoning It In: Self-Service, Telecommunications and New Consumer Labor." PhD diss., New York University, 2010.

Parreñas, Rhacel Salazar. *Servants of Globalization: Women, Migration, and Domestic Work.* Stanford, CA: Stanford University Press, 2001.

Patel, Reena. *Working the Night Shift: Women in India's Call Center Industry.* Stanford, CA: Stanford University Press, 2010.

Patton, Cindy. *Inventing AIDS.* London: Routledge, 1990.

"Philippines: Asia's Knowledge Center." I.T. Action Agenda for the 21st Century. Manila, Philippines: National Information Technology Council, October 1997.

Pinches, Michael. "The Philippines' New Rich: Capitalist Transformation amidst Economic Gloom." In *The New Rich in Asia: Mobile Phones, McDonald's, and Middle-Class Revolution*, edited by Richard Robison and David S. G. Goodman, 105–136. New York: Routledge, 1996.

Pollard, Amy. "Field of Screams: Difficulty and Ethnographic Fieldwork." *Anthropology Matters* 11, no. 2 (2009). http://www.anthropologymatters.com /index.php/anth_matters/article/view/10/10.

Poster, Winifred. "Who's on the Line? Indian Call Center Agents Pose as Americans for U.S. Outsourced Firms." *Industrial Relations* 46, no. 2 (2007): 271–304.

Prendergast, Catherine. *Buying into English: Language and Investment in the New Capitalist World.* Pittsburgh, PA: Pittsburgh University Press, 2008.

Radhakrishnan, Smitha. *Appropriately Indian: Gender and Culture in a New Transnational Class.* Durham, NC: Duke University Press, 2011.

Rafael, Vicente L. *Contracting Colonialism: Translation and Christian Conversion in Tagalog Society Under Early Spanish Rule.* Quezon City, Philippines: Ateneo de Manila University Press, 1988.

Rafael, Vicente L. *White Love and Other Events in Filipino History.* Durham, NC: Duke University Press, 2000.

Raghuram, Sumita. "Identities on Call: Impact of Impression Management on Indian Call Center Agents." *Human Relations* 66, no. 11 (2013): 1471–1496.

Ramos-Zayas, Ana Y. *Street Therapists: Race, Affect, and Neoliberal Personhood in Latino Newark.* Chicago: University of Chicago Press, 2012.

Raymundo, Sarah. "In the Womb of the Global Economy: *Anak* and the Construction of Transnational Imaginaries." *Positions* 19, no. 2 (2011): 551–579.

Reese, Niklas, and Joefel Soco-Carreon. "No Call for Action? Why There Is No Union (Yet) in Philippine Call Centers." *Current Research on South-East Asia* 6, no. 1 (2013): 140–159.

Rivas, Cecilia Maribal. *Salvadoran Imaginaries: Mediated Identities and Cultures of Consumption*. New Brunswick, NJ: Rutgers University Press, 2014.

Roberts, Sarah T. "Commercial Content Moderation: Digital Laborers' Dirty Work." *The Intersectional Internet: Race, Sex, Class and Culture Online*, edited by S. U. Noble and B. Tynes, 147–160. Bern, Switzerland: Peter Lang Publishing.

Rodríguez, Dylan. *Suspended Apocalypse: White Supremacy, Genocide, and the Filipino Condition*. Minneapolis: University of Minnesota Press, 2010.

Rodriguez, Robyn. *Migrants for Export: How the Philippine State Brokers Labor to the World*. Minneapolis: University of Minnesota Press, 2010.

Roediger, David R., and Elizabeth D. Esch. *The Production of Difference: Race and the Management of Labor in U.S. History*. Oxford: Oxford University Press, 2012.

Rofel, Lisa. *Desiring Subjects: Experiments in Neoliberalism, Sexuality, and Public Culture*. Durham, NC: Duke University Press, 2007.

Root, Robin. "'Mixing' as an Ethnoetiology for HIV/AIDS in Malaysia's Multinational Factories." *Medical Anthropology Quarterly* 20, no. 3 (2006): 321–344.

Rosenbaum, Susanna. "Longing and Belonging in America: Immigrants Redefining the Nation." Paper presented at the Annual Meeting of the American Anthropological Association, Washington, DC, November 6–9, 2014.

Ross, Andrew. *Fast Boat to China: Corporate Flight and the Consequences of Free Trade*. New York: Pantheon, 2006.

Ross, Andrew. *No-Collar: The Human Workplace and Its Hidden Costs*. New York: Basic Books, 2003.

Rowe, Aimee Carillo, Sheena Malhotra, and Kimberlee Pérez. *Answer the Call: Virtual Migration in Indian Call Centers*. Minneapolis: University of Minnesota Press, 2013.

Rubin, Gayle. "Thinking Sex: Notes for a Radical Theory of the Politics of Sexuality." In *Pleasure and Danger: Exploring Female Sexuality*, edited by Carol Vance, 267–319. London: Routledge, 1984.

Russell, Bob. *Smiling Down the Line: Info-Service Work in the Global Economy*. Toronto: University of Toronto Press, 2009.

Said, Edward. *Orientalism*. New York: Vintage Books, 1979.

Saloma-Akpedonu, Czarina. *Possible Worlds in Impossible Spaces: Knowledge, Globality, Gender and Information Technology in the Philippines*. Quezon City, Philippines: Ateneo de Manila University Press, 2006.

Salzinger, Leslie. *Genders in Production: Making Workers in Mexico's Global Factories*. Berkeley: University of California Press, 2003.

Sangaramoorthy, Thurka. "We All Have AIDS: Circulations of Risk, Race, and Statistics in HIV/AIDS Prevention." PhD diss., University of California, Berkeley, 2008.

See, Sarita. *The Decolonized Eye: Filipino American Art and Performance.* Minneapolis: University of Minnesota Press, 2009.

Shah, Svati. *Street Corner Secrets: Sex, Work, and Migration in the City of Mumbai.* Durham, NC: Duke University Press, 2014.

Shaw, Angel Velasco, and Luis Francia, eds. *Vestiges of War: The Philippine-American War and the Aftermath of an Imperial Dream, 1899–1999.* New York: New York University Press, 2002.

Sherman, Rachel. *Class Acts: Service and Inequality in Luxury Hotels.* Berkeley: University of California Press, 2007.

Shome, Raka. "Thinking through Diaspora: Call Centers, India, and a New Politics of Hybridity." *International Journal of Cultural Studies* 9, no. 105 (2006): 105–124.

Sicat, Gerardo. "'Successes' and Adjustment in the Philippine Labor Market." University of the Philippines School of Economics, Discussion Paper 2004-3, University of the Philippines, Quezon City, April 2004.

Smith, Linda Tuhiwai. *Decolonizing Methodologies: Research and Indigenous Peoples.* London: Zed Books, 2012.

Smith, Ross. 2005. "Global English: Gift or Curse? The Case against the World's Lingua Franca." *English Today* 82 21, no. 2 (April 2005): 56–62.

Staiger, Janet, Ann Cvetkovich, and Ann Reynolds., eds. *Political Emotions: New Agendas in Communication.* New York: Routledge, 2010.

Stewart, Kathleen. *Ordinary Affects.* Durham, NC: Duke University Press, 2007.

Tadiar, Neferti Xina M. *Fantasy-Production: Sexual Economies and Other Philippine Consequences for the New World Order.* Quezon City, Philippines: Ateneo de Manila University Press, 2004.

Tadiar, Neferti Xina M. "If Not Mere Metaphor . . . Sexual Economies Reconsidered." Special issue, "Toward a Vision of Sexual and Economic Justice," edited by Kate Bedford and Janet R. Jakobsen. *The Scholar & Feminist Online,* no. 7.3 (2009). http://sfonline.barnard.edu/sexecon/tadiar_01.htm.

Tadiar, Neferti Xina M. *Things Fall Away: Philippine Historical Experience and the Making of Globalization.* Durham, NC: Duke University Press, 2009.

Tan, Michael. "AIDS, Medicine, and Moral Panic in the Philippines." In *Framing the Sexual Subject: The Politics of Gender, Sexuality, and Power,* edited by Richard Guy Parker, Regina Maria Barbosa, and Peter Aggleton. Oakland: University of California Press, 2000.

Tan, Winecito. "Consumer Credit in the Philippines." *Bank for International Settlements Papers,* no. 46 (2009): 117–124.

Teehankee, Julio C. "Duterte's Resurgent Nationalism in the Philippines: A Discursive Institutionalist Analysis." *Journal of Current Southeast Asian Affairs* 35, no. 3 (2016): 69–89.

Thompson, Mark R. "Introduction to the Special Issue: The Early Duterte Presidency in the Philippines." *Journal of Current Southeast Asian Affairs* 35, no. 3 (2016): 3–14.

Thrift, Nigel. "The Material Practices of Glamour." In *The Affect Theory Reader*, edited by Melissa Gregg and Gregory J. Seigworth, 289–308. Durham, NC: Duke University Press, 2010.

Tiongson, Antonio T., Jr., Edgardo V. Gutierrez, and Ricardo Gutierrez, eds. *Positively No Filipinos Allowed: Building Communities and Discourse*. Philadelphia: Temple University Press, 2008.

Tolentino, Roland. *National/Transnational: Subject Formation and Media In and On the Philippines*. Quezon City, Philippines: Ateneo de Manila University Press, 2001.

Treichler, Paula. *How to Have Theory in an Epidemic: Cultural Chronicles of AIDS*. Durham, NC: Duke University Press, 1999.

Tsing, Anna. "Supply Chains and the Human Condition." *Rethinking Marxism: A Journal of Economics, Culture and Society* 21, no. 2 (2009): 148–176.

van der Berg, Marguerite. "Boredom and Lethargy in Ethnography." Paper presented at #Ethnography: Trends, Traverses and Traditions, European Sociological Association. University of Amsterdam, Netherlands, August 27–29, 2014.

Vora, Kalindi. *Life Support: Biocapital and the New History of Outsourced Labor*. Minneapolis: University of Minnesota Press, 2015.

Weeks, Kathi. *The Problem with Work: Feminism, Marxism, Antiwork Politics, and Postwork Imaginaries*. Durham, NC: Duke University Press, 2011.

Wissinger, Elizabeth. "Modelling a Way of Life: Immaterial and Affective Labour in the Fashion Modelling Industry." *Ephemera: Theory and Politics in Organization* 7, no. 1 (2007): 250–269.

Wojtyla, Karol. *Love and Responsibility*. Translated by H. T. Willetts. New York: Farrar, Straus and Giroux, 1960. Rev. ed., San Francisco: Ignatius Press, 1993.

Wright, Melissa. *Disposable Women and Other Myths of Global Capitalism*. New York: Routledge, 2006.

Xenos, Peter, and M. Midea M. Kabamalan. "Emerging Forms of Union Formation in the Philippines: Assessing Levels and Social Distributions." *Asian Population Studies* 3, no. 3 (2007): 263–286.

Yellin, Emily. *Your Call Is (Not That) Important to Us: Customer Service and What It Reveals about Our World and Our Lives*. New York: Free Press, 2009.

INDEX

call centers (*continued*)
placelessness of, 113; as postindustrial workplace, 8–9, 30, 51–52; as queer sites, 32, 157–58, 165–73; racialization of, 5, 21, 102; role of, in global economy, 7–9; security protocols in, 27–28; sexuality in, 28, 32, 155–58, 160–73; significance of, in Philippine economy and identity, 2–6, 64–65, 70–71, 74; social relations underlying, 65–70; technological developments in, 19, 194n54; tensions created by, 4, 22, 29–31, 37, 46–47, 62–69, 75–76, 95, 98, 121, 123, 133. *See also* call center work; call center workers; recruitment; training

call center work: as career choice, 66–67, 76–77, 79; colonial recall in, 30–31, 84–90, 107–8; as a dead end, 64–67, 72, 76, 137, 158, 162, 165; deskilling of, 19, 21; difficulty of, 75; Filipino characteristics of, 30, 58–62; lifestyle associated with, 131–43; mobility in, 72–73, 105; mystery concerning, 63–64; nature of, 51–52, 94; popular opinion of, 66–71, 74–75, 132, 137, 158, 167–68; precarity of, 19, 68, 143; promiscuity associated with, 164–70; schedule of, 2, 48; scholarly portrayals of, 8; skills required for, 97–98, 107–8, 119 (*see also* deskilling of); and social reproduction, 165, 168–69; tasks constituting, 63–64; value of, 68, 70–74, 80, 104, 119, 132. *See also* call center workers

call center workers: amenities provided for, 49–51; American animosity toward, 72; burnout experienced by, 47–48; class of, 30–32, 66–70, 73, 77, 142, 144–45, 184; college-like experiences of, 49–51; compared to typical Philippine workers, 10–11; consumption patterns of, 31–32, 132–43, 145, 148, 151–56; criticisms of, 137, 140, 142, 160, 174–80; customers' treatment of, 35, 41, 69–70; debt and financial risk assumed by, 148–50; "development" of, 56–57; emotional labor of, 36, 44–47; empowerment of, 123; entrepreneurship possibilities for, 146–48; and fashion, 151–53; financial habits and practices of, 139–42, 153–56; gay male, 171–73; and HIV/AIDS, 28, 32, 157–60, 162, 168, 171, 174–80; life stages of, 141, 143, 205n4; managers' relations with, 53–56, 59; material circumstances of, 122–23; motivation of, 47–48, 53, 57–58; parents' relations with, 66–67, 77, 167–68; performance evaluation of, 39–44, 53–54; and productive intimacy, 52–58; productivity as ideal of, 32, 142, 151, 153–54; professionalism of, 36, 72; psychosocial environment of, 49–51; racialization of, 18, 21, 102; recruitment of, 95–104, 142–43; relations among, 36–37, 45–53, 57, 138–40, 153, 163–64, 169, 180; resistance and insubordination of, 46; retention of, 48; returning from overseas, 79–80; schedules of, mismatched with social norm, 2, 48; self-perception of, 71–75; shortage of, 77–78; skill development programs for, 78–79, 200n20; social and family relationships of, 48–49, 51, 141; social mobility of, 144–48; stereotype of, 138; stress experienced by, 45–48; subjectivities of, 6, 8, 11; as subject-matter experts, 72, 75–76, 122; teams of, 53; union organizing of, 183–84, 211n1; wages of, 1, 64, 193n43, 198n2; work-

fashion, 151–53

feminization: of call center work, 5, 21, 69, 74–77; of colonial subjects, 82; of customer service work, 18–19; of labor, 4–5, 16, 64, 69, 74; Philippine labor associated with, 4, 16, 19, 185

Filipino/American relatability, 5, 9–11, 83–84; affect and, 9; analytical potential of, 114–17; class and, 123, 129–30; colonial roots of, 13–14, 83–84; communication styles and, 197n18; Filipino adaptability and, 107–8; imaginaries of, 26–27; nationalism and, 95; racialization and, 14, 25, 82–83, 112–13; as social capital, 82–86; transformations in, 6, 7. *See also* Filipinos, character and skills of

Filipinos, character and skills of, 5, 7, 11, 22, 58–62, 83, 87–89, 107, 181–82. *See also* Filipino/American relatability

Fordism, 153–54, 206n17

Foucault, Michel, 143, 197n15

freedom, 169–70

Friginal, Eric, 203n51

gay men, 171–73

gender: capitalism and, 10, 19; deviance and, 32, 157; geopolitical relations and, 15–16, 65, 81; telephone operations and, 16; national reputation and, 4, 8; perceptions as influenced by, 69; social precarity and, 194n53. See also *bakla*; feminization; sexuality and sexual practices

General Electric, 18

Global Competitiveness Assessment Tool (GCAT), 78–79

Goldberg, David Theo, 72

Green, Venus, 18, 193n47

Gregory, Steven, 129

Hall, Stuart, 148

Hardt, Michael, 190n16

health information management (HIM), 3, 22, 78, 81, 181, 186, 189n3

Hegde, Radha, 161–62

Heller, Monica, 7, 21

HIV/AIDS, 28, 32, 157–62, 166, 168, 171, 174–80, 209n32, 210n38

Hoang, Kimberly, 4

Hochschild, Arlie, 43, 102, 173, 196, 198n24

home ownership, 145–46

homework, 186–87

IBPAP (Information Technology Business Process Outsourcing Association of the Philippines), 78–79, 83–88, 195n74, 202n36

India: call centers in, 9, 112–13, 197n12; Philippine competition with, 87, 202n45

Information Technology Business Process Outsourcing Association of the Philippines. *See* IBPAP

International Monetary Fund (IMF), 3, 14–15, 65

interviews, 100–102

inumagan (morning drinking), 46, 138

Jackson, John, 26

James, Selma, 196n6

Jenkins, Jean, 21

kapwa (unity of self with others), 30, 60

knowledge economy, 20–22: in the Philippines, 3, 6, 15–16, 20–22, 70–71, 77–78

knowledge process outsourcing (KPO), 3, 22, 79, 81, 189

Rodríguez, Dylan, 13, 88, 190n7
Rodriguez, Robyn, 16
Root, Robin, 160
Rosenbaum, Susanna, 26
Rubin, Gayle, 210n33

Saloma-Akpedonu, Czarina, 21
savings. *See* money management
See, Sarita, 62
sexuality and sexual practices: call centers and, 28, 32, 155–73; class and, 162; cohabitation and, 163; diversity of, 165–73; as metaphors, 15–16; in the Philippines, 166–71; premarital sex and, 163, 168–69; in Southeast Asia, 165
sexually transmitted diseases, 28, 32
sex work, 15, 157–63
shadow labor, 198n24
Sherman, Rachel, 123
Shome, Raka, 112
small businesses, operated by call center workers, 146–48
social factory, 196n6
socialized workers, 196n6
social mobility, 144–48
social reproduction: call center work and, 165, 168–69; of class, 66–67; of relational labor, 44–51
Spain, 12
Spiff (magazine), 134–36, 150–52, 167–69
subjectivities: of call center workers, 6, 8, 11; capital's use of, 46–47; Filipino, 58–62; neoliberal influences on, 6; work and, 52, 187

Tadiar, Neferti Xina M., 81
Tan, Michael, 157–59
teams, 53. *See also* coaching
Teehankee, Julio, 187
telemarketing, 18

telephone operations, 17–19, 193n47. *See also* call centers
Theory Y management, 48, 54, 197n8. *See also* psychology of the workplace
Thomasites, 13
Thrift, Nigel, 153
training: by American personnel, 118–30; in American culture, 104–17, 119–21; postcolonial issues in, 31; and supervised calls, 38, 120
transnationalism: and constructions of class, 35, 69–70, 127–30; and ethnography, 27–29; and labor migration, 15–16, 20, 79–80; national identity shaped by, 32, 126; and the postindustrial workplace, 8–9, 19, 58, 62, 77; and power, 35, 75, 77, 112–13; scholarship on, 32–33
transwomen, 32, 152, 167, 171–72, 197n11
Treichler, Paula, 159
Trump, Donald, 187
Tsing, Anna, 87

unionization, of call center workers, 183–84, 211n1
United States: aggrieved whiteness in, 31, 126–29, 187; as colonial/imperial power, 5–14, 31, 83–84, 88, 190n7, 192n25; decline of, 12, 89–90, 115; homosexuality in, 210n33; immigration in, 111–12, 114–15; Philippines' relations with, 3–7, 11–16, 111–13, 182, 187–88, 190n7; resistance against, 3–4, 12, 31, 95, 110–11, 114–15; social relations in, 125–26; special nature of Philippines' relationship with, 11, 14, 83, 88, 192n25; training in culture of, 104–21. *See also* Americans; Filipino/American relatability

utang na loob (debt of gratitude), 59–60, 198n19

Vora, Kalindi, 47

Weeks, Kathi, 52
Wissinger, Elizabeth, 153
women: in call centers, 5, 21; characteristics associated with, 17–18; in customer service and telephone operations fields, 5, 17–19; in Filipina labor migrations, 4
workstations, 34, 39
World Bank, 14–15, 65

xenophobia. *See* racism